Jewish Gnosticism, Merkabah Mysticism, and Talmudic Tradition

Jewish Gnosticism, Merkabah Mysticism, and Talmudic Tradition

BASED ON THE ISRAEL GOLDSTEIN LECTURES, DELIVERED AT THE JEWISH THEOLOGICAL SEMINARY OF AMERICA, NEW YORK

by

GERSHOM G. SCHOLEM

Professor of Jewish Mysticism, The Hebrew University, Jerusalem

NEW YORK

THE JEWISH THEOLOGICAL SEMINARY OF AMERICA

5720—1960

Library of Congress Catalogue Card Number: 60-10743.

PRINTED IN THE UNITED STATES OF AMERICA
PRESS OF Maurice Jacobs INC.
224 N. 15TH ST., PHILADELPHIA 2, PENNA.

TABLE OF CONTENTS

PREFACE

This little book consists of the slightly enlarged text of the Israel Goldstein lectures delivered under the auspices of The Jewish Theological Seminary of America in New York during the spring term of 1957. They are supplemented by four appendices, the last of which was kindly contributed in Hebrew by my friend, Professor Saul Lieberman. I owe a debt of gratitude to Professor Lieberman, who took up the point I made in Section VI of this book concerning the age of *Shiur Komah* and established, by an additional thorough analysis of talmudic and midrashic statements on Canticles, the Tannaitic origin of this esoteric teaching.

My thanks are also due to Professor Louis Finkelstein, Chancellor of The Jewish Theological Seminary, for his willingness to undertake the publication of this highly technical little book, which, I hope, will shed new light on aspects of early rabbinic Judaism sorely neglected by earlier Jewish scholars and by students of Gnosticism. Finally, I wish to express my gratitude to Mrs. Stanley Friedman, who contributed greatly to making my English readable.

GERSHOM SCHOLEM

Jerusalem
The Hebrew University
April, 1959

I

GENERAL REMARKS

In speaking of Jewish mysticism in the early talmudic period, especially in the second and third centuries, I do not propose to present a full analysis of all the problems involved in the existence of mystical doctrines of an esoteric character in rabbinic Judaism. As a matter of fact, such an all-inclusive analysis cannot yet be made, for no proper account has been given of all the pertinent facts, all the texts involved, and all the ideas to be explored. I might even say that it is the purpose of these lectures to prove that there is much more to the subject than is immediately apparent. Indeed, I hope to establish proof that new findings, some of which I shall set forth in the following discussion, warrant a reconsideration of the entire problem.

The question of the existence in Jewish circles of a religious movement analagous to what is generally known in the history of the Christian church as Gnosticism has acquired new urgency as a result of the development of research in recent years. Of course, everyone agrees by now that 'Gnosticism,' in the comprehensive sense in which it is used in the history of religion, is a rather loose term. Only a few of the several sects, groups, and tendencies now considered 'Gnostic' were known as such in their own time. But this does not preclude the use of this convenient term for the religious movement that proclaimed a mystical esotericism for the elect based on illumination and the acquisition of a higher knowledge of things heavenly and divine. It is to this knowledge that the very term 'Gnosis,' meaning 'knowledge,' that is to say, knowledge of an esoteric and at the same time soteric (redeeming) character, alludes.

Theories that the origin of Gnosticism is to be found outside the scope of Judaism have been widely discussed. It is one of many marvels confronting the explorer in the field that scholars who have been looking far and wide to establish the source from which it all has come have been remarkably reluctant, or, rather, unwilling to allow the theory that Gnostic tendencies may have developed in the very midst of Judaism itself, whether in its classical forms or on its heterodox and sectarian fringes. The more far-fetched the explanation, the better. The theories of Reitzenstein in particular, on the Iranian origin of Gnosticism, have had considerable influence for some time. Even when, on closer inspection, they have been found disappointing and highly speculative, they still linger on—if only in a somewhat emasculated form. One is often left wondering about the methods used in this approach; and one is no less amazed by the stupendous ignorance of Jewish sources that warps the conclusions and even the basic approach of some of the finest scholars. Since the appearance of the excellent collection of rabbinic source material in Strack-Billerbeck's *Commentary on the New Testament*, we have, furthermore, been vouchsafed a new kind of fake scholarship, one that feeds on this work and takes it for granted that what is not in Billerbeck is not in existence.

On the other hand, the research of several competent scholars has made a case for the theory that Christian Gnosticism was in part preceded by a somewhat similar development in the midst of Judaism. It remains to be seen whether the newly discovered library of Gnostic papyri from Nag-Hammadi, which is likely to revolutionize all Gnostic research, will support this theory. Indeed, it has been said that the Gospel of Truth, the publication of which has just been announced, presents a strictly monotheistic form of Valentinian Gnosticism that must have preceded its dualistic and antinomian evolutions.[1] But, alas, the text, to judge from the translations from the Coptic (with which I am not conversant), is so enormously difficult that judgment must be reserved until a proper discussion of it will have taken place.

The term 'Jewish Gnosticism' can comprise a multitude of meanings. The first question we must ask is whether, after all, there did exist a pre-Christian Jewish Gnosticism that served as a point of departure for early Christian heresies. Second, we must decide whether such Jewish Gnostic teaching had already acquired a dualistic and heretical character. Had it introduced the differentiation between the highest unknown God and the Demiurge, or creator-God, identified with the God of Israel as he is revealed in the Law of Moses; or was this teaching still within the bounds of traditional Jewish concepts? Had it kept its essentially monotheistic character and given no encouragement to tendencies either to diminish the validity of the Law, or, in antinomian circles, to negate it entirely? Finally, there is the fundamental problem of whether evidence exists of a later devel-

[1] Cf. G. Quispel's paper on the doctrine of the Anthropos in these texts, in *Eranos Jahrbuch*, Vol. XXII (1953). The Gospel of Truth (Codex Jung) has been published by Malinine, together with French, German, and English translations (Zürich, 1957). On the whole problem of the Nag-Hammadi papyri, see now Jean Doresse, *Les livres secrets des gnostiques d'Égypte* (Paris, 1958).

opment of this Jewish Gnosticism, one parallel in point of time with those well-known Gnostic streams outside Judaism.

Discussion of these questions has grown considerably during the last few years, and some remarkable contributions to the general problem have been made. What has been lacking, however, is a closer consideration of the extant Jewish sources of esoteric tradition. Too much of what has been said has been of a highly hypothetical, if sometimes quite plausible, character. Nor does this apply only to the writings of Moritz Friedländer, at which many scholars, not always justifiably, have been poking fun.[2]

At this point I cannot avoid a remark about the Dead Sea Scrolls, which have given new impetus to these discussions. The problem of a possible connection between these texts and later Jewish esotericism has not been discussed thus far, although there are several similarities in phraseology and possibly also in technical terminology between some of the texts I will discuss here and the scrolls.[3] As a matter of fact, it has been maintained that "a pre-Christian Judaism of Gnostic character [*gnostisierendes Judentum*] which hitherto could be inferred only from later sources is now attested to by the newly discovered Dead Sea Scrolls."[4] It is said, too, that this Jewish Gnosis is still deeply rooted in the Jewish concept of the Law and in later Jewish apocalyptic.[5] Although such an hypothesis is psychologically and historically quite plausible, I must admit that I have come to view these statements with much skepticism. As a careful reader of these texts, I have not been able to detect those special terms and shades of meaning, read into them by K. G. Kuhn, that give them a specifically Gnostic or pre-Gnostic character. On the other hand, we may well wonder what, precisely, is meant by "the wondrous mysteries" (רזי פלא) of God revealed to the authors of these documents. They are mentioned several times but never explained. Phrases such as this lead to the assumption that there were, indeed, esoteric teachings among the sectarians, although these teachings are not expounded in the literature thus far recovered. The discovery of any new and

[2] Moritz Friedländer, *Der vorchristliche jüdische Gnosticismus* (Göttingen, 1898); *Die religiösen Bewegungen im Judentum im Zeitalter Jesu* (Berlin, 1905).

[3] In Appendix A to my article on the oldest extant (third or fourth century) chiromantic text, הכרת פנים וסדרי שרטוטין, I have shown that the word תולדות is used there in the technical sense of 'nature,' exactly as it is used in the Manual of Discipline; cf. ספר אסף (Jerusalem, 1953), pp. 477–479. The use of רז for 'mystery' is still the same in the scrolls and in the Hekhaloth, rather than סוד, which largely supplanted רז in later times.

[4] R. Bultmann, *Theologie des neuen Testaments* (1951), p. 361.

[5] K. G. Kuhn, *Zeitschrift für Theologie und Kirche*, XLVII (1950), 197 ff.

even small fragment of the scrolls could, of course, alter this state of things, and it is wise to reserve judgment until all the material is available.

It has even been said that the scrolls are essentially mystical documents and that the experiences spoken of in the Scroll of Hymns are genuinely mystical experiences. If so, we would then possess the first documents of Jewish mysticism preserved in Hebrew, and it would be only fair to look for the continuation of this tradition in later Jewish developments. But whether this point, which has been made with great vigor by Theodor Gaster, will prove true, is highly debatable—at least on the strength of the texts published.[6] The uncommonly attractive English translation of the hymns that Gaster has offered in proof of his contention is much more highly strung and eloquent than the rather poor diction of the Hebrew original, and the reader wonders whether Gaster has not considerably overdone the mystical coloring here. I shall not elaborate these points now.

Considerable progress has been made, however, through the closer analysis of early Christian Gnostic teachings and their Jewish implications. A good example of such work is furnished by Ernst Haenchen in his valuable study of the traditions surrounding Simon Magus, of the *Megale Apophasis* ascribed to him, and of the Samaritan origin of mythological Gnosticism as distinct from its philosophical counterpart.[7] It is too often and too easily forgotten in these discussions that in speaking of Samaritans we are speaking of heretical Judaism; and once we admit that such a development could take place within the Samaritan variant of Judaism, the possibility of analagous developments within the main branch of Pharisaic or Ḥasidic Judaism must equally be admitted. In fact, G. Quispel has come to the same conclusion, namely, that the oldest documents of Christian Gnosticism presuppose a Jewish Gnosis in which the figure of the Redeemer has not yet acquired a central place.[8] A similar conclusion was reached earlier by Eric Peterson, who has stressed the existence of such a pre-Christian stratum in Judaism in several of his papers. He has particularly emphasized the point that such a development did not take place in Palestine alone but in Babylonia as well; and that Christian Gnosticism in Babylonia, too, seems to have been preceded by a form of Jewish Gnosticism, one which in this case assimilated

[6] Theodor Gaster, *The Dead Sea Scriptures in English Translation* (1956), especially pp. 6–7.

[7] Ernst Haenchen, "Gab es eine vorchristliche Gnosis?" *Zeitschrift für Theologie und Kirche*, XLIX (1952), 326–349.

[8] "Der gnostische Anthropos und die jüdische Tradition," *Eranos Jahrbuch*, XXII (1953), 194–234.

Jewish and Persian elements and intertwined the one with the other.[9] Indeed, I think it can be shown by a closer study of the much discussed Mandaean texts (in which the Jewish elements are much stronger than generally supposed) that such a process may well have taken place.

Important and promising as all these alleys of inquiry are, it is with that other aspect of the problem, mentioned above, that I propose to deal here. The scholars who have taken part in these discussions have used as their primary sources of Jewish material the apocalyptic literature and some talmudic statements of an esoteric character. The problem of the continuity of Gnosticism within the body of Judaism deserves, however, to be considered from another point of view as well—from the point of view of Jewish esoteric tradition itself. This tradition has not been taken sufficiently into account and most assuredly deserves closer analysis. It is preserved not only in that Greek material which has found refuge or acceptance in Christian writings, as is the case, for instance, with the Jewish mystical prayers discovered by Bousset in the seventh book of the Apostolic Constitutions[10] (a document, incidentally, to which much too little attention has been paid by historians of the Jewish religion). Nor must we confine ourselves, as Peterson did, to the analysis of early Christian apocrypha and pseudepigrapha, or to Greek and Coptic papyri and inscriptions, highly important as these are. But there exists a whole chain of Hebrew and Aramaic texts, preserved, not on the outer fringes of Judaism, but in circles highly conscious of their attachment to rabbinic Judaism. It is these texts, which, if properly considered in connection with all these other sources, will throw new light on the subject we are discussing.

I am speaking of the mystical revelations known as the Hekhaloth Books. This class of writings contains a number of complete books as well as several fragments and amorphous material scattered widely through Hebrew manuscripts. I shall enumerate the most important of these texts, many of which will be examined in the following discussion:

1) The Visions of Ezekiel (ראיות יחזקאל), the main part of which has been recovered by Jacob Mann and S. A. Wertheimer from the Cairo Genizah.[11]

[9] *Zeitschrift für Neutestamentliche Wissenschaft*, XXVII (1928), 90–91. Cf. also p. 84 there.

[10] Wilhelm Bousset, "Eine jüdische Gebetsammlung im 7 Buch der apostolischen Konstitutionen," *Nachrichten von der Gesellschaft der Wissenschaften in Göttingen*; *Phil.-Hist. Klasse* 1915 (1916), pp. 435–485.

[11] S. Wertheimer, בתי מדרשות (new ed.; Jerusalem), II (1953), 127–134.

2) The Lesser Hekhaloth (היכלות זוטרתי), of which only a small part has been published, and that from an atrociously bad manuscript and without recognition of its identity.[12] Extremely difficult as this mostly Aramaic text proves to be, some headway can be made toward restoring a much better text by using the four manuscripts still extant in Oxford, Munich, and The Jewish Theological Seminary of America in New York.[13]
3) The Greater Hekhaloth (היכלות רבתי), which has been published in very bad versions, but which can be restored to a highly readable text by comparing the manuscripts, some of which are quite good.[14]
4) The book, *Merkabah Rabbah* (מרכבה רבה), partly published by S. Musajoff.[15]
5) The titleless Hekhaloth, containing alternate utterances by R. Ishmael and R. Akiba. This text is mostly unpublished but is largely preserved in the four abovementioned manuscripts.[16] It seems that the oldest text of the *Shiur Komah*, of which more

[12] Parts of it are found, under the erroneous title תפלת כתר נורא, in an important collection of Merkabah texts culled from several manuscripts and published by Solomon Musajoff (Jerusalem, 1921) as ס' מרכבה שלמה. See fol. 6a–8b. Adolph Jellinek, in his Introduction (p. xliv) to Vol. VI of his בית המדרש, was the first who recognized the true identity of the היכלות זוטרתי. This true piece of information was not used by Odeberg, who mistakenly identified the Lesser Hekhaloth with a piece belonging to the book *Merkabah Rabbah*; cf. his Introduction to *3 Enoch or the Hebrew Book of Enoch*, ed. and trans. H. Odeberg (Cambridge, 1928), p. 104.

[13] Oxford, Neubauer 1531, fol. 38a–46a; Munich 22, fol. 160b–164; Munich 40, fol. 94a–98a; The Jewish Theological Seminary of America (New York) 828 (according to the numbers in the typewritten handlist prepared by the late Professor Alexander Marx), fol. 16b–18b, 23a–25a.

[14] The least objectionable of these editions of היכלות רבתי is to be found under the title פרקי היכלות רבתי in S. Wertheimer's בתי מדרשות, I (1950), 63–136. The two volumes of this collection of Wertheimer's papers, in a revised and augmented version, contain much other valuable material pertaining to the literature of Jewish Gnosticism. In the following observations and quotations I use the text of היכלות רבתי established for a critical edition by Ch. Wirszubski and myself. The oldest manuscripts speak of these books as הלכות היכלות רבתי וזוטרי :הלכות, quoted in Judah ben Barzilai's פירוש ס' יצירה, p. 101.

[15] In מרכבה שלמה, fol. 1–6. It is also called there רזו של סנדלפון, but this subtitle obviously refers to a part of the whole. The text is contained in several other manuscripts (e. g. J. Th. Sem. 828, fol. 38b–43a; Munich 40, fol. 109–113) where no title is mentioned, but where, at the end, we read סליק מרכבה רבה. (מרכבה רבה and מרכבה זוטא are mentioned in MS Sassoon 290 in the Sassoon Library, London. Cf. תרביץ, XVI, 206.)

[16] In Appendix C I have transcribed this text from two MSS, Oxford 1531, fol. 50a–60a and J. Th. Sem. 828 (see note 13), fol. 29a–35a, which contains several paragraphs lacking in MS Oxford.

will be said in these lectures, was originally a part of the *Merkabah Rabbah* but was later transmitted in the manuscripts as a separate unit.

6) The chapter on physiognomics and chiromancy, which originally made part of the Hekhaloth traditions. I published the remaining fragment some years ago.[17]
7) The Book of the Hekhaloth (ספר היכלות), first published by Jellinek, and later, under the title *3 Enoch or the Hebrew Book of Enoch*, by Hugo Odeberg, who also included an English translation. This is the only longer text that has been given a scholarly treatment.[18] It belongs to a later stratum than the preceding texts in this list.[19]
8) The Treatise of the Hekhaloth, *Massekheth Hekhaloth*, a short description of the throne and the Merkabah-world. It is apparently the latest of these texts. It was reprinted by Jellinek and translated into German by A. Wünsche.[20]

All these texts, with the exception of the first one, purport to be revelations about the heavenly chariot, the *Merkabah*, vouchsafed to the Tannaim R. Ishmael and R. Akiba and transmitted by them. Such revelations are therefore related to the old traditions about the *Merkabah* (first to fourth centuries C. E.), small fragments of which are to be found in the talmudic treatise *Ḥagigah* (fols. 12–16a) and in scattered places all over talmudic and midrashic literature. The first text, too, although not ascribed to Ishmael or Akiba covers some aspects of the same field in a different manner.[21]

The problem vital for our consideration is, of course, how close the relation actually is between these texts, which give rather elaborate and detailed accounts of the Merkabah-world, and the talmudic traditions. Are they later developments, written by people who had

[17] Cf. הכרת פנים וסדרי שרטוטין in ספר אסף (Jerusalem, 1953), pp. 459–495, where I discussed the age of this text and other pertinent questions concerning it.

[18] *3 Enoch or the Hebrew Book of Enoch* (Cambridge, 1928). Cf. the writer's *Major Trends in Jewish Mysticism* (3rd ed.; New York, 1954), pp. 357–358.

[19] Odeberg's dating (third century) is unacceptable. The fifth to sixth century would be nearer the mark. The author of this text already reinterprets, and wrongly, some older Merkabah traditions that a third century writer could not have misunderstood. But much of the material is old and is important. The trouble is that Odeberg has based his edition on a particularly bad manuscript and one has to reconstruct the good readings (already partly found in Jellinek's scattered editions of most of the book) from the critical apparatus.

[20] Jellinek, בית המדרש, II (1853), 40–47, and August Wünsche, *Aus Israels Lehrhallen*, III (1909), 33–47.

[21] Cf. the discussion in Section VII.

no direct contact with the old Merkabah speculations and visions, but who used them only in a fanciful way, to supplement by their own inventions traditions that were lost? Or do we really have here, at least in part, a true reflection of these traditions?

The answer to these questions has something to do with yet another question, namely, why have not these texts attracted closer attention at the hands of scholars? The reason is simply that most scholars, from the very beginning of nineteenth century Jewish studies, have continually underrated the antiquity of these texts (of which only numbers 3, 7 and 8 were known to them) and have continually relegated them to early medieval times, thus precluding their correct evaluation. This attitude was somewhat understandable as a reaction of the emergent historical criticism against the pretensions of Kabbalistic and mystical pseudepigraphy, and took place at a time when relatively little was known about the religious syncretism of the late Hellenistic and early Christian period. The striking similarities between the literary physiognomy of some of these texts and some of the so-called magical papyri escaped them, as did their close relation to other sources from this period. The one notable exception to this unhappy state of things was provided by Moses Gaster, whose fine intuition and wide knowledge in these fields was, however, warped by a considerable weakness of philological method and precision. This lack has prevented his ideas from being discussed seriously.[22]

The entire problem presented by this material has been reconsidered in my book *Major Trends in Jewish Mysticism*, where I have shown[23] that the most important of these texts are undoubtedly much older than hitherto presumed. My findings and analyses, as far as I am aware, have been widely accepted. But further research on these questions has yielded new results. The truth of the matter is that in many respects I was not radical enough. I dated the oldest of these texts from the fourth and fifth centuries, although stating that they contained some material which was much older and which presented striking parallels to Gnostic teachings and practices. In these lectures I should like to discuss some of these new results, deepening, and in some cases supplementing my former studies.

[22] Cf. M. Gaster's paper on *Shiur Komah* in his *Studies and Texts in Folklore, Magic, Hebrew Apocrypha, etc.*, II (1928), 1330–1353, reprinted from *MGWJ*, Vol. XXXVII (1893).

[23] Especially in the Second Lecture, "Merkabah Mysticism and Jewish Gnosticism," pp. 40–79.

II

THE HALAKHIC CHARACTER OF HEKHALOTH MYSTICISM

Before I proceed, however, one other observation must be made. The question of the existence of a dualistic heretical Gnosis within Judaism has been much disputed—especially in Moritz Friedländer's prolific writings, where quite a grain of truth has been overshadowed by many inconsequential and misleading statements. It would, of course, be very important to have documentary proof of the existence of such radical dualism from Jewish sources. The talmudic statements on the *Minim*, however, about which we have a large and sometimes quite fanciful literature, are capable of supporting several different interpretations, since it is not at all clear whether some of the most important talmudic passages refer to Judeo-Christians or to Gnostics of an antinomian bent, and even, in the latter case, whether to Jewish or to gentile Gnostics.[1]

This doubtful state of things would be radically and most happily altered were we able to accept the interpretation offered by M. André Dupont-Sommer of an Aramaic inscription found by him on a silver splint. He dates this text, with some probability, in the early third century, but both his reading and his interpretation of the text make it a dualistic document full of rather curious content. According to his reading the inscription plainly indicates a dichotomy between the highest God and the God of Israel—exactly the position taken by many Gnostics for whom the God of Israel, or the Demiurge, was a being of inferior status in the hierarchy of heavenly beings. Since the Jewish character of this particular inscription is unmistakable, M. Dupont-Sommer's conclusions, if true, would be highly significant for every discussion of Jewish Gnosticism. A careful examination, alas, reveals that the inscription contains no trace of Jewish heterodoxy at all. Correctly interpreted, it reads like a perfectly orthodox Jewish

[1] Travers Herford, *Christianity in Talmud and Midrash* (1903), and, lately, Marcel Simon, *Verus Israel* (1948), pp. 214–238, defended the Christian character of the most controversial passages on the *Minim*—against Friedländer. I am not at all convinced that they are right in most cases. In many it seems obvious that Jewish sectarians were meant, and a rather forced interpretation had to be applied in order to transform them into Christians.

incantation, although highly significant and yielding unexpected results in other respects.[2]

The texts of Merkabah mysticism that have so far come to our knowledge also display what I have called an orthodox Jewish tendency, and are in no way heretical. By this I mean that although they do expound some ideas of a highly mystical character, these texts adhere strictly to monotheistic concepts. Some of these mystical ideas and the problems deriving from them will be discussed later, namely, the doctrine of the mystical body of God, the frequent use of secret or mystical names of God, the difficulties arising from such use, and the consequent blurring, in some instances, of the borderline between these names of God and the names of the angels. These mystical aspects, however, do not detract from the basic fact that the theology presented, or rather implied, here does not conflict with the biblical concept of God, even though it may conflict with some later philosophical concepts of medieval Judaism. There is no reason to assume that the names of great heroes of talmudic learning, such as Ishmael and Akiba, were used by the authors of these writings to cloak unorthodox teachings. If what these texts present is Gnosticism—and their essentially Gnostic character cannot in my opinion be disputed—it is truly rabbinic Gnosis, and the illuminations and revelations granted to the adepts are such as conform to the Jewish vision of the hierarchy of beings. Indeed, all these texts go to great lengths to stress their strict conformity, even in the most minute detail, to halakhic Judaism and its prescriptions.

An excellent illustration of this attitude is to be found in Chapter 18 of the Greater Hekhaloth, in a description of the procedure by which the adepts recall their teacher and master, R. Neḥuniah ben Hakanah, from ecstasy to a normal state of consciousness. R. Neḥuniah is pictured as seated in the temple of Jerusalem, sunk in ecstasy, describing to his pupils, who are standing about and taking down his words, the visions he beholds of the secret chambers of the Merkabah. R. Neḥuniah stands, as it were, before the throne of God. But a problem arises about the meaning of an expression he uses to describe the activities of the gate-keepers of the sixth heavenly palace. These gate-keepers are said to threaten the destruction, on their own initiative and without asking permission of their superiors, of "all those who *do and do not* go down to the Merkabah."[3] The pupils, unable to

[2] See Appendices A and B.

[3] Cf. Chap. 17:6: מפני ששומרי פתח היכל הששי היו משחיתים ביורדי מרכבה ולא ביורדי מרכבה שלא ברשות, והיו מצוים עליהם [scil. על המלאכים] ומכין אותם ושורפין אותם ומעמידים אחרים במקומם, ואף אחרים העומדים תחתיהם כך היא מדתם, שאינם מתייראים ומעלין על לב לומר:

understand this mystifying formula, turn to R. Ishmael saying, "See him, and bring him back, that he may return to us from the vision which he beholds of the Merkabah, that he may tell us who he is who *does and does not* go down to the Merkabah." And this is how R. Ishmael describes his procedure:

> Immediately I took a piece of very fine woolen cloth and gave it to R. Akiba, and R. Akiba gave it to a servant of ours saying: "Go and lay this cloth beside a woman who immersed herself and yet had not become pure, and let her immerse herself [a second time]. For if that woman will come and will declare the circumstances of her menstrual flow before the company, there will be one who forbids [her to her husband] and the majority will permit. Say to that woman: 'Touch this cloth with the end of the middle finger of your hand, and do not press the end of your finger upon it, but rather as a man who takes a hair which had fallen therein from his eyeball, pushing it very gently.' " They went and did so, and laid the cloth before R. Ishmael. He inserted into it a bough of myrtle full of oil that had been soaked in pure balsam and they placed it upon the knees of R. Neḥuniah ben Hakanah; and immediately they dismissed him from before the throne of glory where he had been sitting and beholding:
>
> Wonderful loftiness and strange dominion,
> Loftiness of exaltation and dominion of majesty,
> Which come to pass before the throne of glory,
> Three times each day, in the height,
> From the time the world was created and until now, for praise.[4]

What is important here is not the set of fictitious circumstances attending this procedure, but, rather, the cumulative effect of all

למה אנו נשרפים וכי מה הנאה יש לנו שאנו משחיתים ביורדי מרכבה ולא ביורדי מרכבה שלא ברשות? ועדיין כך היא מדתם של שומרי פתח היכל שישי.

[4] I am using a draft of an English translation of the Greater Hekhaloth prepared several years ago by Dr. Morton Smith, who has kindly put it at my disposal. The Hebrew text is: אמר ר' ישמעאל: מיד נטלתי מטלית של פרהבא ונתתיה לר' עקיבא ור' עקיבא נתנה לעבד שלנו לומר: לך והעמד מטלית זו אצל אשה שטבלה ולא עלתה לה טבילה והטבילה. שאם תבוא אותה האשה ותאמר מדת וסתה לפני חבורה בידוע שאחד אוסר והרב מתירין. אמרו לה לאותה אשה: געי בה במטלית זו בראש אצבע צרדה של ידך ואל תדרסי ראש האצבע עליה אלא כאדם שנוטל נימא מגלגל עינו שנפלה לו מדחף אותה ברמיזה. הלכו ועשו כן והניחו את המטלית לפני ר' ישמעאל. נעץ בה מורבייא של הדס מלאה פלייטון ששרוי באפלסמון נקי והניחו על ארכובותיו של ר' נחונייא בן הקנה, ומיד פטרוהו מלפני כסא הכבוד שהיה יושב ורואה

בגאוה מופלאה ושררה משונה
בגאוה של רוממה ושררה של זהיון
שמתרגשות לפני כסא הכבוד
שלש פעמים בכל יום ויום במרום
משנברא העולם עד עכשיו לשבח.

(The last five lines constitute a formula used several times in the Greater Hekhaloth.)

these provisions, demonstrating that even the slightest possible suspicion of impurity, defined according to strictest rabbinic law, is enough to have the ecstatic dismissed from before the throne. Examples of this attitude abound in these texts,[5] affirming the fact that their writers lived near the center of rabbinic Judaism, not on its fringes.

Furthermore, whereas some of these writings are concerned with descriptions of the ascent and the heavenly peregrinations of the ecstatic, others of them have quite a different purpose. Their goal is not to aid the adept in attaining the vision of the Merkabah, but, rather, to aid him in acquiring a perfect knowledge of the Torah and to protect him from its loss through forgetfulness. Instead of the angelological details of the celestial hierarchy of such interest to the Greater Hekhaloth (or to the so-called Hebrew Book of Enoch), it is only one angel who commands the attention of the other writings, namely, the Prince of Torah (שר תורה); the angel who can grant perfect knowledge of all the fields of the Law, both in its exoteric and its esoteric aspects.

It is not clear whether we are dealing here with two different aspects of the same thing, developed in different circles but more or less at the same period, or whether these two attitudes represent different developments at different times. The second hypothesis, which has much to commend it, would, of course, put these incantations or conjurations of the Prince of Torah into a later period, when the ecstatic ascent had already lost much of its freshness and had been superseded by a greater stress on the magical elements—which, to be sure, the ascent had also contained. Yet quite similar procedures already appear in magical papyri from the fourth century,[6] and the figure of the Prince of Torah, mostly called Yophiel (יופיאל), makes its appearance in the Aggadah at an early period.[7] The very

[5] According to Chap. 20:1, only those can go down to the vision of the Merkabah who fulfill two qualifications: "... he who reads the Bible and *studies* Mishnah, Midrash, Halakhoth, and Aggadoth ... and he who *fulfills* all which is written in the Torah and keeps all the prohibitions [הזהרות] of statutes and judgments and laws which were declared to Moses on Sinai."

[6] K. Preisendanz, *Papyri Graecae Magicae*, I (Leipzig, 1928), 14.

[7] In the preface to the early geonic book שמושי תורה (a biblomantic text) the angel is called יפיפיה שר של תורה; cf. Jellinek, בית המדרש, I, 64. (This seems to be 'Iφιαφ in Preisendanz, *op. cit.*, II [1931], 160, in a half-Jewish incantation from the fifth century.) יופיאל is mentioned at the end of our version of the היכלות רבתי (Chap. 30), which section belongs to a separate composition on the שר תורה. The Pseudo-Jonathan Targum (ed. Ginzburger, p. 366) on Deut. 34:6 mentions מטטרון יופיאל אוריאל ויפיפיה as רבני חכמתא, "Princes of Wisdom" (חכמה=תורה!). In אותיות דר' עקיבא, in S. Wertheimer, בתי מדרשות, II, 354, Metatron is called both מלאך שר התורה and

fact that such a figure could appear in the Aggadah at all presupposes a function of his which could not have been far removed from what we actually find in some of the Hekhaloth writings. An angel who is delegated over the Torah cannot be an angel whose sole function is to keep the Torah in its heavenly archives, but one who is also responsible for distributing its knowledge among men. It is, therefore, quite plausible that procedures for getting this angel to impart some of his treasures to the students of the Law could have been very old, and that these procedures could have used for this purpose some of the paraphernalia of the ecstatic ascent to heaven. When either R. Ishmael or R. Akiba describes his ascetic preparations and his performance in asking for the revelations of the Prince of Torah, he uses the same materials used by the Greater Hekhaloth in the description of the ascent. Our first hypothesis, however, holds true only for a part of these traditions, and we may safely assume that many of the injunctions for a perfect knowledge of the Law do in fact belong to a later stage. The more intricate the study of Halakhah and Aggadah became, the more such preternatural help was deemed highly desirable. As a matter of fact, we have a long chain of such prescriptions, reaching from the Lesser Hekhaloth[8] and the Sar Torah (at the end of the Greater Hekhaloth)[9] through the time of the Geonim[10] and of the German Ḥasidim of the Middle Ages.

מלאך שר החכמה. In the Merkabah text transcribed in Appendix C, יופיאל is mentioned as שר של תורה (MS Oxford 1531, fol. 53a).

[8] As a sort of preface to the Lesser Hekhaloth, we read (MS Oxford 1531, fol. 38a): בשעה שעלה משה למרום אל האלהים לימדו הקב"ה: כל אדם שיהא לבו שונה [MS J. Th. Sem.: שוגה] הזכר עליו את השמות האלו בשם בארי אבהאי האי מרמראות סמוסלם אברי ואנכיבון שיתפסו בלבבי כל מה שאני שומע ו[א]למד מקרא ומשנה תלמוד הלכות והגדות ולא אשכח לא בעולם הזה ולא בעולם הבא. בא"י למדני חוקיך. The magical names *μαρμαραωθ* and *σεμίσελαμ* occur very frequently in the magical papyri. If *σεμισελαμ* is indeed the Hebrew שמש עולם, then the word has returned to these Jewish circles from Greek sources without being recognized as Hebrew!

[9] It is obvious that the last chapters (27–30) of the Greater Hekhaloth, which contain the שר התורה, are not an original part of the compilation. They describe in very dramatic fashion and poetic style the revelation of the ways to conjure the שר תורה, granted by God to Israel at the time the Second Temple was built. In our texts the readings שר תורה and סוד תורה have sometimes become confused. The dialogues between God, Israel, and the angels (who wish to prevent the divulgence of the mystery) have considerable literary merit. As an introduction to theurgic practice they are parallel to the Midrash מעין החכמה, which was originally written as an introduction to the theurgic ס' שמושי תורה.

[10] Cf. the writer's article, סדרי דשמושא רבא, in *Tarbiz*, XVI (1945), 196–209 which also contains (pp. 206–209) a recipe for a conjuration of the Princes of the Torah on the night of יום הכפורים from MS Sassoon 290 in London.

III

THE FOUR WHO ENTERED PARADISE AND PAUL'S ASCENSION TO PARADISE

If we wish to inquire into the antiquity of the tradition preserved in the Hekhaloth literature, we have not only to consider the many points of contact between these texts and their parallels in the Hellenistic and early Christian literature, but we have also to look for internal evidence in talmudic writings to give us a clue as to the period in which some of these Hekhaloth traditions may have originated. By analyzing the talmudic story of the four who entered Paradise, I have proved in my previous book, *Major Trends in Jewish Mysticism*, that the true understanding of this highly significant anecdote about R. Akiba and his colleagues can be achieved only when we relate it to some pertinent statements in the Greater and Lesser Hekhaloth. In the story, as it is told in the Talmud (*Ḥagigah* 14b), R. Akiba warns his colleagues: "When you come to the place of the pure marble plates, do not say 'Water! Water!' For it is said: He that telleth lies shall not tarry in my sight." I have shown[1] that the later Merkabah mystics still understood perfectly the meaning of this enigmatic passage—that it referred to the dangers confronting the mystic in his ascent through the seven palaces of the seventh heaven, which is called *'Araboth.* The pertinent passage in the Hekhaloth texts is to be found in the Munich manuscript (it is quoted in *Major Trends in Jewish Mysticism*): "At the gate of the sixth palace it seemed as though hundreds of thousands of waves of water were storming against him, and yet there was not a drop of water, only the ethereal glitter of the marble plates with which the palace was tessellated." That the traditions of the Hekhaloth and of the talmudic Baraitha could thus supplement and explain each other was offered as proof that we are dealing with one and the same continuous stream of tradition.

I should like to add now that in the Lesser Hekhaloth, in which R. Akiba always speaks in the first person, we receive even more

[1] *Major Trends in Jewish Mysticism*, pp. 52–53. A. Neher's hypothesis about the eschatologic meaning of the warning אל תאמרו מים מים has not convinced me; cf. his article, "Le voyage mystique des quatre," *Revue de l'Histoire des Religions*, CXL (1951), 59–82.

information. The talmudic tale mentions Ben Azai, Ben Zoma, and Aḥer as Akiba's companions on his journey to heaven. Of Ben Azai it is said that he saw and died, of Ben Zoma, that he saw and was afflicted (that is to say, went out of his mind). In The Jewish Theological Seminary of America manuscript of the Lesser Hekhaloth we find two further statements. The one that is also found with some variants in the other manuscripts reads:

> Ben Azai was deemed worthy and stood at the gate of the sixth palace and saw the ethereal splendor of the pure marble plates. He opened his mouth and said twice, "Water! Water!" In the twinkling of an eye they decapitated him and threw eleven thousand iron bars at him. This shall be a sign for all generations that no one should err at the gate of the sixth palace.[2]

The other even more elaborate version, to be found at the beginning of the text according to this manuscript, seems to adapt this additional information to that of the Babylonian Talmud:

> Ben Azai beheld the sixth palace and saw the ethereal splendor of the marble plates with which the palace was tessellated and his body could not bear it. He opened his mouth and asked them [apparently the angels standing there]: "What kind of waters are these?" Whereupon he died. Of him it is said: Precious in the sight of the Lord is the death of his saints. Ben Zoma beheld the splendor of the marble plates and he took them for water and his body could bear it not to ask them, but his mind could not bear it and he went out of his mind . . . R. Akiba ascended in peace and descended in peace.[3]

It is interesting to note that this interpretation of Ben Azai's ecstatic death stands somewhat in contrast to the assumption that he who asks the fatal question about the waters is a wretch, perhaps a descendant of those who kissed the Golden Calf, and unworthy to see "The King in His beauty," as the elaboration of this episode in yet another passage of the Lesser Hekhaloth has it.[4] If the tradition

[2] I am quoting some variant readings of the MS Oxford 1531 in brackets: א"ר עקיבא בן עזאי [פלני אלמני] זכה ועמד בפתח היכל השישי וראה זיו אויר אבנים [אבני שיש טהור] ופתח פיו [שתי פעמים] ואמר מים מים. בהרפסת העין חתכו את ראשו והטילו עליו אחד עשר אלף מגזרי ברזל. בסימן הזה יהיה לדורות שלא יתעה אדם בפתח היכל הששי

[3] MS J. Th. Sem. 828, fol. 16b: בן עזאי הציץ בהיכל הששי וראה זיו אויר אבני שיש שהיו סלולות בהיכל ולא סבל גופו ופתח פיו ושאלם מים הללו מה טיבן ומת עליו הכתוב או' יקר בעיני יהוה המותה לחסידיו. בן זומא הציץ בזיו באבני [!] השיש וסבר שהוא מים וסבל גופו שלא שאלם אבל לא סבל [!] דעתו ונפגע יצא מדעתו . . . ר' עקיבא עלה בשלום וירד בשלום.

[4] Cf. the full text in *Major Trends*, p. 361. It is part of the Lesser Hekhaloth in all the manuscripts (e. g. Oxford 1531, fol. 43a–b, J. Th. Sem. 828, fol. 23a). This is the passage which Hai Gaon quotes as part of the היכלות זוטרתי; cf. Benjamin

about Ben Azai in the passage just quoted is authentic, then the elaboration must date from a later time; for it does not fit him, who, in the biblical verse applied to him, is called one of the Ḥasidim, or saints of God. On the other hand, if we consider as genuine the statement that the rejected mystic is descended from the worshippers of the Golden Calf, which in view of its bold, radical tone I am rather inclined to do, then we have to consider the statement that follows Ben Azai's question, "What kind of waters are these," as an additional aggadic development which throws no further light on the genuine tradition about the mystical journey of the four sages.

Another point should be raised, moreover, with regard to this Baraitha. In its insistence on the dangers implicit in the ecstatic ascent to heaven, it is not only connected with the tradition preserved in the Hekhaloth, but, under a different aspect, seems to be connected with a famous passage in Paul's second Epistle to the Corinthians. The Baraitha speaks of four who entered Paradise, the Hebrew word *pardes* (פרדס) apparently being used in its two meanings, the general one of 'orchard,' and the specific one of 'Paradise' as a technical term both in Hebrew and in Greek.

That the biblical word *pardes* was, in fact, used as the technical term for the heavenly paradise in the oldest Jewish esoteric writings has now been finally proven by findings made in the Qumran caves. J. T. Milik has published two fragments of an Aramaic text of the Book of Enoch (comprising Chapters 32:2 and 77:3) in which the heavenly "paradise of righteousness" of the Greek and Aethiopian versions is indeed called *pardes kushṭa*.[5]

The talmudic story makes use of the first meaning of *pardes* (orchard) by saying that Elisha Aḥer, who became a heretic, or *min*, cut down the saplings—whatever this metaphor may signify.[6] On the other hand, it is clear from the context that this orchard is a

---

Lewin, *Oṣar Hageonim* on *Ḥagigah* (part of תשובות), p. 14. Lewin was not aware of the existence of MSS of the היכלות זוטרתי.

[5] Cf. *Revue Biblique*, LXV (1958), 71 and 76. See also note 10 of this section.

[6] The metaphor is also used in connection with Adam's fall. Cf. בראשית רבה, ed. Theodor, Par. XIX, p. 172: שלא תעשה את הגדר יותר מן העיקר שלא יפול [!] ויקצץ את הנטיעות. Jacob Levy's explanation of נטיעות as 'metaphysical speculations' in his talmudic dictionary (III, 381) is certainly wrong. Better is A. Marmorstein's observation (*Religionsgeschichtliche Studien*, II [1912], 68): "*Wie sie* [the rabbis] *denjenigen verdammten, der den Zaun einreisst, so warnten sie stets vor der Beschädigung der Pflanzen.*" מקצץ הנטיעות may indeed have a meaning similar to פורץ גדרן של חכמים. נטיעות are, then, the commandments around which a סייג לתורה or a גדר is erected. But in other passages the pious ones are called God's נטיעות and the phrase מקצץ כל נטיעותיו is applied to their deaths (*Yerushalmi*, *Berakhoth* II, 8).

heavenly abode. Rashi, who certainly followed in the tradition of the Merkabah mystics, explains the words "entered *pardes*" (נכנסו לפרדס) as "ascended to heaven by means of a sacred name."[7] Even R. Akiba, upon entering this *pardes*, encountered ministering angels who wanted to eject him or bar him from continuing on his way.[8] This proves, in my opinion, that the Baraitha uses the same terminology as Paul, who, speaking of his visions and revelations, says: "I know a man belonging to the Messiah, who, fourteen years ago, was caught up to the third heaven—whether in the body or out of the body, I do not know, God knows. And I know that this man was caught up into Paradise—whether in the body or out of the body, I do not know, God knows—and he heard things that cannot be told, that man may not utter [II Corinthians 12:2–4]." It is obvious that Paul, who wrote these lines about the year 58 C. E., was speaking of an idea with which his readers were familiar, a Jewish conception that he, as well as his readers in Corinth, had brought over into the new Christian community. The same idea was also used, at about the same time, by the author of the Slavic Book of Enoch, who seems to have been a Hellenistic Jew writing during the second half of the first century.[9] Describing Enoch's rapture, the author has him say: "They [i. e. the men] carried me up to the third heaven and set me down in the midst of Paradise [Chapter 8]." In the apocryphal Life of Adam and Eve, God, after Adam's death, sends the Archangel Michael up into the Paradise in the third heaven to fetch three linen sheets with which to shroud Adam's body. In the Apocalypse of Moses, which represents a parallel version of the Life of Adam and Eve, Adam himself is "carried into Paradise up to the third heaven" after his death.[10] The familiar idea that the ecstatic sees in his lifetime what other people see only after death recurs, therefore, in Paul's

[7] עלו לרקיע על ידי שם.

[8] *Ḥagigah* 15b.

[9] The proofs for a Christian origin, adduced by A. Vaillant in his recent critical edition of this book (Paris, 1952), are singularly weak. They consist of parallels to New Testament phrases (not actual quotations) that could at the time have been used by anyone.

[10] Cf. Kautzsch, *Apokryphen* und *Pseudepigraphen*, II, 519 and 527 (Apocalypse of Moses, Chaps. 13 and 37) and the version translated by M. Hack in Kahana, הספרים החצונים, I, 1 (1937), 16. In the Life of Adam and Eve, Chap. 25, it is even said that after the fall, but before Adam was cast out from God's presence, he had a similar experience: he was caught up into the "Paradise of Righteousness" and had a vision of God on His throne, a vision of the Merkabah and its "fiery wheels." The same term (παράδεισος τῆς δικαιοσύνης) is used in the Greek text of Enoch 32:3, and corresponds, as I remarked above, to the Aramaic term פרדס קושטא.

as well as the rabbis' journey to heaven. There is, however, a significant difference. Whereas Paul is "caught up" to Paradise, the rabbis "enter" it. But this, of course, may be due to the metaphorical use of Paradise as an orchard. In Chapters 19–20 of the Greater Hekhaloth, the mystic is taken up and transported in a "chariot of light"[11] before the throne of glory.

Such ecstatic journeys are well-known in Jewish literature from the days of the early apocalypticists to those of the Hekhaloth. The heroes change, but the basic idea remains: under the guidance of angels, man beholds (in his body or out of his body) those mysterious realms which God permits him to see. In the Greek text of the Testament of Levi (2:5) we are told that Levi's journey took place in a 'sleep' (ὕπνος)—which may be, actually, nothing but the ecstatic trance of the visionary. The seven heavens are opened to him and the angel says "Enter" in the same manner in which the angel at the sixth gate admits the Merkabah mystic when he has passed all trials. In the Aramaic fragment of this Testament, which seems to be of considerable age and reminds us in some respects of the Genesis Apocryphon among the Dead Sea Scrolls, it is even said that this trance of Levi's lasted for two whole weeks.[12] Paul's testimony is a link between these older Jewish texts and the Gnosis of the Tannaitic Merkabah mystics. It has nothing to do with the novel and partly bizarre interpretations that later Patristic tradition, unaware of the Jewish background of Paul's saying, read into his words.[13]

Another link of this type, which is at the same time a parallel to Paul's passage, is contributed by a quotation from the lost Apocalypse of Zephania supplied by Clement of Alexandria.[14] If this Apocalypse is a Jewish source—which is not quite certain, although I can detect no Christian elements in its language and terminology—it must have existed in Tannaitic times. Here we read: "And the spirit carried me and caught me up into the fifth heaven, and I beheld angels that are

[11] קרון של נוגה. The Lesser Hekhaloth use the Aramaic equivalent עגלא מן נורא (in what seems to me a rather irregular use of the preposition מן instead of די). Cf. Section X, n. 22.

[12] ונגדו שבעתין מן לותי ואנה אתעירת מן שנתי. Cf. R. H. Charles, *The Greek Versions of the Testaments of the Twelve Patriarchs* (1908), p. 246.

[13] Cf. Ildefonse de Vuippens, *Le Paradis Terrestre au troisième Ciel: Exposé historique d'une conception chrétienne des premiers siècles* (Fribourg, 1925). The author has assembled very interesting later material. His own interpretation of the original meaning of the passage in Paul seems to me completely wrong.

[14] Montague R. James, *The Lost Apocrypha of the Old Testament: Their Titles and Fragments* (London, 1920), p. 73; Emil Schürer, *Geschichte des jüdischen Volkes* (4. *Auflage*), III (1909), 367.

called Lords [κυρίοι][15] . . . as they are dwelling in Temples of Salvation and singing hymns to the ineffable and most high God." In the clause I have omitted it is stated, in addition, that each of the angels has a crown set upon his head, as well as a throne shining seven times brighter than the light of the sun.

The language and terminology of the entire passage seem to accord much more with that of the Hekhaloth literature than with that of the older apocalypses with which the passage has been compared. The Greek term *ναοί*, especially in the phrase *ἐν ναοῖς σωτηρίας*, which has a very Semitic ring, seems to represent the precise Greek counterpart of the Hebrew term *Hekhaloth—Hekhal* meaning both 'palace' and 'temple.' Furthermore, just as we have the king dwelling in the Palaces of Silence, of Holiness, and of Purity in the Greater Hekhaloth, so we have here the "Temples [or Palaces] of Salvation." As a matter of fact, the Lesser Hekhaloth contain a paragraph (MS Oxford 1531, fol. 45a) that speaks of a Metatron-like figure whose function is to "arrange the throne and to clothe [the glory with] the garment and to adorn the *Ḥashmal* and to open the Gates of Salvation [*sha'arei yeshu'ah*]." It can be supposed that these "Gates of Salvation" are connected with the "Palaces" or "Temples of Salvation" mentioned in the Apocalypse of Zephania. The crowns of the angels are described very often in the Hebrew texts;[16] and as for the angelic hymns, I shall turn to them presently. Even if we should assume that we are dealing here with an early Christian apocalypse, this quotation would still prove how much common ground existed between the ideas and terminology used in such early Christian texts and the Hekhaloth literature. And, as we shall see, it stands to reason that this common ground was Jewish.

[15] Cf. the category called *κυριότητες* in Paul's Epistle to Collossae 1:16. These are perhaps the שרי מלכיות in 3 Enoch 16:1.

[16] On the crowns of the angels, cf. Chap. 18 of the Hebrew Book of Enoch (Odeberg, *3 Enoch or the Hebrew Book of Enoch*, pp. 52–64), and Chaps. 12:3 and 16:1. On the *θρόνοι* (angels possessing thrones), cf. Odeberg's Introduction, p. 142. Odeberg paid no attention to the passage from the Apocalypse of Zephania.

IV

THE MERKABAH HYMNS AND THE SONG OF THE KINE IN A TALMUDIC PASSAGE

There is still more material that is of great importance for the correct dating of some of the Hekhaloth material. Indeed, for the dating of at least one stratum of the Greater Hekhaloth this material is decisive.

The Greater Hekhaloth presents us with a large number of Hebrew hymns, which it treats in an unusual manner: the very same hymns are characterized by the text as representing two different types of songs. On the one hand, the hymns are addressed to the throne and to Him who sits upon it, and are described as celestial songs of praise sung by "the Holy Living Creatures" (*Ḥayyoth ha-Kodesh*) who, in Ezekiel 1:5 ff., are the bearers of the throne. On the other hand, these same hymns are the ones the mystic is instructed to recite before and during his ecstatic ascent to heaven (which, in a very curious and so far unexplained change of phraseology, is always referred to in this text as a *descent* unto the Merkabah[1]). The hymns describe, in a plethora of solemn phrases, the spirit of majesty and solemnity that permeates the heavenly realm, "the Palaces of Silence" in which God's Shekhinah dwells, and express, too, the ideas of the writers about the many different angelic hosts and their part in the

[1] The context clearly shows that ירד למרכבה is used even where, immediately afterward, the ascent (עליה) of the mystic is mentioned. In an eschatological context we find the expression ירד לגן עדן, although an *ascent* to Paradise is indicated. Thus we find אלו יורדין לגן עדן ואלו יורדין לגיהנם in *Ruth Rabbah,* at the very beginning of the Midrash. Since the ark containing the scrolls of the Torah is like the throne, the talmudic phrase יורד לפני התבה (for prayer) may have influenced the other one, i. e. יורד למרכבה. There is a marked difference between the היכלות זוטרתי and היכלות רבתי in this connection. The former does not use the phrase ירד למרכבה, and when it does speak of ירידה, actual descent after the vision is meant. At the end of this text we read: א"ר עקיבא: כשפירשתי מידת עליית וירידת המרכבה הזאת קבעו לי ברכה בכל יום ויום בבית דין של מעלה ובבית דין של מטה ועוד אמ"ר עקיבא נמה לי בת קול מתחת כסא הכבוד ואמרה לי: ידיד שמצטער במידת עליית וירידת המרכבה לפני, קבעתי לו ברכה שלש פעמים בכל יום ויום בבית דין של מעלה ובבית דין של מטה, והבית ששונים אותו אוהב אני אותו ופודיהו אני. But in the corresponding passage of the היכלות רבתי (Chap. 14:2) we find: ר' נחונייא בן הקנה יושב ומסדר לפניהם את כל דברי מרכבה ירידה ועליה, היאך יורד מי שיורד והיך עולה מי שעולה. On the other hand, the היכלות רבתי still retains several instances of the original usage.

celestial liturgy.[2] Their immense solemnity of style is unsurpassed in Hebrew hymnology. In the strangely vacuous sublimity and the august repetitiousness of their diction they reflect marvelously the religious mood of those who conceived them. They are, indeed, outstanding paradigms of what Rudolf Otto has called "Numinous Hymns."[3]

Let me quote three short examples:

I (Chapter 2:4)

משבח ושירה של יום ויום
מגילה ורינה של עתים ועתים
ומהגיון היוצא מפי קדושים
ומניגון המתגבר מפי משרתים
הרי אש וגבעות להבה
נצברות ונגנזות ונתכות בכל־יום
כדבר שנאמר קדוש קדוש קדוש וכו'

From the praise and song of each day,
From the jubilation and exultation of each hour,
And from the utterances which proceed out of the mouth of the holy ones,
And from the melody which welleth out of the mouth of the servants,
Mountains of fire and hills of flame
Are piled up and hidden and poured out each day.

II (Chapter 7:4)

עטורי פאר, מוכתרי כתרים
מרננים עליון בשיר גילה
רוממו אתם לאדון להבה
כי בשכינת שכינה, הדר הדרי
חדרי חדריו אתם חונים
הפליא את־שמכם משם משרתיו
הבדיל אתכם ממשרתי מרכבה.
המזכיר שם אחד מכם—
אש לוהטת, להבה סובבת
שלהבת מקפת, גחלי זיו מנתזות.

O wreathed in splendor, crowned with crowns,
O chorister of Him on high,
Extol the Lord enthroned in flames
For in the presence of the Presence,

[2] All these hymns end with the *trishagion* of Isa. 6:3 and are therefore *Kedushah*-hymns. In many of them, however, this refrain is introduced quite artificially and without any reference to the text of the hymn itself.

[3] R. Otto, *The Idea of the Holy*, trans. John W. Harvey (1923), p. 34.

In the inmost glory
Of the inmost chambers
You set up your posts.
Your name He distinguished from His servant's name,
From the Chariot's servants He set you apart.
Him who the name of one of you mentions
The flame surrounds, a leaping fire,
Around him burning, glowing coals.*

III (Chapter 8:1)

מבטלי גזירה, מפירי שבועה
מעבירי חימה, משיבי קנאה
מזכירי אהבה, מסדרי ריעות
לפני הדר גאון היכל נורא:
מה לכם שאתם נוראים
ופעמים לכם שאתם שמחים
מה לכם שאתם מרננים
ופעמים לכם שאתם מבוהלים:
אמרו:
כשאופני גבורה מרכבה מקדירין
עומדים אנו בבהלה גדולה
וכשזוהרי שכינה מרכבה מאירין
אנו שמחים שמחה רבה.

O you
Who
Annul the decree, undo the oath,
Remove the wrath, avert the ire,
Recall the love, in order to set it
Before the splendor of the Temple of our Awe:
What is it with you that you fear
While there are times when you rejoice?
What is it with you that you sing
While there are times when you're aghast?
They said:
When the Ofanim of Might the Chariot overcast
In fearful dread we stand;
But when the sparks of Shekhinah the Chariot set in light
We're gay, O very gay.

While scholars had not yet formed a soundly established theory of the origin and earliest development of the liturgical poetry of the

* This and the following translation are the work of Dr. Judah Goldin, which he has kindly put at my disposal.

Synagogue, the antiquity of these hymns was vastly underrated. To the extent that they were considered at all, they were ascribed to the seventh or eighth century, if not to a later period. In view of the fact that the Palestinian *piyyut* certainly represents a later stage of development than the Hekhaloth hymns, and that we now know that the emergence of the Palestinian *piyyut* took place several centuries before the eighth, this notion has become altogether untenable. We do not have to depend upon the results of contemporary studies of the earliest *piyyutim*,[4] however, in order to determine the period in which the hymns were composed. Although the inference from such studies will be important, we have more direct testimony.

When I enlarged upon the nature and importance of these hymns in *Major Trends in Jewish Mysticism*, I still did not have the courage to date them earlier than the fifth century;[5] although I was, naturally, well aware that hymns of the angels before the throne, and especially those of the *Ḥayyoth*, the bearers of the throne, were an authentic motif of the esotericism of the Jewish apocalypticists. Such hymns are mentioned not only in the Apocalypse of John (14:2–3), but also in the Apocalypse of Abraham (Chapter 18)—a text that more closely resembles a Merkabah text than any other in Jewish apocalyptic literature.[6] The latter has even preserved (in Chapter 17) the full text of a hymn sung by the throne to God.[7] It is difficult to say, however, whether the text of this hymn as it is preserved in the Slavic version goes back to a Hebrew hymn or to a Greek one substituted for the original Hebrew. Yet even though it would seem a little

[4] Cf. J. Schirmann, "Hebrew Liturgical Poetry and Christian Hymnology," *Jewish Quarterly Review*, XLIV (1953), 123–161.

[5] *Major Trends*, pp. 57–60.

[6] Cf. the *ἄγγελοι . . . ὑμνοῦντες θεὸν ἄρρητον* in the Apocalypse of Zephania, quoted in Section III. The Hermetic book Poimandres (§ 26) has a similar idea of the hymns of the holy ones. Cf. also A.-J. Festugière, *La Révélation d'Hermès Trismégiste*, III (1953), 133–137, who quite unnecessarily assumes pagan sources for the concept although conceding the Jewish origin of the New Testament references to this idea. R. Reitzenstein, *Poimandres* (1904), pp. 292–296, has published a later text, which mentions the hymns of the Archangels received by Moses on Mount Sinai as a *phylakterion* against all evil spirits. Since a magical Archangel-book by Moses is already quoted in a Leiden papyrus of the fourth century (K. Preisendanz, *Papyri Graecae Magicae*, II [1931], 128), the reference might be to some old Jewish source parallel to the ס' שמושי תורה. Hans Bietenhard, *Die Himmlische Welt im Urchristentum und Spätjudentum* (1951), in the chapter, "der himmlische Lobgesang," pp. 137–142, knows nothing of the Hekhaloth literature.

[7] Cf. the Greater Hekhaloth, Chap. 24:1: "When he [the initiate to the Merkabah] stands before the throne of glory, he begins and recites the song that the throne of glory sings each day."

difficult to reconstruct a Hebrew text here, it is significant that a Tannaitic tradition of the second century C. E. explains the enigmatic term *Ḥashmal* (beryl) in Ezekiel 1:16 as an abbreviation of *Ḥayyoth Esh Memalleloth*, "Fiery Living Creatures who utter" (namely, words of praise);[8] for these creatures correspond exactly to the "Four Fiery Living Creatures who sing" in Chapter 18 of the Apocalypse of Abraham. Indeed, it is the very existence of this kind of material that gives us good reason to assume the existence of a continuous tradition concerning these hymns possessed, in turn, by both the apocalypticists and the Tannaim.

If we then inquire as to whether the talmudic tradition and the Hekhaloth hymnology were similarly related, an affirmative answer can now be given. In a talmudic passage of which, to the best of my knowledge, no satisfactory interpretation has yet been offered, I have been able to discover definite proof that hymns of the type preserved in the Greater Hekhaloth were surely known in the third century C. E. The passage in question is found in *'Abodah Zarah* 24b, and parallel passages in *Bereshith Rabbah*, Par. LIV, and *Seder Eliyahu Rabbah*, Chapter 12.[9] It deals with the meaning of I Samuel 6:12: "And the kine took the straight way to the way of Beth Shemesh," drawing the cart upon which the Ark of the Lord had been placed. Several talmudic sages in this passage explain the Hebrew *vayisharnah ha-paroth* by an ingenious play of words, taking *vayisharnah* as connected, not to the root *yashar* (straight on), but to the root *shir* (to sing). According to their interpretation, the kine sang a hymn of praise (אמרו שירה). The question is then raised: What was the song they sang? Some second and early third century rabbis identify their song, quite simply, with some well-known psalm (like Psalm 98) or with the Song of Moses at the crossing of the Red Sea. There is nothing particularly exciting about this exegesis.[10] R. Isaac Napḥa, however, a Palestinian Amora of the middle of the third century, ascribed to the kine a song of a very different nature. In this song the kine are said to be addressing the Ark. And this is what they sing:

[8] *Ḥagigah* 13b. Cf. also *'Abodah Zarah* 3b, where it is mentioned that God listens several hours each day to the song of the *Ḥayyoth* (יושב ושומע שירה מפי החיות).

[9] Ed. Theodor, p. 581, and ed. Friedmann, p. 68. Theodor, *loc. cit.*, has noted the various readings.

[10] R. Meir identified the song with שירת הים, R. Simeon ben Lakish with Psalm 98 (מזמורא יתמא), R. Eleazar with Psalm 99, and R. Samuel bar Naḥmani with Psalm 93.

רוני רוני השיטה[11]
התנופפי ברוב הדרך
המחושקת ברקמי זהב
המהוללה בדביר ארמון
המפוארה בעדי עדיים.[12]

Rejoice, rejoice acacia-[shrine]
Stretch forth in the fullness of thy majesty
Girdled in golden embroidery
Praised in the recesses of the palace
Resplendent in the finest of ornaments.

Now this seems to me a most significant hymn. The choice of words, the majesty of phrase, and the lyrical rhythm are strongly reminiscent of the Hekhaloth hymns I have been describing. Why did R. Isaac Napḥa put such a hymn into the mouths of the kine? The answer is as clear as it has been overlooked up to date: this is an imitation of the setting in the Hekhaloth hymns. Just as the Holy Living Creatures, bearing the throne, sing hymns to the throne, so do these kine, bearing the Ark, sing hymns to the Ark. It would be utterly unnatural to suppose that the great hymns to the throne in the Hekhaloth imitate this curious hymn of the kine, but it is perfectly reasonable to assume the contrary. As a matter of fact, we find at least two lines of this little hymn almost prefigured in two corresponding hymns preserved in the Greater Hekhaloth. The text reads: "R. Ishmael said: 'What is the wording of the songs[13] which a man must recite when he descends unto the Merkabah? He opens up and recites the beginnings of the songs.' "[14] And the very first hymn begins with the following words:

[11] Another very good reading is רומי רומי (rise, rise), instead of רוני.

[12] In *SER*, Chap. 12, the last line reads differently: המאופדת בין שני הכרובים, and similarly in *BR*, Par. LIV: המעולפת מבין שני הכרובים. *BR* quotes the lines as Elijah's teaching and does not mention Isaac Napḥa. A later reference in *Midrash Shmuel* is already full of corrupt readings and I have not used it here.

[13] The correct reading is: מה הפרש שירות. The *Hif'il*, הפריש, instead of the *Pi'el*, פרש, is used in other Merkabah texts, too. Cf. the ראיות יחזקאל, in Wertheimer, בתי מדרשות, II, 130: על תניי אני מראה לך המרכבה שלי כדי שתפריש להם לישראל. The same usage is found in the Greater Hekhaloth, Chap. 22:3: אלו שהפרשתי שמותם.

[14] פותח ואומר ראשי שירות. This seems to me a close parallel to the important statement about the procedure of the Merkabah teaching found in the *Yerushalmi*, *Ḥagigah* II, 1: כיצד הוא עושה? בתחלה רבו פותח לו ראשי פסוקים ומסכים. ראשי שירות is parallel to ראשי פסוקים and ראשי פרקים. I have considered the possibility that ראשי שירות may mean 'the main songs' or 'the summaries of the songs,' as in the Greek *κεφάλαια*, but Professor S. Lieberman has convinced me that this is an untenable proposition; cf. his forthcoming commentary on *Tosefta Shabbath* I, 12.

תחילת שבח וראשית שירה
תחילת גילה וראשית רנה
משוררים השרים המשרתים בכל־יום
ליהוה אלהי ישראל ולכסא כבודו
הם מנשאים גלגל כסא כבודו:
רנן רנן מושב עליון
הריע הריע כלי חמדה[15]
שנעשה בהפלא ופלא.
שמח תשמח מלך שעליך
כשמחת חתן בבית חופתו.

The beginning of praise and the commencement of song
The beginning of jubilation and the commencement of exultation
Are sung by the princes who serve each day
The Lord God of Israel and the throne of His glory.
They bear up the wheel of the throne of His glory, singing:
"*Rejoice, rejoice, supernal dwelling!*
Shout, shout for joy, precious vessel!
Made marvelously and a marvel.
Surely thou shalt gladden the king who sitteth upon thee
[with a joy] as the joy of the bridegroom in his bridechamber."

It is clearly to be seen that we have here a precise parallel between the throne, the supernal dwelling, and the Ark, made of acacia wood, upon which the Shekhinah rests.

In Chapter 24 of the Greater Hekhaloth there is a long hymn addressed by the throne to God as *Yoṣer Bereshith*, the term used in these texts for the creator of the world, or Demiurge. This very colorful and important hymn opens with lines that also remind us of the talmudic hymn:

מלך מפואר המעוטף בתפארת
המהודר ברקמי שיר
המעוטר בהוד והדר
עטרת גאות וכתר נוראות.

Resplendent king, robed in splendor
Glorified with embroideries of songs[16]
Crowned with magnificence and majesty
A crown of sublimity and a diadem of fearfulness.

[15] כלי חמדה as an epitheton of the throne is also found in *Merkabah Rabbah*. Cf. מרכבה שלמה, fol. 5a: אמר: עקיבא בני, כסא הכבוד זה שאני יושב עליו, כלי חמדה שהכינה ידי. The continuation of the text in מרכבה שלמה, fol. 5a–b, contains a very corrupt version of the hymn from the Greater Hekhaloth quoted above.

[16] One wonders whether the phrase רקמי שיר (parallel to the more concrete

The fact that a third century rabbi puts a hymn of this literary type into the mouths of the kine is proof that such hymns were current in his time, and perhaps for some time before. But we can go further than this. It can be distinctly shown that R. Isaac Napḥa was not only aware of a general literary type, but had a particular interest in the songs of the Heavenly Living Creatures. In *Sanhedrin* 95b he is quoted as saying of the soldiers in Sennacherib's army who were besieging Jerusalem (II Kings 19:35), that God "opened their ears and they heard the song of the Beasts [*Ḥayyoth*] and died." He was, therefore, well acquainted with the idea of heavenly songs to which only the initiate could listen without endangering his life. Moreover, his very acquaintance with this concept, which, although not recorded in the Hekhaloth texts, is perfectly consistent with their trend of ideas, confirms the impression that he was deeply steeped in Merkabah mysticism.

The conclusion to be drawn from this discussion is clear. To the extent that they represent the type of song that I have characterized, there is no reason for dating the Hekhaloth hymns later than the third century. This conclusion, of course, has tremendous implications, for then the content of these hymns, describing the world of the Merkabah, must automatically be given the same early date. It is clearly to be inferred, moreover, that this type of hymnology had its origin in Palestine.

In this connection another fact gains additional importance. One of the most famous hymns of the early Synagogue is the prayer for the New Year service ascribed to the Babylonian teacher Rab, of the first generation of Amoraim. The hymn begins with the words:

עלינו לשבח לאדון הכל
לתת גדולה ליוצר בראשית

We have to praise the Lord of all
To enhance the greatness of the *Yoṣer Bereshith*,

and not only continues in the same rhythm as many of the Merkabah hymns,[17] but uses, too, several expressions and metaphors char-

---

רקמי זהב) does not reflect the etymological meaning of the Greek word ὕμνος, *gewebte Rede*; cf. H. Ehrlich, *Rheinisches Museum*, LXII (1907), 321. If we assume that the Palestinian author of these hymns was familiar with Greek rhetoric, he might have used המהודר ברקמי שיר as a highflown phrase meaning 'glorified with hymns.' (I owe this remark to an observation made by Professor Shalom Spiegel.)

[17] These hymns consist mostly of double verses containing 4 plus 4 words, 4 plus 3 words, or 3 plus 3 words. Only some of them reveal a more complicated structure. They use the biblical *parallelismus membrorum*.

acteristic of them.[18] Since we know that Rab was an exponent of Jewish mystical traditions, which he had brought over from Palestine,[19] it is now no longer strange to find that in the alternating utterances ascribed to R. Akiba and R. Ishmael in one of the Hekhaloth writings, a large part of this prayer is put into the mouth of R. Akiba, speaking in the first person singular.[20] I do not argue that this is an authentic tradition going back to Akiba, but I do maintain that it is extremely significant that the Merkabah mystics who composed and compiled these hymns in the third and fourth centuries could consider the *'Alenu* hymn as related to their own hymnology.

The fact that both the type of hymn found in the talmudic passage discussed above and the *'Alenu* belong to the third century, in addition to the fact that earlier rabbis mentioned in the same passage do not seem to be acquainted with this kind of hymnology, allows us to surmise that it only evolved in the third century, superceding those earlier forms referred to in the apocalyptic literature. This lack of awareness of the parallel between the song of the kine and the Hekhaloth hymns is especially notable in the case of R. Meir, for this teacher was positively attracted by speculations about the seven heavens and the realm of the divine throne. It is he to whom the Baraitha about the seven heavens is attributed in *Aboth de Rabbi Nathan* (Chapter 37); and it is he who compared the blue color of the fringes (ציצית) to that of the sea, the heaven, and, finally, the throne of glory (*Sotah* 17a). But, after all, this amounts to an *argumentum e silentio*, and I offer it with all due reservation. I think,

[18] Such as יוצר בראשית, מושב יקרו, and שכינת עוזו. To יוצר בראשית, cf. the Greater Hekhaloth, Chap. 22:4, and *Shiur Komah* in מרכבה שלמה, fol. 38b (where R. Abraham ben David, ראב"ד, still had the correct reading: שיעורו של יוצר בראשית; cf. the writer's ראשית הקבלה [1948], p. 76). To מושב יקרו, cf. מסכת היכלות, published under the title מעשה מרכבה by Wertheimer in בתי מדרשות, I, 56: כסא הכבוד מתוקן למושב יקרו, and *Shiur Komah* in מרכבה שלמה, fol. 32a–b and 34a: מבית מותב יקריה ולעילא קי"ח אלף פרסאות. It is also mentioned in two other hymns, both of the Hekhaloth type. In מרכבה שלמה, fol. 41b (=ס' רזיאל [1701], fol. 39a), there is a hymn that reads:

ברוך שמו במושב הדרו
ומבורך בתפארת עזו.

And in a hymn preserved in the מדרש אלפא ביתות, in Wertheimer, בתי מדרשות, II, 423, we find:

שם מרכבתו על גלגלי אוכלה
ומושב יקרו על כרובי להבה.

שכינת עוזו is found in the Lesser Hekhaloth, MS Oxford 1531, fol. 42b: ושכינת עוזו בין פיסת יד.

[19] Cf. W. Bacher, *Die Agada der babylonischen Amoräer*, (*zweite Auflage*; 1913), pp. 16–21.

[20] Cf. the text in Appendix C—from MS Oxford 1531, fol. 51a–b (§ 5).

however, that we need not have such reservations with regard to the main point of my contention, to wit, that such a highly important stratum as the hymnology of the Hekhaloth belongs to the early talmudic period.

It remains to be seen whether this style of angelic hymnology has some historical connection with the Dead Sea Scrolls. In a summary report on the small fragments of many of the scrolls, published in 1956, it is said that some of them contain a "type de liturgie angélique (peut-etre associé à une forme ancienne de la vision de la Merkabah)."[21] It will be of great importance if this claim should be substantiated by forthcoming publications from the fragments. As a matter of fact, several years before this report was published Professor Saul Lieberman ventured the suggestion that the hymn in *'Abodah Zarah* 24b (the relation of which to the Merkabah hymns had not yet been indicated) could, according to the style and choice of words, be connected with some documents belonging to the Dead Sea sectarians.[22]

Regarding the probability of a relationship between the angelic hymns in the Hekhaloth and those in older texts of Jewish character, one more detail to be found in both the earlier and the later hymns may be mentioned. In the description of the celestial *Kedushah* (Isaiah 6:3) preserved in the Hekhaloth texts, we read:

> The Holy Living Creatures do strengthen and hallow and purify themselves, and each one has bound upon its head a thousand thousands of thousands of crowns of luminaries of divers sorts, and they are clothed in clothing of fire and wrapped in a garment of flame and cover their faces with lightning. And the Holy One, Blessed be He, uncovers His face. And why do the Holy Living Creatures and the Ophanim of majesty and the Cherubim of splendor hallow and purify and clothe and wrap and adorn themselves yet more? Because the Merkabah is above them and the throne of glory upon their heads and the Shekhinah over them and rivers of fire pass between them. Accordingly do they strengthen themselves and make themselves splendid and purify themselves in fire seventy times and do all of them stand in cleanliness and holiness and sing songs and hymns, praise and rejoicing and applause, with one voice, with one utterance, with one mind, and with one melody.[23]

[21] *Revue Biblique*, LXIII (1956), 65.

[22] S. Lieberman, *Procedings of the American Academy for Jewish Research*, XX (1951), 404: "Certainly this style is not what we generally identify as rabbinic."

[23] MS J. Th. Sem. 828, fol. 8a in a MS of היכלות רבתי. Menaḥem Recanati, פירוש התפילות, fol. 38a, quotes this piece from ספר היכלות. The last sentence reads in Hebrew: וכולם עומדים בטהרה ובקדושה ואומרים שירה וזמרה שבח וצהלה וקולם בקול אחד בדבור אחד בדעת אחת ובנעימה אחת.

Now this idea of their singing "with one voice"[24] already occurs in the Ascension of Isaiah in Chapters 7:15, 8:18, and 9:28. These chapters belong, to be sure, to the Christian part of this apocalypse, but there is good reason to assume that the angelology used was of a Jewish character. And, in fact, that the angels sing in this manner is also mentioned in the Slavic Enoch (19:6), in which I, for one, cannot detect any Christian elements. Moreover, it would seem that the same detail was taken over both by the Hekhaloth traditions and by the earliest Christian liturgy. In one of the oldest hymns introducing the main mystery of the Mass, all kinds of angels, cherubim, and serafim praise God's glory, *quia non cessant clamare cotidie, una voce dicentes: Sanctus Sanctus Sanctus Dominus Deus Sabaoth, etc.*[25]

[24] קול אחד in this sense is good Hebrew. Cf. שמות רבה, Par. XLII, 1: כאילו בקול אחד.

[25] Quoted by Joseph Kroll, *Die Lehren des Hermes Trismegistos* (1928), p. 309.

V

SOME OLD ELEMENTS IN THE GREATER HEKHALOTH

The Hekhaloth books, I have said, describe at great length the ecstatic ascent of the soul to heaven. Although the details of this ascent in the Greater Hekhaloth differ in many ways from those in the Lesser ones, it is difficult to decide whether either of these two texts represents an earlier stage of tradition or whether both are parallel versions of only slightly different groups. Still, both texts together present us with such an abundance of particulars, in contradistinction to the talmudic material, that we begin to wonder about the relation of these Hekhaloth traditions to the talmudic injunction against precisely this kind of revelation. Tannaitic tradition has it that a pupil who is found worthy to begin a study of mystical lore is given *Rashei Perakim* only.[1] Instead of these "beginnings of chapters," whose function is only to point to the subject matter to be dealt with and leaves to the student the task of proving his understanding, the Hekhaloth texts omit nothing at all that is relevant. We may safely say that such an additional step indicates a post-Tannaitic composition, even though much of the material itself may belong to the Tannaitic period—which, of course, was, at the same time, the flowering season of Gnosticism.

Particularly fine examples of the kind of detail I refer to can be found in Chapters fourteen to twenty-one of the Greater Hekhaloth, which set forth an extremely specific, even meticulous, account of a mystical ascent. The Palestinian character of these chapters is unmistakable, both in language and background. Such, for example, is the use of the Hippodrome in Caesarea as a measure for the size of the mangers set before the fiery horses of heaven that serve the gate-keepers. These gate-keepers stand in their places,

> angry and war-like, strong, harsh, fearful, terrific, taller than mountains and sharper than peaks. Their bows are strung and stand before them; their swords are sharpened and in their hands. Lightnings flow and issue forth from the balls of their eyes, and balls of fire from their nostrils, and torches of fiery coals from their mouths. They are equipped with helmets and

[1] Cf. n. 14, Section IV.

> with coats of mail, and javelins and spears are hung upon their thews . . . the horses upon which they ride stand beside mangers of fire full of coals of juniper and eat fiery coals from the mangers, [taking] a measure of forty bushels of coals in one mouthful. And the measure of the [content of the] mouth of each horse is [the content of] three mangers such as a manger of Caesarea, and the measure of each manger is the measure of the gate of Caesarea; and there are rivers of fire beside the mangers, and their horses drink as a measure of the fullness of the water-pipe which is in the Valley of Kidron which brings and contains all the rain water of all Jerusalem.[2]

The "fiery horses" seem to be an elaboration of the horses who carried the prophet Elijah up to heaven, and the forbidding aspect of their appearance reflects the dangerous passage that awaits the adept, especially at the seventh and last palace. As for the Hippodrome, although it is known from Josephus,[3] it is never, as far as I know, mentioned in talmudic or midrashic literature. This illustration, like the one about the Valley of Kidron, is, therefore, not based on a literary source, but on a concrete Palestinian reality known to the writer.

After passing through the seven heavens, the mystic must penetrate the seven resplendent palaces of the seventh heaven itself before arriving at the throne of God and attaining the vision of the man-like figure seated upon the throne of glory (Ezekiel 1:26). I shall have more to say about this figure presently. But before we, too, arrive at this final vision, it should be remarked that some of the details of the pilgrimage of the soul in ecstasy, all of which are highly formal and very technical, are also known to us from other Gnostic texts. For example, all the different versions of the Hekhaloth lay great emphasis upon the knowledge of various seals (חותמות), described as magical names either of the angels or of aspects of the godhead, that must be shown as passports to the gate-keepers at the entrances to the seven palaces.[4] Seals closely paralleling these are to be found in

[2] Chap. 15:8: ובפתח היכל שביעי זעופין ועומדים כל הגיבורים, עריצים, עזים וקשים, נוראים ומבוהלין, גבוהים מהרים ולטושין מגבעות, קשתותם דרוכות והן בפניהם, חרבותם לטושות והן בידיהם, וברקים טורדים ויוצאים מגלגלי עיניהם וכוכיות של אש מחוטמיהם ולפידי גחלים מפיהם, וכובעים ושיריונות הן מעוטרין, ורמחים וחניתות תלויין להם בזרועותיהם.

Chap. 16:1: סוסים שרוכבים עליהם עומדים על אבוסי אש מלאים גחלי רתמים ואוכלים גחלים מתוך אבוסיהם כשעור ארבעים סאה גחלים בפה אחד. ושעור פה כל סוס וסוס שלשה אבוסים מאבוסיה של קיסרי ושעור כל אבוס כשעור פתח של קיסרי. ונהרי אש בצד אבוסיהם והיו שותים כל סוסיהם כשעור מלוא אמת המים שיש בנחל קדרון שמוציאה ומחזקת כל מימי גשמים של כל ירושלים.

[3] Josephus, *Antiquities*, xvi.5.1.

[4] Cf. the passages on חותמות in היכלות רבתי, Chaps. 17–19. היכלות זוטרתי, MS Oxford 1531, fol. 44a has: א״ר עקיבא: חזור ותפוס לך שמות שבעת שרים . . . וחיתומיהן, שם

the Coptic Gnostic sources coming from the Valentinian school, such as the Pistis Sophia and, especially, the books of Jeû.[5] The Coptic manuscripts, however, still retain geometric figures of a rather complicated structure (strangely reminiscent of mental images used in some yoga techniques and called *yantras*), which were to be impressed upon the mind and produced at the right moment together with the mystical names. The Hebrew manuscripts have no longer preserved this part of the description.

In other sources of Valentinian Gnosis, particularly those of the school of Markos, the soul, as it journeys through the seven heavens, has recourse also to Aramaic formulae in a Greek context as a means of appeasing the inimical powers of the Demiurge. In similar manner, the Hebrew text of the Hekhaloth makes use of Greek formulae to describe the interchange of formal greetings between the archons at the highest gates and the soul.[6] Furthermore, the archon, or ruler, at the sixth hall, who in one aspect goes by the name of Dumiel ("the mystical silence [*dumiyah*] permeating the palaces"), is at the same time the ruler of the four elements, and in this aspect goes by a secret name, the etymology of which can still be clearly recognized. We cannot say as much for most of these names, which give the impression, rather, of having been born, not from some natural language, but by a process of glossolalia. Suppressed emotion is released in a stream of mystical language—names and words that resemble only in a vague way the general tenor of known languages such as Greek, Hebrew, or Coptic. But in the instance to which I refer, such is not the case. The name אבירגהידרפיר was obviously composed from the Greek names of the four elements, *aèr*, *gè*, *hýdor*, *pýr*.[7] The Hebrew transliteration of *aèr* as אביר instead of אויר[8] represents the Palestinian manner of transliteration.

The point I wish to make is this: In the few details I have described,

---

כל אחד ואחד אתָ מראה לו חותמו והוא מכניס אותך להיכלו. But in the detailed description we always read the phrase: אתה מראה לו חותם וטבעת שחקוק עליה [then the name follows]. In another text (to be found in Appendix C) from MS Oxford 1531, fol. 53a, we read יכוין לבו בתפלתו ויחתום עצמו בחותמות שלו; fol. 54a: א"ר ישמעאל: ז' חותמות חתמתי עצמי בשעה שירד פרקדס מלאך הפנים. Cf. also מרכבה רבה in מרכבה שלמה, fol. 1b: יפתח וישביע כי נתחזק וחתם [צ"ל ויחתום] עצמו בשם של מ"ב אותיות.

[5] Cf. on some aspects of these contacts between the Coptic Gnostic writings and their Hekhaloth counterparts, the writer's article "Über eine Formel in den koptisch-gnostischen Schriften und ihren jüdischen Ursprung," *Zeitschrift für die neutestamentliche Wissenschaft*, XXX (1931), 170–176.

[6] Cf. *Major Trends*, p. 362.

[7] The manuscripts read אבירגהידרהים. In the היכלות זוטרתי the last element (הים instead of פיר) has become יהו, an element of the Tetragrammaton.

[8] Cf. J. Hans Lewy in *Tarbiz*, XII (1941), 163–167.

we have demonstrable proof of contact with non-Jewish conceptions; and every analysis of these texts furnishes still more material of the same character. But it is essential to note that this contact is always with Hellenistic (specifically, Hellenistic-Egyptian) elements, and that not a single Christian element appears in them. There is no reason whatever to assume that Christian descriptions of such ascents to heaven have been judaized. The logical conclusion seems to be, given the historical circumstances, that, initially, Jewish esoteric tradition absorbed Hellenistic elements similar to those we actually find in Hermetic writings. Such elements entered Jewish tradition before Christianity developed, or at any rate before Christian Gnosticism as a distinctive force came into being. Later, when Judaism and Christianity finally parted ways, these elements, whose development, once borrowed, had been within and in the manner of a distinctly Jewish esotericism, were taken over into Christianity and into early Gnostic circles, rather than the reverse. It is difficult to assume that during the period of extreme strain between the Synagogue and the Church in the second century, Jews who were bent upon keeping their distinctly Jewish character would borrow from Christian circles. And indeed, as I have said, there is no evidence for such borrowings. The contrary, however, would be easily explained by the steady stream of converts from Judaism into Christianity, some of whom could have been recipients of Jewish esoteric doctrine. I shall return to this point, to which I attach much relevance, at a later stage.[9]

The process of development just outlined would explain such facts, as, for instance, the presence of obviously Jewish elements of esoteric teaching in the *Excerpta ex Theodoto*, a collection made by Clement of Alexandria from the writings of one of the outstanding pupils of the Gnostic Valentine. The Jewish elements in these fragments, curiously overlooked by the two scholars who have edited and commented upon them in our generation,[10] clearly represent a deterioration of the Jewish tradition, which has here been partly misunderstood or reinterpreted and partly put into false contexts. It is as a result of this process that the Demiurge (which is, for the Gnostic, in a

[9] See the end of Section VI.

[10] Robert Casey, *The Excerpta ex Theodoto* (1933) and Marc Sagnard, *Les Extraits de Théodote* (1949). Some of these Jewish elements have been rightly pointed out by Henri Marrou in *Revue du Moyen Age Latin*, V (1949), 169. §§ 37–39 of the *Excerpta* are all soaked with Merkabah mysticism. From a comparison of § 38 with § 62 it becomes clear that in the Jewish material that was used, the terms ὁ τόπος (=המקום) and ὁ δημιουργός (=יוצר בראשית) were identical. This, of course, is what would be expected in a non-dualistic Jewish source.

pejorative sense, identical with the God of Israel) comes to be called in these fragments "the Space." This phrase is nothing but a Greek translation of one of the most outstanding Jewish designations of God, and one which came into general use in the first century before Christianity sprang up.[11] The use in the *Excerpta* has no other parallel in literature but this one. Nor is there any other parallel in literature of the use in the *Excerpta* of the stream of fire that issues forth from beneath the throne (*θρόνος τοῦ τόπου*; corresponding to the Hebrew כסאו של מקום) and flows down unto Gehenna, which reads exactly like the corresponding talmudic statement in *Ḥagigah* 13b; or for the concept of the curtain hung before the throne of God to prevent the pneumatic elements from being annihilated by His sight. This curtain is frequently mentioned and described in some detail in the Hekhaloth literature;[12] but what in the Hekhaloth refers to the highest possible sphere to which the mystic may attain, in the Christian Gnostic text is relegated to a rather lower realm in the hierarchy of supernal beings.

[11] Cf. the analysis by A. Spanier, "Die Gottesbezeichnungen המקום and הקדוש ברוך הוא in der fruhtalmudischen Literatur," *MGWJ*, LXVI (1922), 309–314, and by A. Marmorstein, *The Old Rabbinic Doctrine of God*, I (London, 1927), 108–147. Philo, *de somniis*, I, 63, and *de fuga*, 75, uses *topos* as an allegorical designation of God Himself. But these are isolated instances, caused by the exegetical context and needs of Philo's homilies, and do not reflect general usage on Philo's part.

[12] On this פרגוד, cf. *Major Trends*, pp. 72 and 367; A. Marmorstein's references in *Jahrbuch für Jüdische Volkskunde*, II (1925), 379; and Odeberg, *3 Enoch*, on Chap. 45 of the text, p. 142. In the אותיות דר' עקיבא the curtain is called פרגוד של מקום, the same phraseology as in *θρόνος τοῦ τόπου*. Cf. Jellinek's text in בית המדרש, III, 44; but Wertheimer in בתי מדרשות, II, 388, has: פרגוד של הקדוש ברוך הוא.

VI

THE AGE OF *SHIUR KOMAH* SPECULATION AND A PASSAGE IN ORIGEN

At the end of his journey the Merkabah mystic beholds not only a vision of the world of the Merkabah and the throne of God, but also a vision of Him who sits upon that throne—a vision in which He appears to the mystic in "a likeness as the appearance of a man [Ezekiel 1:26]." Whereas all the other visions are of things created, however high their rank, this final vision is of the divine glory itself. The doctrine which grew up around this vision, the doctrine of the mystical "body of God," *Shiur Komah*, is of special importance in establishing the antiquity of some parts of the Hekhaloth writings.

The doctrine is contained in a fragment of a most puzzling character, the age of which has been the subject of much dispute. It appears, like all these texts, in a pseudepigraphical setting, and is attributed to Tannaitic authorities of the second century, especially R. Akiba and R. Ishmael, to whom it was said to have been revealed.[1] It consists of the description of the limbs of God in the figure of a man and reads like a deliberate and excessive indulgence in anthropomorphism. Small wonder that it has deeply shocked later and more sober Jewish thought. Small wonder also that it was hailed by the Kabbalists of the Middle Ages as the profound symbolic expression of the mysteries of what could be called the Kabbalistic *pleroma*.[2] Jewish apologetics has always tried to explain it away.[3] The measurements

[1] Two parallel versions of שעור קומה are published in מרכבה שלמה: a) fol. 32a–33b, in the name of R. Akiba; b) fol. 34a–43a (several fragments), in the name of R. Ishmael. A large portion of these latter fragments are hymns and prayers the relation of which to שעור קומה is doubtful, but which do belong to the Hekhaloth literature. Another fragment attributed to R. Akiba is to be found on fol. 44a–b. Some fragments of Akiba's שעור קומה are also to be found in היכלות זוטרתי. The oldest manuscript known to me is a Genizah fragment in Oxford, Hebr. C 65 (not catalogued in Cowley's), which consists of one leaf, partly damaged, and written in the eleventh century. The original full text of this MS corresponded to מרכבה שלמה, fol. 36a–40b, and contained much better readings. See also the old פירוש on *Shiur Komah* in the writer's ראשית הקבלה, pp. 212–238 (based on the text current in Germany in the thirteenth century).

[2] Cf. the general characterization of these fragments in *Major Trends*, pp. 63–67, which I presuppose here.

[3] A. Schmiedl, *Studien über jüdische, insbesondere jüdisch-arabische Religionsphilosophie* (1869), pp. 249–251.

of every limb, and, especially, of the most minute parts of the head are given; and at the same time we are instructed in the secret names of each limb, names which are constructed of seemingly incomprehensible combinations of letters.[4] The whole doctrine is linked, not only in the separate fragment of it that has come down to us under the title *Shiur Komah* (literally, "The measurement of the body"), but also in the small fragment incorporated into the Greater Hekhaloth,[5] to the description of the figure of the lover in the Song of Songs: "My beloved is white and ruddy . . . his head is as most fine gold, his locks are curled and black as a raven. His eyes are like doves, etc. [5:11–16]"[6] Almost all the extant texts of the Hekhaloth books contain some more or less outspoken reference to this doctrine, which is further embellished by several allusions to a *ḥaluk* (garment), a robe of glory with which this mystical body of God is apparently clothed (and about which I shall say something in Section VIII).

The question that concerns us is this: Is this doctrine, which gives a bodily appearance to the *Kabod*, 'the glory of God' (also described as the גוף השכינה, 'the body of the Shekhinah'), an early ingredient of Jewish mystical teaching later adopted by some Christian Gnostic circles? Or is it a later recrudescence of an extravagant anthropomorphism of which the earlier mystical tradition of the rabbis of the first and second centuries is innocent? It is true, of course, that a close parallel to the *Shiur Komah* is to be found in the Gnostic Markos' description of the "Body of Truth" (σῶμα τῆς ἀληθείας). This text, written in the latter part of the second century, has impressed many readers as giving some older symbolism an allegorical interpretation of a rather Kabbalistic character.[7] But the source from which Markos could possibly have gotten the material he interpreted accord-

[4] The Genizah fragment of שעור קומה seems to have retained these *ephesia grammata* in much better shape. Sometimes the structure of a name that is hopelessly corrupt in the later MSS is still clearly recognizable; e. g. the name of the right arm is here גבדהוזיא and is obviously constructed on an alphabetic principle, like the names of the limbs in the fragments of Markos the Gnostic. The printed version (מרכבה שלמה, fol. 37b, l. 14) has גברהזזיא.

[5] היכלות רבתי, Chap. 10; מרכבה שלמה, fol. 38a; היכלות זוטרתי, MS Oxford 1531, fol. 45a.

[6] This explains the fact that God is called in several of these fragments by the specific name *Jedidiah*, as for example, ידידיה מרי עלמא (in היכלות רבתי), or ידידות (in מרכבה שלמה, fol. 34b; cf. also the writer's ראשית הקבלה, p. 221). ידידיה also appears in היכלות זוטרתי, MS Oxford 1531, fol. 43a.

[7] Irenaeus, *Adversus Haeres.*, I.14.2. The names of the limbs are αω, βψ, etc., i. e. אתב"ש—combinations! Cf. also Moses Gaster, "Das Schiur Komah," in his *Studies and Texts*, II, 1330–1353, particularly p. 1344. Gaster, many mistakes notwithstanding, was basically right in his defense of a high age for the שעור קומה.

ing to his own fancy has remained an unsolved riddle. This problem can now be resolved, in my opinion, in favor of our first hypothesis, to wit, that the teachings of the *Shiur Komah* do indeed represent a second century Jewish tradition.

The existence of this tradition in that period is attested to by Origen in a curious passage in the introduction to his commentary on the Song of Songs; and I wish here to offer my own interpretation of this passage. Origen writes:[8]

> It is said that the custom of the Jews is that no one who has not reached full maturity is permitted to hold this book in his hands. And not only this, but although their rabbis and teachers are wont to teach all the scriptures and their oral traditions [*Mishnayoth*; Origen uses the Greek term *deuteroses*] to the young boys, they defer to the last [in the original: *ad ultimum reservari*] the following four texts: The beginnings of Genesis, where the creation of the world is described; the beginning of the prophecy of Ezekiel, where the doctrine of the angels is expounded [in the original: *de cherubim refertur*]; the end [of the same book] which contains the description of the future temple; and this book of the Song of Songs.

There is no doubt but that this quotation refers to the fact that esoteric teachings were connected with the four texts enumerated. We know from the Mishnah that the creation and the first chapter of Ezekiel were considered texts of esoteric character par excellence, and were, therefore, forbidden to be taught publicly or before a man had reached a distinguished station in life.[9] With reference to the last chapters of Ezekiel, it is possible that these chapters could have been linked to apocalyptic speculations, and the fact that they obviously contradict statements about the temple formulated in the Torah would naturally have tended to limit their study. It may well be, although we have no definite knowledge, that the contradictions between the two sources were resolved in some kind of esoteric teaching. On the other hand, the book of Canticles was interpreted by the Synagogue as an allegory of the love between God and the Community of Israel and was considered a legitimate text for study for all groups. It was, in fact, a favorite subject for the public aggadic teachings of the rabbis in the second and third centuries.

Thus far, no satisfactory explanation has been offered for Origen's

[8] "Prologus in Canticum," in *Patrologia Latina*, ed. Migne, XIII, 63. What I call the original is, of course, the Latin translation of the lost Greek text.

[9] *Ḥagigah* 13a; cf. the condition laid down in *Kiddushin* 71a for the transmission of the Tetragrammaton (another piece of secret lore), where the candidate is required to be עומד בחצי ימיו.

inclusion of this book in his list. A. Marmorstein and S. Lieberman have tried to interpret it in the light of some much later midrashim of a pseudepigraphical character that would place the study of the Song of Songs in the same category as the study of the Merkabah, and that state that it was no longer fit for public study during the period of Exile because the handmaid (meaning the Christian Church) had usurped the place of the mistress (the Community of Israel).[10] Saul Lieberman has rightly observed that this must be understood as a reference to the fact that the Church had begun, in the third century, to interpret the Song of Songs as an allegory of the love of Christ and the Church. While Lieberman's interpretation holds good for these later pseudepigraphical statements, it can hardly be accepted as an explanation of Origen's original statement. Origen refers to something current in Jewish usage; but the rabbis before his time could not have known about a Christological interpretation of Canticles that might have caused them to declare the book unfit for general study. They could not have known of such a Christological interpretation for the simple reason that it gained acceptance in the Church only through Origen's famous commentary itself.[11] We cannot assume that the Synagogue in the second century, or at the beginning of the third century, could have relegated a book to oblivion because it was given a Christological interpretation that actually came into general use only at a later time.

It seems to me, therefore, that Origen's statement calls for another explanation. I have said that the Song of Songs—because it contained a detailed description of the limbs of the lover, who was identified with God—became the basic scriptural text upon which the doctrine of *Shiur Komah* leaned. But it is clear that the authors of our fragments of *Shiur Komah*, instead of interpreting the Song of Songs as an allegory within the framework of the generally accepted midrashic interpretations, saw it as a strictly esoteric text containing sublime and tremendous mysteries regarding God in His appearance upon the throne of the Merkabah. Indeed, by virtue of these strange revelations *Shiur Komah* comes to be considered, in the fragments that

[10] These midrashim are quoted from unknown sources in a Hebrew and Arabic commentary on Canticles from the thirteenth or fourteenth century that was published by M. Friedlaender in *Festschrift zum 80. Geburtstage Moritz Steinschneiders* (1896), Hebrew Section, pp. 52–53. Cf. A. Marmorstein, "Deux Renseignements d'Origène concernant les Juifs," *REJ*, LXXI (1920), 195–199; and Saul Liberman, מדרשי תימן (Jerusalem, 1940), pp. 13–17.

[11] Hippolytus of Rome interpreted Canticles in a similar vein some time before Origen, but his work never gained the authority of the latter's commentary; cf. Friedrich Ohly, *Hohelied-Studien* (Wiesbaden, 1958), p. 15.

have been preserved, as the deepest chapter opened up to the Merkabah mystic for his inspection and speculation. For, as the Lesser Hekhaloth puts it, *Shiur Komah* speaks of "God who is beyond the sight of His creatures and hidden from the angels who minister to Him; but who has revealed Himself to R. Akiba in the vision of the Merkabah."[12] R. Ishmael and R. Akiba are even made to promise the initiate, who is encouraged to study this "Mishnah" every day after his prayer,[13] that "Whoever knows the measurements of our Creator and the Glory of the Holy One, praise be to Him, which are hidden from the creatures, is certain of his share of the world to come."[14]

The Song of Songs, then, in order to have been included in Origen's list, must have been known in Palestine in his time, and even for some time before, as a text linked to esoteric teachings about the appearance of the Divinity; just as, in general, the doctrine of the Merkabah was linked with the first chapter of Ezekiel. Moreover, if it is thus true that Origen's statement and our fragments of *Shiur Komah* explain each other, there can no longer be any valid reason to assign a late date to the sources from which these fragments derive.[15]

The only conclusion to be reached from these analyses is that at least three particularly important parts of the Hekhaloth literature must be acribed to either the Tannaitic or the early Amoraic period. These three parts, or, rather, strata, are:

1. The description of the ascent to heaven and its dangers, connected with the talmudic passage concerning the four who entered paradise.
2. The celestial hymns preserved in the Greater Hekhaloth.
3. The *Shiur Komah.*

Moreover, in the light of the foregoing remarks, we may even draw some further conclusions. S. Lieberman was the first scholar who saw that a Baraitha quoted in the treatise *Bekhoroth* 44a, according to which the length of the nose is like the length of the little finger, was identical with a statement in the main fragment of the

[12] Lesser Hekhaloth, MS Oxford 1531, fol. 45b.

[13] המשנה הזו שנה אותה בכל יום אחר התפילה; in the Lesser Hekhaloth, *ibid.*, fol. 45a.

[14] מרכבה שלמה, fol. 38b.

[15] Professor S. Lieberman has kindly put at my disposal a searching study of Tannaitic and early talmudic statements concerning Canticles as an esoteric text, which can be found as Appendix D to this volume. His contribution greatly strengthens the view of the Tannaitic origin of the *Shiur Komah* Gnosis taken in these pages.

Shiur Komah.[16] As long as the age of the *Shiur Komah* could not be determined, this could be explained as a mere coincidence or, perhaps, as a quotation from the Baraitha in the *Shiur Komah.* With our present knowledge, however, we may assume that the true relation of the two passages is just the reverse. That is to say, the application of this rule about the nose in a halakhic context was but a quotation from the *Shiur Komah*, the composition of which preceded the talmudic speaker, who quotes it, quite rightly, as a Baraitha.

It may be appropriate to observe here as well that the Judeo-Christian, possibly Ebionitic, source of the Pseudo-Clementinian Homilies knows of a similar teaching according to which God has bodily form (*morphē*).[17] Again, this Judeo-Christian tradition and the *Shiur Komah* explain each other. It may therefore be surmised that the Gnostic Markos took the variant of the *Shiur Komah* that he used for his doctrine of the "Body of Truth" from sources of a strictly Jewish character.

A criterion for the time at which such Jewish Gnostic traditions were taken over by non-Jews, and especially by Christian Gnostics, is furnished by the following facts. I have shown in *Major Trends in Jewish Mysticism* that Jewish speculation about Metatron as the highest angel who bears, in a way, the name of God, and who is called יהוה הקטן or אדני הקטן (the Lesser Tetragrammaton), was preceded by an earlier stage in which this Angel of High was not called Metatron, but Jahoel; a fact which explains the talmudic references to Metatron much more convincingly than any of the older attempts.[18] (The statement that Metatron "has a name like the name of his Master"[19] is incomprehensible except when it is understood to refer to the name Jahoel). Now, whereas this Jewish speculation about Jahoel was taken over by early Christian tradition and by those pagan circles in Egypt, strongly influenced by Jewish esoteric traditions, who have left us the magical papyri,[20] the metamorphosis of Jahoel into Metatron has left no imprint on Christian speculation or on those syncretistic magical recipes and incantations as we have them in Greek and

[16] מרכבה שלמה, fol. 38a. Cf. Saul Lieberman, שקיעין (Jerusalem, 1939), p. 12. The *Shiur Komah* fragment reads: אורך החוטם כאורך אצבע קטנה.

[17] *Pseudo-Clementian Homilies*, ed. Rehm (1953), p. 59 (3:7), and especially pp. 232–233 (17:7–8).

[18] *Major Trends*, pp. 68–69.

[19] *Sanhedrin* 38b: מטטרון ששמו כשם רבו.

[20] Forms like Jaoel, Joel, and Jael all represent the same name. The origin of the name might be traced to a period when יהו was still used as an independent name of God. In the Elephantine papyri we frequently find the combination יהו אלהא. From this form to יהואל was a short step.

Coptic. There can be no doubt, for instance, that the concept of Jahoel as we find it in Chapter 10 of the Apocalypse of Abraham[21] was an esoteric one and belonged to the mystical teachings on angelology and the Merkabah. The borrowings from esoteric Judaism about Jahoel must have been made, therefore, before the metamorphosis into Metatron took place. This brings us back again into the late first or early second century and makes a case for connecting the Hekhaloth strata of the late second or early third century with this even earlier stage of Jewish Gnosticism, one which was striving equally hard to maintain a strictly monotheistic character. The continuity of tradition at these several stages is, consequently, to be taken into account no less than the fact that novel elements, too, made their appearance.

[21] In this Jewish book he is said to be the guide of Abraham, in the same fashion in which Metatron is R. Ishmael's guide in the Hebrew Book of Enoch, and is defined by the same formula that is later used in connection with Metatron: "a power in virtue of the ineffable Name that is dwelling in me." The context of the book plainly contradicts Box's assumption that "the name Yahoel (Jaoel) is evidently a substitute for the ineffable name Yahweh, the writing out of which in full was forbidden." Cf. G. H. Box, *The Apocalypse of Abraham* (1919), p. 46.

VII

SOME REMARKS ON METATRON AND AKATRIEL

I have mentioned the concept of Metatron and I should like at this point to add some further remarks concerning this angel. It is a curious fact that although the only three passages of the Babylonian Talmud which mention Metatron[1] do not use the term "Lesser Jaho" or "Jao" in describing him, they can best be explained by presupposing this idea. Since the idea of the "Lesser Jaho" appears not only in the Hekhaloth literature, especially where it deals with Metatron, but also in Coptic Gnostic literature (as has been shown by Odeberg[2]), it must date back to the early stage of Metatron speculation, when such speculation was still concerned with the angel Jahoel. Incidentally, it should also be noted here that although the three talmudic passages about Metatron recur in the Book of Hekhaloth (also called the Hebrew Book of Enoch), no use is ever made, in this and similar texts, of the passage in *Siphre* on Deuteronomy 34:4 (§338) that has frequently been quoted in modern discussions of the function of Metatron and the meaning of his name.[3] I think there can be no doubt that the interpretation according to which "The Finger of God became a Metatron to Moses and showed him the whole land of Israel," is a medieval misunderstanding of a good text. The original text has no relation whatsoever to the idea of Metatron.[4] If there had been a Tannaitic tradition to the effect that

[1] Cf. סנהדרין 38b; חגיגה 15a; and עבודה זרה 3b.

[2] Odeberg, *3 Enoch*, pp. 188–192. The references to the appellative יהוה הקטן in the literature of the Hekhaloth are numerous. Cf. Odeberg, *op. cit.*, p. 33, and the writer's remarks in *Major Trends*, p. 366.

[3] Odeberg, in his Introduction to *3 Enoch*, pp. 91–92, and the scholars quoted by him in connection with the discussion of the name Metatron, pp. 127–131. Odeberg's contention that Chaps. 41–48 of 3 Enoch are paralleled in the passage in *Siphre* both in "ideas and mode of expression" is more than doubtful. The text of the passage, established by him as "evidently the right reading," has no critical value; cf. the apparatus in Louis Finkelstein's critical edition of the *Siphre* (1939), *ad loc.*, p. 388.

[4] אצבעו של הקב"ה היתה לו מטטרון למשה. Here מטטרון is just another spelling for the well-known word מטטור or מטטורין. In Latin or Greek words in rabbinic texts the plural is frequently used instead of the singular. There is nothing in the authentic sayings about Metatron that justifies the derivation of the name from *Metator*, which, however, was the etymology accepted (or introduced) by the medieval German Ḥasidim and the Kabbalists.

Metatron had shown the Land of Israel to Moses before his death, the author of the Book of Hekhaloth, which deals extensively with all aspects of the concept of Metatron, would certainly not have neglected to make use of it; as, in fact, he did make use of the other, authentic talmudic statements. The highly forced interpretations of Odeberg notwithstanding, this passage has to be excluded from every serious discussion of the meaning of Metatron.

Equally misleading are Odeberg's oversimplified assertions identifying Metatron with the Prince of the World (שר העולם). It is well-known that in the talmudic and midrashic passages that mention the "Prince of the World" he is never identified with, or even brought into relation to, Metatron. Passages like *Yebamoth* 16b and others, which attribute certain biblical verses to the Prince of the World, are never mentioned in Merkabah literature. In fact, the sources for the identification with Metatron mentioned (and rejected) in the *Tosafoth* to *Yebamoth* and alluded to by Maimonides[5] have been a matter of speculation.[6] It is Odeberg's contention that one of the fragments of *Shiur Komah* speaks of Metatron as Prince of the World.[7] As a matter of fact, nothing of the sort is to be found in the versions of *Shiur Komah* known to me, and especially not in the book, *Raziel* (fol. 31), quoted by him. On the other hand, it is true that functions ascribed to the Prince of the World in Chapters 30 and 38 of the Book of Hekhaloth, or 3 Enoch, are ascribed to Metatron himself in a later version of the Metatron teaching—without, however, dentifying him as the Prince of the World.

It is my thought that the process by means of which these two figures were merged must have taken place in circles that identified Michael with this title. For it is a fact that many things which had been said about Michael in earlier aggadic sources were transferred by the Merkabah mystics to Metatron. This process of identification can be traced at least to the third or fourth century.

The most important extra-talmudic source for this transformation is the Visions of Ezekiel.[8] I see no reason to consider this important text as a later pseudepigraphon. Whereas great and well-known talmudic heroes appear as the principal speakers in all the other texts

[5] Maimonides, *Guide to the Perplexed*, II, Chap. 60. The identification of the שר העולם with the active intellect shows that what he had in mind was a philosophical interpretation of the concept of Metatron.

[6] Cf. Manuel Joël, *Blicke in die Religionsgeschichte*, I (1880), 126–128; L. Ginzberg, *Legends of the Jews*, V, 29 and VI, 150.

[7] Odeberg, in his Introduction to *3 Enoch*, p. 104.

[8] ראיות יחזקאל; see no. 1 in the list of Merkabah texts mentioned in Section I.

about the Merkabah, no such show is made here. Only cursorily, and, as it were, in passing, are their ideas on some questions mentioned. The authorities quoted here are Palestinian rabbis of the fourth century, some of whose names are not at all familiar. One of these, a little-known Amora named Inyanei bar Sasson, or Sisson, appears, in fact, in a passage of the Palestinian Talmud (*Yoma* III, 7) concerning the tradition of the ineffable name of God. He is called there R. Inyanei bar Sossai, or Sissi, and is said to have offered to pass on to R. Ḥanina in Sepphoris the knowledge of the esoteric name, but to have desisted when he discovered his son hiding under the bed.[9] This independent testimony confirms his interest in esoteric knowledge.

The Visions of Ezekiel set forth a description of the seven heavens that is parallel to, if somewhat different from, the familiar account found in *Ḥagigah* 12b (which, in an old parallel passage in *Aboth de R. Nathan*, Chapter 37, is ascribed to the Tanna R. Meir). Not only is the sequence of the names of the heavens a little different from that in *Ḥagigah*,[10] but it is further stated that God created a Merkabah in each of the seven heavens, not only in the highest one. It is noteworthy that this new information, too, is quoted in the Visions in the name of R. Meir.[11]

Since everything in the heavenly realm has a secret name in this literature, it is not surprising that these new Merkabahs also have names, or that—in a manner quite unlike that of the reticent talmudic Baraitha—these names are revealed to us. In some fourth and fifth century Greek charms of protection, heavily tinged with Jewish elements, even the secret names of the rulers of the abyss and the six heavens (corresponding to the seven heavens of the Merkabah traditions) are mentioned. The names of the new Merkabahs are apparently Hebrew, some of them representing the names of well-known angels, like Raphael, Suriel, and Yophiel or Yephephiyah, and some

[9] ר' אינייני בר סוסיי סליק גבי ר' חנינא דציפורין. אמר: איתא ואנא מסר יתיה לך. עאל ליה בריה תחות ערסא עטש ושמע קליה. אמר: מה אתון נהיגין גביכון ברמיו? אזיל, לא לך ולא ליה. The parallel passage in *Koheleth Rabba* III, 11, is told quite differently, but the main motif remains. Cf. W. Bacher, *Die Agada der palästinensischen Amoräer*, III, 546–547 and 673, on the many variants of this rabbi's name. That he was concerned with mystical speculations about the names of God is proved also by a saying of his on Ex. 3:14 in *Shemoth Rabba*, Par. III, 4.

[10] There are variations in the names and order of the seven heavens in all the parallel passages (including ויקרא רבא, Par. XXIX, 11 and סדר רבה דבראשית, ed. Wertheimer, בתי מדרשות, I, 39–43). Even in the text of ראיות יחזקאל there are contradictory statements.

[11] Cf. Wertheimer, בתי מדרשות, II, 130: אמר ר' לוי משום ר' יוסי מעוניה שאמר ר' מאיר: שבעה רקיעים ברא הקדוש ושבעה מרכבות בהן.

of them consisting of magical names of uncontested Aramaic or Hebrew etymology, such as Marmaraoth and Muriatha.[12] This type of secret name abounds both in the Hebrew and Aramaic Hekhaloth texts and in the Greek and Coptic magical papyri.

We read the following in the Visions about the third heaven, called *Zebul* (in the parallel recension in *Ḥagigah* 12b it is considered the fourth), where Michael, "the Great Prince," stands and makes an offering in the celestial temple:[13]

> And what is there in *Zebul*? R. Levi said in the name of R. Ḥama bar Ukba, who said it in the name of R. Joḥanan: The Prince [obviously Michael, as in the talmudic passage] is not dwelling anywhere but in *Zebul* and he is the very fullness of *Zebul* [i. e. fills all of it?] and before him are thousands of thousands and myriads of myriads who minister to him. Of them it is said by Daniel: I beheld till thrones were placed, etc.; a fiery stream issued, etc. [7:9–10]. And what is his name? *Kimos* [or *Kemos*], קימוס, is his name. R. Isaac said: *Ma'atah* [or *Me'atah*], מעתה, is his name. R. Inyanei bar Sisson said: *Bizbul* [meaning: in *Zebul*] is his name. R. Tanḥum the Old said: *'Atatiyah*, אטטיה, is his name. Eleazar Nadwadaya[14] said: *Metatron*, like the name of the [divine] Dynamis. And those who make theurgical use of the [divine] Name say: *Salnas*, סלנס, is his name, *Kasbak*, קסבק [a different reading: *Baskabas*], is his name, similar to the name of the Creator of the World. And what is the name of the Merkabah of *Zebul? Halwaya*, הלויה, is its name.

This passage proves not only that the figures of Metatron and Michael were indeed consolidated, but that they were still identical as late as the fourth century and that Metatron was but a secret name of Michael, on an equal footing with his other secret and unexplained names. (The theurgists, משמשין בשום, already had a tradition about his magically effective names). Our passage states at the same time, however, that the name Metatron is also like the name of God—here called the Dynamis. This is a Palestinian parallel to the state-

[12] Cf. K. Preisendanz, *Papyri Graecae Magicae*, II, 160, and the parallel text quoted by him. The Greek Σουριήλ represents the Hebrew סוריאל (well-known from the Hekhaloth tradition) rather than צוריאל.

[13] Wertheimer, בתי מדרשות, II, 132–133: ומה יש בו בזבול? אמר ר' לוי משם ר' חמא בר עוקבא שאמר משם ר' יוחנן: השר אינו שרוי אלא בזבול והווה מלואו של זבול ולפניו אלפי אלפים וריבי רבבות המשמשין אותו, עליהם אמר דניאל חזה הוית עד די כרסון וג' נהר די נור נגד, ומה שמו קימוס שמו. ר' יצחק אומר מעתה שמו, ר' עינייני בר ססון אומר בזבול שמו. ר' תנחום הזקן אומר אטטיה שמו. אלעזר נדודיה אומר מיטטרון כשם הגבורה, ומשמשין בשום אומרים סלנס שמו קסבק [בסקבס] שמו בשום יוצר העולם. ומה שמו של מרכבה של זבול? הלויה שמה.

[14] Professor Lieberman thinks this indicates his home: Eleazar from Nadwad (or Narwad, נרוד). A place of this name is mentioned in some rabbinic sources; cf. Samuel Klein, "Narbatta," *MGWJ*, LXXIV (1930), 373.

ment made in the Babylonian Talmud (*Sanhedrin* 38b) by the Babylonian teacher R. Idith (late third century?), that the name of Metatron is "like the name of his master. For it is written: For my name is in Him [Exodus 23:21]." This formula must have developed at an earlier time than our passage; and, as a matter of fact, there are passages in the Hekhaloth books regarding mystical names said to be secret names of the Dynamis. We should, nonetheless, be careful not to rationalize the name of Metatron in this context, and the very continuation of the sentence should serve as a warning: Metatron is as much a secret name of the Dynamis as, according to the practitioners of magic, or theurgists, *Kasbak* is a name "similar to the name of the Demiurge [*Yoṣer 'Olam*]."

Only some of the names given in our passage, such as *'Atatiyah* and *Metatron*, have been incorporated into the lists of mystical or secret names of the angel Metatron that are preserved in the Hekhaloth literature. These lists, for the most part, are headed by the names Metatron and Jahoel.[15] On the other hand, these lists also contain names mentioned by the Babylonian Talmud as mystical names of an anonymous angel identified by Rashi with Gabriel.[16] It seems, therefore, that the later traditions about Metatron, developed after the time when the Jahoel concepts flourished, comprised elements of the teaching concerning both archangels, Michael and Gabriel, unless we assume that Rashi's identification was mistaken.

We may, accordingly, speak of two stages through which the traditions concerning the seven heavens have gone. The first knows nothing of Metatron and, forming a part of teachings not confined to the esotericists alone, do not mention secret names that may have magical connotations. The second stage, however, introduces these magical elements and puts Metatron in the place of Michael. Whether this transformation took place during the Tannaitic period is difficult to say. It may well be the case if we consider the tradition about the seven Merkabahs ascribed to R. Meir as genuine, as I am inclined to do. On the other hand, the testimony regarding the secret names mentioned in the passage quoted from the Visions is identified with teachers who lived as late as the third and fourth centuries. Still, there is no reason to assume that secret names of this type were

[15] אטטיה is mentioned in the list found in אותיות דר' עקיבא, in Wertheimer, בתי מדרשות, II, 353. Odeberg's text, incorporated in his late MS of *3 Enoch* (Chap. 48), has the corrupt readings חטטיה and, later on, עטטיא.

[16] *Sanhedrin* 44b. These names are found among the secret names of Metatron in the *Merkabah Rabbah*, מרכבה שלמה, fol. 5a. One could argue that they were actually never names of Gabriel but of Michael or Metatron.

introduced into Judaism only then; indeed, there is every reason to assume that they were much older.

I shall discuss this question in Section IX in another connection, but I should like to stress here a point that, as far as I can see, has been generally overlooked. In Josephus' account of the Essenes, it is said that the members of this group took a formidable oath to divulge neither the books belonging to their sect nor the names of the angels. It has been generally assumed that the names of the angels alluded to in this passage of the *Bellum Judaicum* are names similar to those in the Book of Enoch, that is to say, they are names having a more or less understandable etymology, sometimes simply referring to the function assigned to the particular angel. The possibility must be considered, however, that the oath referred to the secret names of the angels rather than to their "official" ones; names that for the most part have no visible etymology and that were largely used for magical purposes. To assume the truth of this possibility would lead to the further assumption that such traditions about secret names of angels (and of the Divinity, for that matter) as abound in the Hekhaloth books and the Visions of Ezekiel are but a continuation of the tradition of the Essenes of the first century C. E. That the secret names and *nomina barbara* of the Hekhaloth books are of the same type as those used in the magical papyri indicates that there was common ground for some of these traditions.

But let us return to the problem of the Prince of the World. It is the linking of Metatron to Michael that may account for Metatron's identification with the Prince of the World. Moreover, this identification can now be demonstrated to have been known to Jewish mystical tradition in Babylonia, at least in the post-talmudic period. In a Palestinian source, Chapter 27 of *Pirke R. Eliezer*, Michael is still given the attribute of שרו של עולם; yet from the same period we have testimony in which it is Metatron who is called the "Great Prince of the whole World" (מטטרון איסרא רבא דכולי עלמא). This phrase can also be found on one of the "magic bowls" containing Aramaic incantations, most of which date from the sixth to the eighth centuries. Published only twenty years ago,[17] the text from this particular bowl is the oldest source we have that clearly identifies Metatron as the Prince of the World.

In approximately the same period, the Jewish Gnostic book,

[17] Cyrus Gordon, who published the text in *Archiv Orientální*, IX (1937), 95, gave an incorrect interpretation of איסרא. Metatron is called שרא רבא (=איסרא רבא on the bowl) in the Targum of the Merkabah-chapter, Ezek. I, in Wertheimer, בתי מדרשות, II, 139; and השר הגדול על כל השרים in שעור קומה, cf. מרכבה שלמה, fol. 39b.

Raza Rabba (The Great Mystery), was written—we do not know whether in Palestine or in Babylonia. (I have published some fragments of this text in an appendix to my book on the beginnings of the Kabbalah.) Here, in a tradition ascribed, pseudepigraphically, to R. Akiba, the Prince of the World is introduced as quoting the verse "In wrath remember compassion [Habakuk 3:2]" at the hour when he offers the souls of the righteous as a celestial offering.[18] Whether the author thought of Michael or Metatron in this connection cannot be decided, and, as a matter of fact, does not make any difference in the light of what we have seen. Indeed, if the main fragment of the *Shiur Komah* as we have it already existed in the third century, then the identification of Michael and Metatron in their function as celestial High Priest[19] can be assigned an earlier date than that of the Amora R. Inyanei bar Sasson, or Sisson, in the Visions of Ezekiel; for Metatron is described at some length in the *Shiur Komah* as the celestial High Priest of the heavenly tabernacle.

In the passage of the *Shiur Komah* to which I refer, this heavenly tabernacle is called משכן מטטרון, but in a parallel passage it is called משכן הנער (the tabernacle of the youth)[20]; *Na'ar*, according to 3 Enoch 3:2, being the predicate by which Metatron is called by God. It is by no means clear whether this predicate has anything to do with the verse of Psalms 37:25, "I have been a youth and now I am old," which, in *Yebamoth* 16b, is put into the mouth of the Prince of the World because only he, having been present during the history of creation from its beginning to its end, could have spoken these words.[21] This interpretation of the term, however, stands in sharp contrast to the explanation offered in 3 Enoch 4:10: that it is "because I am small and a youth among them [i. e. the angels] in days, months, and years, that they call me youth." It is obvious that the concept of Metatron as a transformed Enoch is incompatible with the concept of the Prince

[18] The writer's ראשית הקבלה, pp. 235–236: א"ר עקיבא: מאי דכתיב ברגז רחם תזכור? פסוק זה שר העולם אמרו בשעה שמקריב לפניך נשמות הצדיקים.

[19] Michael as High Priest was known to the Jewish source used in the Gnostic *Excerpta ex Theodoto*, § 38; only "the Archangel [i. e. Michael]" enters within the curtain (καταπέτασμα), an act analogous to that of the High Priest who enters once a year into the Holy of Holies. Michael as High Priest in heaven is also mentioned in *Menaḥoth* 110a (parallel to *Ḥagigah* 12b) and *Zebaḥim* 62a. The Baraitha in *Ḥagigah* is the oldest source.

[20] Cf. מרכבה שלמה, fol. 40a and מדרש במדבר רבה, Par. XII, 15 (on Num. 7:1), where משכן הנער is mentioned. *Shiur Komah* is, of course, very much older than the medieval *Bemidbar Rabbah*.

[21] In *Ḥullin* 60a, the idea that the Prince of the World was present at the hour of creation is applied to Ps. 104:31.

of the World as conceived in the talmudic passage; but the latter would not be incompatible with a concept of Metatron based on his identification with Michael.

It should also be observed that the explanation quoted above from 3 Enoch concerning the predicate 'youth,' is contradicted by the statement in the preceding chapter of the same book (and by the *Shiur Komah* fragment, too[22]) that maintains that not the angels, but God Himself prefers to call Metatron by this particular name rather than by his seventy secret names (corresponding to the seventy languages of the world). It should also be borne in mind that *Na'ar* means in Hebrew not only 'youth,' but also 'servant'; and it can be proven that it was in this capacity, as servant before the throne or in the celestial tabernacle, and not because of his youth as compared to the age of the highest angels, that Metatron was called *Na'ar*. For in one of the oldest fragments of the *Shiur Komah* that we possess, which is partly written in Aramaic, the term *Na'ar* is rendered *Shammasha Reḥima* (the beloved servant). The passage reads: "R. Akiba said: Metatron, the beloved servant, the Great Prince of Testimony [שמשא רחימא שרא רבא דסהדותא], said to me . . . "; and what follows is a description of the measures of the glory when it dwells upon the throne of glory.[23]

If, therefore, the hypothesis about the basic age of the *Shiur Komah* fragments that I have advanced is acceptable, and Metatron as High Priest instead of Michael was known even before the fourth century, then the possibility has to be considered that the author of the talmudic passage used Psalm 37:25 as he did precisely because he knew of the function of the Prince of the World as a High Priest or servant on high. The author of the passage in *Yebamoth* is R. Samuel ben Naḥman, the famous Palestinian Amora of the third century, whose preoccupation with mystical lore is well attested to and generally admitted by talmudic scholars. This, of course, would indicate that, albeit in a playful manner, R. Samuel was referring to Metatron, whom he already knew from another context as *Na'ar*, youth or servant.

We have necessarily, then, to differentiate between two basic aspects of Metatron lore, which in our Hekhaloth literature, as far as it deals specifically with Metatron, have already been combined and to a certain extent confused. One aspect identifies Metatron with Jahoel or Michael and knows nothing of his transfiguration from a

[22] Cf. מרכבה שלמה, fol. 39b: והנער קומתו מלא עולם וקורא אותו הקב"ה נער.

[23] MS J. Th. Sem. 828, fol. 19a: אמר ר' עקיבא: אמ' לי מטטרון שמשא רחימא שרא רבא דאסהדותא [other texts: דסהדותא] מעיד אני עדות זו ביהוה אלהי ישראל חייא וקיימא. In the corresponding version, מרכבה שלמה, fol. 32a, the salient words are lacking.

human being into an angel. The talmudic passages concerned with Metatron are of this type.[24] The other aspect identifies Metatron with the figure of Enoch as he is depicted in apocalyptic literature, and permeated that aggadic and targumic literature which, although not necessarily of a later date than the Talmud, was outside of it. When the Book of Hekhaloth, or 3 Enoch, was composed, the two aspects had already become intertwined and the writer presented explanations belonging to the second aspect for material clearly belonging to the first. Thus, for example, it is obvious that the predication of Metatron as the Lesser Jaho, which was taken over by the Christian Gnostics of the second century, was based on the original speculation about the angel Jahoel. But the author of 3 Enoch, or his sources, had already forgotten this origin of the name Lesser Jaho, and proceeded to give an explanation of it that accorded with his account of Enoch's transfiguration. The explanation that only after this metamorphosis did God proclaim Metatron "in the presence of all His heavenly household" as יהוה הקטן, was, of necessity, unconvincing.[25]

I should like to add to these remarks about Metatron some new material concerning the well-known Baraitha in *Berakhoth* 7a about Akatriel or Akhtariel. There, in a manifestly apocryphal passage, R. Ishmael is made to say: "Once I entered the Holy of Holies to burn incense [in his unhistorical role as High Priest] and I beheld Akatriel Jah, the Lord of Hosts, sitting on a high and sublime throne, and he spoke to me thus: 'Ishmael, my son, give me your praise [or: blessing].' " Whether this name, Akatriel, represents the name of an angel or the name of God Himself in one of the aspects of His glory as it is revealed upon the throne, cannot be decided on the merits of the talmudic passage alone. As a matter of fact, medieval commentators disagreed sharply in their interpretations and R. Ḥananel already mentions both interpretations in his commentary on *Berakhoth*.[26]

[24] The passage in *Ḥagigah* 15a, however, can also be interpreted in another way: Since Metatron is pictured as a heavenly scribe (למכתב זכוותהון דישראל), this may refer to the tradition about the ascension of Enoch, to whom a similar function is indeed ascribed in the Book of Jubilees 4:23: "We conducted him into the Garden of Eden in majesty and honor, and behold there he writes down the condemnation and judgement of the world, and all the wickedness of the children of men." The two functions supplement each other. But the parallel proves less than it seems to prove, since both the Apocrypha and the Hekhaloth books know several angelic scribes; cf. Odeberg, *3 Enoch*, Introduction, p. 59. In any case, the Palestinian Targum on Gen. 5:24, speaking of Enoch's transfiguration into Metatron, calls him, expressively, ספרא רבא, 'the great scribe.'

[25] 3 Enoch, Chap. 12:5; cf. Odeberg, p. 33.

[26] Cf. also שאלות ותשובות הגאונים, Lyck, no. 116. R. Ḥananel says: יש אומרים אכתריאל מלאך הוא ואנו לא קבלני אלא הכבוד הוא.

In the talmudic and exoteric aggadic literature Akatriel is spoken of no more, but R. Nissim of Kairawan testified that he had found the phrase "I beheld Akatriel" in "some Aggadahs."[27] These Aggadahs must have been of an esoteric character; and we find, indeed, that some of the Hekhaloth texts do mention the name and yield some further information. In 3 Enoch, whose original title was the Book of Hekhaloth, Akatriel is mentioned only once, and it seems significant that the name is not to be found in the long list of heavenly archons recorded in Chapters 17 and 18 of this book. But in some of the manuscripts there is an additional chapter about Moses' ascension to Heaven[28] which runs as follows: When Moses ascended to Heaven, his prayers were heard, and "He who sits upon the Merkabah opened the windows that are above the heads of the Cherubim and a host of 180,000 advocates and the Prince of the Countenance, Metatron, with them, went forth to meet Moses." Metatron and the angels engaged in a discourse about the glory of God and, the text continues, "In this moment Akatriel Jah JHWH of the Hosts spoke [literally: answered, i. e. their prayers] and said to Metatron, the Prince of the Countenance: 'Let no prayer that he prays before me return void. Hear his prayer and fulfill his desire, great or small.' Forthwith, Metatron, the Prince of the Countenance said to Moses: 'Son of Amram! Fear not, for God has already found delight in thee.'" Although Odeberg's remarks in his commentary on this text, connecting this name with Kabbalistic speculations concerning the first *Sephirah Kether*, are irrelevant,[29] it is still true that Akatriel must be understood here as one of the names of God as He appears on the throne, and not as the name of an angel. When Metatron has heard His warning, he announces to Moses that God [*Elohim*] delights in him. The voice of Akatriel is the voice of Him who sits upon the throne. Why it is so called is not explained.

A very different meaning is given to Akatriel, however, in a piece called The Mystery of Sandalphon.[30] We read in the Oxford man-

[27] B. Lewin in אוצר הגאונים on ברכות has omitted this quotation, found in Abraham Epstein, *Das talmudische Lexikon* יחוסי תנאים ואמוראים (1895), p. 26 and S. A. Poznanski, לקוטים מן ספר מגלת סתרים, p. 9.

[28] In Odeberg's edition, Chap. 15B. I have also found this paragraph in a 14th century manuscript (formerly in the Library of the Jewish Community in Vienna, Schwarz, No. 32) which contains some chapters of this Hebrew Enoch book.

[29] Odeberg has indulged in Kabbalistic (and pseudo-Kabbalistic) speculations about the meaning of Metatron which have no reference to historic facts, especially in his Swedish article on the concept of Metatron in early Jewish mysticism, *Kirkohistorisk Årsskrift*, XXVII (1928), 1–20. He has misled not a few scholars.

[30] Sandalphon is mentioned in the Merkabah traditions in *Ḥagigah* 13b as

uscript (1531) of the Hekhaloth: "Elisha ben Abuya [the fourth of the sages to enter Paradise] said: 'When I ascended unto Paradise, I beheld Akatriel JHWH, the Lord of Hosts, who is sitting at the entrance of Paradise, and 120 myriads of ministering angels surround him.' "[31] It is obvious that this passage, which combines the talmudic account of the journey of the four sages to Heaven with novel elements, describes Akatriel as an angel and corresponds to the description R. Nissim gives of Akatriel as "an angel like Michael and Gabriel."[32] Akatriel (substituting here for Metatron, who is mentioned in the *Ḥagigah* passage) is, in this version, encountered at the gate of Paradise[33] immediately after the ascent to Heaven. He does not sit upon a throne to be reached only at the end of a long journey through the palaces and chambers of Paradise, but, rather, his place is at the very entrance to Paradise itself—a position that would seem to imply a status inferior to that pictured in the talmudic passage.

Obviously, the truth of the matter is that there were different traditions regarding Akatriel. In a passage of a Hekhaloth text appearing in the Oxford manuscript but belonging to another composition, an incantation of Auzhaya (**אוזהיא**), the Prince of the [divine] Countenance, calls upon him "in the name of Atbaḥ Ah, the Lord of Hosts, and in the name of Tikarathin, the Lord of Hosts, and in the

---

standing behind the Merkabah wreathing crowns for his master. Cf. also in *Pesikta Rabbathi*, ed. Friedmann, 97a, on Sandalphon: גבוה מחבריו מהלך ת"ק שנה ומשתמש אחר המרכבה; and *Midrash Konen*, in Jellinek's בית המדרש, II, 26, where Sandalphon is called a *meturgeman*, a 'translator,' mediating between Israel and their Father in heaven, wreathing crowns for the Master of Glory (God) from Israel's prayers.

[31] MS Oxford 1531, fol. 60a: אמר אלישע בן אבויה: כשהייתי עולה בפרדס ראיתי את אכתריאל יה [MS J. Th. Sem. 828, fol. 35a adds: אלהי ישראל] י"י צבאות שהוא יושב על פתח פרדס וק"כ רבוא של מלאכי השרת מקיפין לו [MS J. Th. Sem. 828: מוקפין לי] שנ' אלף אלפין ישמשוניה וריבוא ריבוון וכו'. כיון שראיתי אותם נבהלתי ונרתעתי ודחקתי את עצמי ונכנסתי לפני הקב"ה. אמרתי לפניו: רבונו של עולם כתוב בתורתך הן ליו"י אלהיך השמים ושמי השמים וג'. וכת' מעשה ידיו מגיד הרקיע, אחד בלבד. אמר לי אלישע בני, כלום באתה להרהר אחר מדותי, לא שמעת [the MSS have: שמעתי] משל שמושלין בני אדם. The end of the fragment is not preserved. The title, רזו של סנדלפון (not the piece which is found under this title in מרכבה שלמה 1a) is lacking in the MS J. Th. Sem., where the paragraph just transcribed follows immediately after the end of the text transcribed in Appendix C and has been joined to it. The copyist of the MS J. Th. Sem. says: לא מצאתי המשל.

[32] R. Nissim says: פירשו רבותינו כי הוא מלאך כמו מיכאל וגבריאל. This corresponds to the appearance of Akatriel as an angel in the 8th century apocalyptic piece published by Chaim M. Horowitz, בית עקד האגדות (1881), where we read on p. 59, "R. Ishmael said: Akatriel Jah JHWH Zebaoth put it to me this way." But in what follows, p. 60, the name Metatron appears instead of Akatriel.

[33] The Hebrew term פתח פרדס (without the article!) proves that *pardes* is indeed used as a technical term for paradise, just as another writer would have said פתח גן עדן and not פתח גן העדן.

name of Akatriel JHWH, the God of Israel, which is sealed upon the crown and engraved [or: expounded] upon His throne."[34] This passage points to a conception that, again, is quite different from the aforementioned ones. The Aramaic definition of the name Akatriel would seem to indicate clearly that it is the secret name of a crown (תגא). But of whose crown? Of the crown of one of the angels—and we know already that all of them have crowns—or of the crown of Him who sits and is revealed upon the throne? The end of the quotation seems to point in the second direction. The name Akatriel is explicitly engraved upon "*His* throne," which can be nothing but the throne of the divine glory. In this connection Akatriel is neither an angel nor God Himself; it is one of the secret names of His various paraphernalia as He appears upon the throne. To define Akatriel in this way, as the secret name of the crown, seems both a plausible and a rational explanation of its etymology.[35]

Incidentally, the Hekhaloth terminology regarding the secret name or names of the crown may throw new light on the phrase **אשתמש בתגא** ("to make theurgic use of the crown"), as it is found in *Aboth* I, 13. *Taga* (תגא), the crown, has been more or less rightly explained as a paraphrase of the ineffable name,[36] but in view of the foregoing we may say even more precisely that it represents the crown on which the ineffable name is engraved. Such a "Crown of the ineffable name"

[34] MS Oxford 1531, fol. 49b–50a and MS J. Th. Sem. 828, fol. 27a: בשם אטבח אה יהוה צבאות ובשם שריה יהוה צבאות ובשם תיקרתין יהוה צבאות ובשם אכתריאל יוי אלהי ישראל דמחתם על תגא ומפרש בכורסיה [MS J. Th. Sem.: אכתריאל יה יהוה צבאות אלהי ישראל מחתם על תגא]. The secret name of God, תיקרתין (Thikarathin or Thikarthin), might be identified with a name preserved in a Coptic charm of largely Jewish character quoted in E. Goodenough's monumental work, *Jewish Symbols in the Greco-Roman Period*, II (1953), 176, after other Jewish names of God: "We praise thee *Thrakai* who has stretched out the earth as a cover over the abyss."

[35] Osias Schorr's etymology of אכתריאל in החלוץ, X, 70, is untenable: אכתרי אל from the Greek ὀχϑηρός, 'the Most High.' William Rosenau, "Some Notes on Akteriel," *Paul Haupt Festschrift* (1926), pp. 103–105, has "guessed" the correct explanation without being aware of the existence of the various passages in the Merkabah literature and without mentioning Rashi, from whose commentary he took it.

[36] Cf. J. Goldin's translation of *The Fathers According to R. Nathan* (1956), p. 71 and *Major Trends*, p. 358. Instances of השתמש (or Aramaic אשתמש) as a term for theurgic practice are: (1) שבת, fol. 88a: רז זה שמלאכי השרת משתמשים בו; (2) R. Abbahu in מדרש תהלים on Ps. 16: הכבוד גילה [rejoiced] בשעה שהקטנים הוגים להשתמש בו; (3) *ibid.* on Ps. 36: שני דורות נשתמשו בשם המפורש; (4) *Targum Koheleth* 3:11: אילו הוה מסיר [שמא מפרש] ביד אינשי הוה משמש ביה ומשכח בגווה מה דעתיד למהוי בסוף יומיא; (5) היכלות רבתי, Chap. 28:2: להשתמש בכתר נורא; (6) 3 Enoch 5:4: כל המשתמש בזיו השכינה, and 5:9. In ראיות יחזקאל (see quotation above) the magical theurgists are called משמשין בשום.

is indeed mentioned in *Pirke R. Eliezer.*[37] This tradition, according to which the name Akatriel and not the Tetragrammaton was sealed upon the crown, seems to have originated in a circle whose members either knew of the saying of R. Ishmael as recorded in the Talmud, and transferred the name of the crown to the crown itself; or else speculated about the secret name of the crown and transferred it subsequently to the Divinity, as the talmudic passage appears to imply. Later, it was apparently transformed into nothing more than the name of an angel, as we find it in The Mystery of Sandalphon. But the heart of the matter is that in all these cases the material preserved in the Hekhaloth literature supplements the sparse information provided in the Talmud and must be considered as essentially of the same period.[38]

[37] Chap. 4: עטרת נתונה בראשו וכתר שם המפורש על מצחו.

[38] The concept of Akatriel as a manifestation of the *Kabod* as it is revealed to Israel is still reflected in a passage of the late מדרש בראשית רבתי, ed. Albeck (1940), p. 41. Here, Prov. 30:4 is said to refer to אכתריאל יה זיו מתוקן לישראל.

VIII

SOME AGGADIC SAYINGS EXPLAINED BY MERKABAH HYMNS. THE GARMENT OF GOD

In order to further establish my point, to wit, the age of the traditions contained in the esoteric texts we are discussing, let me give another example of the way in which the material found in these texts amplifies and often explains the exoteric passages in the Talmud and the Midrash related to them. The *Aggadath Shir ha-Shirim* on Song of Songs seems to be one of the oldest of the midrashim and has preserved material of great importance. In it we read the following statement by R. Ḥaninah, the nephew of R. Joshua, a rabbi of the second century:

> There are rivers of fire which pass before the Shekhinah like streams of water mingled with fire. When permission was given to Gabriel to burn the whole army of Sennacherib, permission was given to the Leviathan to destroy all the rivers, and therefore it is said: The flashes thereof are flashes of fire, a very flame of God [Song of Songs 8:6].[1]

This passage is remarkable in three respects. It teaches us, first of all, that the fiery stream mentioned in Daniel 7:10 had already been replaced in the second century by a plurality of such rivers. This leads us to conclude that the many passages referring to these rivers and the bridges spanning them to be found in the Hekhaloth texts may therefore be considered as representing Tannaitic tradition.[2] In 3 Enoch 33:4–5 we find, for example:

> And underneath the feet of the *Ḥayyoth* seven fiery rivers are running and flowing, and the breadth of each river is 365,000 parsangs and its depth is 248,000 parsangs; its length is immeasurable and uncountable, and each river turns round in a bow in the four directions of *'Araboth*,[3] etc.

Chapter 37 of this book uses the same terminology as *Aggadath Shir ha-Shirim*—with the exception that the rivers here pass between the

[1] אגדת שיר השירים, ed. Schechter (1897), ll. 1335 ff.: יש נהרות של אש שהן עוברין לפני השכינה כנהרות של מים ומעורבים באש וכשנתנה רשות לגבריאל לשרוף את כל חיל סנחריב ניתנה רשות ללויתן לחבל את כל הנהרות; לכך נאמר רשפיה רשפי אש, שלהבה יה.

[2] Such a piece on the bridges over the fiery streams is to be found in Jellinek's בית המדרש, VI, 153, which he copied from the Hekhaloth MS Munich 40. In MS Oxford 1531 it is found on fol. 50a–b.

[3] *'Araboth*: the name of the seventh heaven in all Merkabah traditions.

four camps of the Shekhinah rather than before it. The manuscript of the Greater Hekhaloth in The Jewish Theological Seminary of America tells us that the angels step down from the heavens "into rivers of fire, rivers of flame, and rivers of burning, and immerse themselves in them seven times and examine themselves in fire 365 times."[4] In the same manner the fiery horses of heaven drink from streams of fire which flow through their troughs.[5] The very important Merkabah text quoted by some medieval authorities under the title *Ma'asseh Merkabah* and published in Appendix C of this book, abounds in descriptions of these rivers and their bridges. The existence of the single Tannaitic passage from the Midrash, quoted above, proves that there is no reason to assign the esoteric material concerning these rivers to later periods.

We learn, in addition, that the statement in this passage about Leviathan and his destructive power, an idea which is extremely uncommon in rabbinic tradition, supports the contention that when the Christian Gnostics, and especially the sect of the Ophites, adopted such a view of Leviathan, they took it from Jewish sources. And, finally, it is worthwhile mentioning that we are told in other midrashic sources that R. Ḥaninah, the nephew of R. Joshua ben Ḥananiah, entertained relations with Gnostic heretics (*Minim*).[6] Now this destructive aspect of Leviathan was suppressed by the exoteric Jewish Aggadah (leaving only faint traces in the Talmud)[7] and was only resuscitated by the medieval Kabbalists; especially by the sources from which the brothers Jacob and Isaac Cohen of Soria derived their traditions. In my studies of their writings, I have characterized these sources as essentially Gnostic.

Yet another example of the relationship between exoteric and esoteric material is provided by the concept of the garment of light in which God shrouds Himself, whether it be in the hour of creation or in His appearance on the throne of the Merkabah. In both instances the anthropomorphic nature of this idea is obvious, as is its relation to the *Shiur Komah* speculations.

Much ink has been spilled on the midrashic account of the conversa-

[4] MS J. Th. Sem. 828, fol. 8a: יורדים כתות כתות... של מלאכי השרת מן רקיע ורקיע לתוך נהרי אש ונהרי להבה ונהרי שלהבת ומטבילין עצמן בהם שבע פעמים ובודקין עצמן באש שלש מאות וששים וחמשה פעמים. This addition to the main text of the Greater Hekhaloth, Chap. 11, is published in another version in Jellinek, בית המדרש, III, 161–163.

[5] Cf. the passage from Chap. 16 of the Greater Hekhaloth quoted in Section V, n. 2.

[6] Cf. *Koheleth Rabba* I, 8. Cf. Travers Herford, *Christianity in Talmud and Midrash* (1903), pp. 211–215.

[7] *Baba Bathra* 74b; cf. L. Ginzberg, *Legends of the Jews*, V, 43–45.

tion between R. Simeon ben Yehoṣadak and R. Samuel ben Naḥman, who is pictured there as a recipient of secret lore. The account reads as follows:

> R. Simeon asked: "As I have heard that you are a master of Aggadah, tell me whence the light was created." R. Samuel said: "The Holy One, blessed by He, wrapped Himself in a white garment [other texts have: as in a garment] and the splendor of His glory shone forth from one end of the world to the other." He said this in a whisper. R. Simeon was bewildered by this. "Is this not said explicitly in Scripture: He covereth Himself with light as with a garment [Psalms 104:2]?" R. Samuel replied: "As I have heard it in a whisper, I told it in a whisper."[8]

No elaboration of the point which R. Samuel ben Naḥman wished to make is found in the older midrashim. Only the *Pirke R. Eliezer* state in Chapter 3: "Whence were the heavens created? From the light of the garment with which He was robed; He took and stretched it like a garment."[9] Curiously enough, this garment is not connected, neither in these aggadoth nor in the Hekhaloth texts, with the "garment white as snow" in which, according to Daniel 7:9, the "Ancient of Days" is clothed when He sits upon the throne.

It is in the Hekhaloth, however, that we gain additional insight into the ideas which lie behind R. Samuel bar Naḥman's words. Nor is this surprising, since there is but little doubt that to "whisper" is a technical term for the communication of esoteric doctrine.[10] The hymns in the Greater Hekhaloth, which, as I have said, reflect teachings current in at least the third century C. E., provide us with several passages that mention the garment of God as a matter of course and as something generally known to the initiate. This garment is always designated in the Hekhaloth by the rabbinic term *Ḥaluk*

[8] In *Bereshith Rabbah*, ed. Theodor, pp. 19–20, and the numerous parallel passages noted by the editor. Cf. on this Aggadah, V. Aptowitzer, "Licht als Urstoff," *MGWJ*, LXXII (1928), 363–370; Robert Eisler, *Weltenmantel und Himmelszelt* (1910), pp. 224–227; Alex. Altmann, "A Note on the Rabbinic Doctrine of Creation," in *Journal of Jewish Studies*, VII (1956), 195–206.

[9] G. Friedlander's translation (1916), p. 15. The Hebrew has: מאור לבושו של הקב"ה שהוא לבוש לקח ממנו ופרש כשמלה.

[10] It is true that in a passage of the Palestinian Talmud quoted in Theodor's notes (Pal. *Beṣah*, end of Chap. 1) the same formula, כשם ששמעתיה בלחישה וג', occurs in a purely halakhic context and was therefore not confined to esoteric utterances. But we know from *Ḥagigah* 13a, where are listed the five qualities by which the recipient of secret lore is to be distinguished, that נבון לחש (i. e. "one who understands things said in a whisper") is one of them. Hai Gaon explains this in one of his *responsa*: ובלחישות לוחשין לו וכללות נותנין לו והוא מבין בהם ומן השמים מראין אותו בסתרי לבבו; cf. B. Lewin, אוצר הגאונים on חגיגה, p. 12.

(חלוק), a term specifying a particular kind of garment, i. e. a long shirt-like robe, and not by the biblical term *Lebush* (לבוש), which may refer to any kind of garment at all. The heavenly bearer of this *Ḥaluk*, one of the principal objects of the Merkabah vision, is not simply called God, but "Zoharariel, Lord, God of Israel," in accordance with the prevailing habit of the Hekhaloth texts of invoking God by one of His secret names. These names, of which only a very few have a plausible etymology, may designate different aspects of the divine glory in its appearance upon the throne.[11] They are particularly problematical in that they are not easily distinguishable from the names of the highest angels, who are also called "Lord God of Israel" from time to time in this kind of text.

This is what we read in Chapter 3:4 of the Greater Hekhaloth:

מידה של קדושה, מידה של גבורה
מידה נוראה, מידה מבוהלה
מידה של רתת, מידה של זיע
מידה של בהל, מידה של חלחלה
מידה של חלוק של זהרריאל יהוה אלהי ישראל
שמעוטר ובא על כסא כבודו
וחקוק ומלא כולו מבפנים ומן החצון יהוה יהוה
ועיני כל בריה אינה יכולה להסתכל בו
לא עיני בשר ודם ולא עיני משרתיו
והמסתכל בו והמציץ והרואה אותו
אוחזות מחזוריות לגלגלי עיניו
וגלגלי עיניו מפלטין ומוציאין לפידי אש
והן מלהטין אותו והן שורפין אותו
כי האש היוצא מן האדם המסתכל
היא מלהטת אותו והיא שורפת אותו.
מפני מה? מפני [מידה] של חלוק של זהרריאל יהוה אלהי ישראל
שמעוטר ובא על כסא כבודו.

A quality of Holiness, a quality of power,
A quality of fearfulness, a quality of sublimity,
A quality of trembling, a quality of shaking,
A quality of terror, a quality of consternation,
Is the quality of the Garment of Zohorariel JHWH, God of Israel,
Who comes crowned to the throne of His glory.

[11] Such names are e. g. טוטרוסיאי ה' אלהי ישראל; טעצש ה' אלהי ישראל (cf. *Major Trends*, p. 363); טרקליי ה' אלהי ישראל; אדירירון ה' אלהי ישראל; רוזיי ה' אלהי ישראל. Cf. many names of this kind in Appendix C of this volume.

And it [the *Ḥaluk*] is every part engraved from within and from without JHWH JHWH
And of no creature are the eyes able to behold it,
Not the eyes of flesh and blood, and not the eyes of His servants.
And as for him who does behold it, or sees or glimpses it,
Whirling gyrations[12] grip the balls of his eyes.
And the balls of his eyes cast out and send forth torches of fire
And these enkindle him and these burn him.
For the fire which comes out from the man who beholds,
This enkindles him and this burns him.
Why is this? Because of [the quality] of the Garment of Zoharariel JHWH, the Lord of Israel,
Who comes crowned to the throne of His glory.

The first fact that presents itself with regard to this hymn is that the vision of the garment apparently arouses the same numinous qualities as are aroused by the vision of the mystical "body of the glory" itself; and that it therefore stands to reason that the description of the garment was a part of the *Shiur Komah* traditions. The visionary was taught to expect such a garment of light covering the glory. This cosmic raiment, similar to the Tables of the Covenant in the aggadic descriptions, is engraved and filled on both sides with repetitions of the Tetragrammaton (which might mean that the name of God penetrates the garment and shines from both sides);[13] and the vision of it induces in some way the same mystical experience which, according to 3 Enoch 15:1, transformed the human Enoch into the angel Metatron. In both cases it is said that the eyeballs are transformed into torches of fire. This is not, it is to be noted, a description of dangers confronting the mystic, but of a mystical transfiguration taking place within him. What is a permanent transfiguration in the case of Enoch, however, is only a temporary experience in the case of the Merkabah mystic (similar to those experiences described by Philo and analyzed by Hans Lewy, *Sobria Ebrietas* [1929], pp. 5–12).

I have just described this garment as 'cosmic.' It is true that in the hymn I have just quoted no such role is assigned to it, but in the other two hymns in which the garment is mentioned its cosmic function is clearly indicated. Chapter 4:2 of the Greater Hekhaloth reads:

[12] מחוורריות (the reading of the best MSS) seems to be a *hapaxlegomenon.*

[13] In the theurgic ritual described in the ספר המלבוש, a text apparently from the early post-talmudic period, the magic garment in which the initiate robes himself is inscribed in a similar manner; cf. the writer's description of this ritual in *Eranos Jahrbuch* 1950, XIX (1951), 148–149. On the writing on the Tables, cf. L. Ginzberg, *Legends of the Jews*, III, 119 and VI, 49.

מי כמלכנו, מי כיוצרנו, מי כיהוה אלהינו
חמה ולבנה מפליט ומוציא כתר ראשו.
כימה וכסיל וכוכב הנוגה
מזרות וכוכבים ומזלות
טורדין ויוצאין מחלוק שלו
שמעוטר ויושב בו על כסא כבודו.

Who is like unto our King? Who is like unto our Creator? Who is like unto the Lord our God?
The sun and the moon is cast out and sent forth by the crown of His head.
The Pleiades and Orion and the Planet of Venus
Constellations and stars and zodiacal signs
Flow and issue forth from the garment of Him
Who is crowned and [shrouded] in it, sits upon the throne of His glory.

Here we learn that the stars were created by the light that issues from His *Ḥaluk*. Nor is this just a poetic *façon de parler*, but it connects well with the Aggadah told by R. Samuel. God wrapped Himself in this garment in the hour of creation just as He does every time He steps down to sit on His throne. Moreover, we may infer from the use of the present tense that new stars and constellations are continuously created from the light of the garment. The mythical implications of this idea of a cosmic garment are clearly to be seen.[14]

The parallel drawn in this hymn between God's crown and His garment is also to be found in the very colorful hymn on creation preserved in Chapter 24:3 of the Greater Hekhaloth:

מלך המלכים
אלהי האלהים ואדוני האדונים
המסובב בקשרי כתרים
המוקף בענפי נגידי נוגה
שבענף [שבכנף?] הודו כסה שמים
ובהדרו הופיע ממרומים
מיופיו נתבערו תהומות
ומתארו נתזו שחקים
וגאים מפליט תארו
ואיתנים מפוצץ כתרו
ויקרים טורד חלוקו

[14] Cf. the rich Greek material assembled by Robert Eisler in *Weltenmantel und Himmelszelt*, pp. 49–112 ("Der Gottheit lebendiges Kleid"), and the Iranian material to be found on many pages of R. C. Zaehner, *Zurvan, a Zoroastrian Dilemma* (1955).

וכל עצים ישמחו בדברו
וירננו דשאים בשמחתו
ודבריו יזלו בשמים
טורדין ויוצאין בלהבי אש
חדוה נותנין לשוחריהם
ושלוה למקיימיהם.

King of Kings, God of Gods and Lord of Lords[15]
He who is surrounded with chains of crowns
Who is encompassed by the cluster of the rulers of radiance,
Who covers the Heavens with the wing of His magnificence,
And in His majesty appeared from the heights,
From His beauty the deeps were enkindled,
And from His stature the Heavens are sparkling
His stature sends out the lofty,
And His crown blazes out the mighty,
And His garment flows with the precious.
And all trees shall rejoice in His word,
And herbs shall exult in His rejoicing,
And His words shall drop as perfumes,
Flowing forth in flames of fire,
Giving joy to those who search them,
And quiet to those who fulfill them.

I think it is obvious that the term *To'ar* (stature) here has the same meaning as *Komah* in *Shiur Komah*. The whole hymn describes the wonders of creation stemming from God's majesty, His beauty, His stature, His crown, and His garment. All these terms occur again in a passage of the *Pesikta Rabbathi* (ed. Friedman, fol. 98b), that tells us that on Sinai God opened the seven heavens and revealed Himself to Israel "in His beauty, His glory [*Kabod*], His stature [*To'oro*], and His crown and the throne of His glory." Only the garment has been replaced by the throne! We have, therefore, a definite connection between the *Shiur Komah* texts, the hymns of the Merkabah, and the Aggadah which the mystically minded R. Samuel ben Naḥman received "in a whisper." All this becomes even more significant if we recall that R. Samuel ben Naḥman lived in Palestine during the period in which, as I have shown, the type of Merkabah hymn preserved in the Greater Hekhaloth originated.

In a paragraph of the Lesser Hekhaloth, which is ascribed to R. Ishmael and may not be part of the original text but a fragment of

[15] Cf. Deut. 10:17. The same formula was used in a Merkabah description that underlies the Apocalypse of John 20:16.

some other Hekhaloth text, there is a description of an archon that has bearing on our subject. R. Ishmael, speaking of a second archon, called מגהשה (variant reading: מנחשה), says:

> There is no creature among all His servants who calls him by this name, but you call him מגהשה because he is second in rank to *Hadariron* [variant reading: *Hadrion*], the good majesty [*Hadar*], the pure majesty, the majesty of splendor, the light of Jah [variant reading: *Oriah*], the light of פנהודי [?; *Panhodi*, face of my majesty?] Jah Jah JHWH Lord of Israel. And he stands at the first gate and ministers at the great gate, and when I saw him, my hands were burned and I was standing without hands and without feet until I saw Panaion the Archon, one of the highest servants, and he stands before the throne of glory facing the . . . [?] whose name is like His name and it is one and the same name. And he stands at the throne of glory and clothes [the glory with] the garment [*Ḥaluk*] and adorns the *Ḥashmal* and opens the Gates of Salvation to show favor and loving kindness and mercy to all those who ascend to the Merkabah.[16]

Whether the name Panaion (פנייון), which is mentioned nowhere else in these texts, is just another secret name of Metatron, remains to be seen. I do not think that it is composed of the Greek πᾶν and αἰών. The ending is the Greek syllable *-on* used in many of these names, and the beginning may have reference to the word *panim* (face) in the term *Sar ha-Panim* (the Prince of the Divine Countenance), a term that denotes a whole class of the highest angels, including Metatron. The function assigned to this angel is a new one. The garment of the glory does not permanently rest upon it; but when the divine glory descends upon the throne it is wrapt in it by this archon. Nevertheless, the existence of the garment is always taken for granted and never explained, even though, in this form of the tradition, it is no longer a cosmic garment, but one which can be manipulated and administered.

[16] היכלות זוטרתי, MS Oxford 1531, fol. 45a (MS J. Th. Sem. 828, fol. 23a): א״ר ישמעאל על מי שתק השר שהוא קורא אותו מגהשה [MS. J. Th. Sem.: מנחשה] שאין כל ביריא בכל משרתיו שיקרא אותו בשם הזה ואתה קורא אותו מגהשה מפני שהוא שיני להדרירון הדר טוב הדר טהור הדר זיו אור יה יה יה אלהי ישראל [MS J. Th. Sem.: הדר זיואי אוריה אור גיהוי פנהודי יה יה יהוה אלהי ישראל] והוא עומד בפתח ראשון ומשמש בשער הגדול וכשראיתיו נשרפו ידיי והייתי עומד בלא ידים ובלא רגלים עד שנראה לי פנייון [MS J. Th. Sem.: פני יוון] השר, [MS J. Th. Sem.: אחר] ממשרתי עליונים והוא עומד לפני כסא כבוד נוכח דיבר שרפים [MS J. Th. Sem.: דבר שריפיתיש] ששמו כשמו ושם אחד הוא, והוא עומד בכסא [מכסא] הכבוד ומתקן את הכסא ומלביש את החלוק ומהדר את החשמל ופותח שערי ישועה להראותו חן וחסד ורחמים לכל העולין למרכבה. The archon Hadariron is mentioned in other passages of this book and also in the Alphabeth of R. Akiba, found in Wertheimer, בתי מדרשות, II, 350. In a very old פיוט he is called הדרירון; cf. M. Zulay in ידיעות המכון לחקר השירה העברית, VI (1946), 236, and the literature quoted by him.

The garment also makes its appearance in one of the magical papyri. In a protective charm that shows strong Jewish influence (I have quoted part above[17] in another context), we read an incantation invoking the rulers of Heaven and earth "through the power of Jao, the strength of Sabaoth, and the garment of Elohim [*τὸ ἔνδυμα τοῦ 'Ελωὲ*], and the rules of Adonai, and the garland of Adonai."[18] All these attributes are obviously Jewish, the garland substituting for the *'atarah*, the crown of God. Whether the connection between the garment and the name 'Elohim' has any reference to the cosmic role this name plays in the creation in Genesis 1 cannot be ascertained but may be surmised. Certainly it presents a pertinent parallel to the *Ḥaluk* of the Hekhaloth.

In a Coptic Christian charm containing a particularly great wealth of Jewish material, the garment (in the phrases of Daniel 7:9) and the crown are equally invoked.[19]

It seems that in some Hekhaloth texts there were yet additional references to this garment. The seventeenth century Kabbalist, R. Abraham Yakhini, in one of his manuscripts, the book *Razi Li*, quotes a Midrash obviously borrowed from one of the Hekhaloth texts transmitted in the name of Akiba:

> R. Akiba said: "In the hour when Israel said *'Az yashir* [the introduction to the song at the Red Sea, Exodus 15:1], God wrapped Himself in a garment of magnificence [*Ḥaluk shel Tiphereth*], on which were engraved all the [words] *'az* [meaning: then] which are found in the Torah."[20]

The language of this apocryphal quotation is indeed that of the Hekhaloth or of some expanded version of the *Midrash Alpha Bethoth*. Instead of the Tetragrammaton, significant words of the Torah are now said to be woven into, or, rather, engraved upon, the garment.

[17] See Section VII, note 12.

[18] K. Preisendanz, *Papyri Graecae Magicae*, II, 161.

[19] Cf. the text in Goodenough, *Jewish Symbols*, II, 184.

[20] MS J. Th. Sem., Adler Collection 2360, fol. 97a: אמר רבי עקיבא: בשעה שאמרו ישראל אז ישיר לבש הקב"ה חלוק של תפארת שהיו חקוקין עליו כל אז שבתורה. In *Mishnah Sotah* 5:4 there is a saying of R. Akiba referring to Ex. 15:1, but it does not deal at all with the אז in the verse.

IX

THE RELATIONSHIP BETWEEN GNOSTIC AND JEWISH SOURCES. JEWISH SOURCES ON THE OGDOAS. YALDABAOTH AND ARIEL. ELIJAH AND LILITH

Since it is my aim to consider not only the relationship between the Hekhaloth writings and the talmudic tradition, but also the relationship between these texts and elements of Gnostic teaching, I should like to draw attention to a very significant detail of such teaching preserved in some of the Hebrew Hekhaloth material.

It is generally known that Gnostic speculation about the aeons of the *pleroma* was especially concerned with the power of the eighth heaven, a power beyond the reach of the other seven heavens comprising the cosmological scheme of things. This power was called the *Ogdoas*, that is to say, the number eight.[1] In accordance with the astrological system of seven heavens and seven spheres current in the Hellenistic world and taken over both by Hermetic and Gnostic writings, talmudic tradition, too, knows of seven heavens. In fact, the collection of esoteric traditions preserved in the second chapter of *Ḥagigah* has even retained (fol. 13a) a reference to an eighth heaven. R. Aḥa ben Jacob, a Babylonian scholar (ca. 300 C. E.), states there that in addition to the seven heavens described in earlier traditions, there exists yet another one—above the heads of the Holy Living Creatures, the *Ḥayyoth*. For this he invokes Ezekiel 1:22: "And the likeness of the firmament upon the heads of the beasts is as the color of the terrible crystal." Since the *Ḥayyoth* are located in the seventh heaven, there must still be another firmament (*Rakia'*) above it.

The eighth heaven to which R. Aḥa refers is the place where the most hidden mysteries are to be found, and, consequently, speculation about it is forbidden. Ben Sira's admonishment, "Have no dealings with hidden mysteries [3:22]," is quoted in the Talmud specifically in this connection. In character, then, this heaven is strictly parallel to that of the Hellenistic highest heaven, the *Ogdoas*. For it is there that the Gnostics of the Valentinian school placed the divine wisdom,

[1] Wilhelm Bousset, *Hauptprobleme der Gnosis* (1907), pp. 12–19; Josef Kroll, *Die Lehren des Hermes Trismegistos* (1928) pp. 303–308; A.-J. Festugiére, *La Révélation d'Hermés Trismégiste*, III (1953), 131–132.

called *Sophia Achamoth*[2] (which was also called *Ogdoas*); while the Hermetic writings placed God even above the *Ogdoas*.[3] The question, therefore, that the talmudic statement poses for us is whether the thought expressed by the Babylonian rabbi was his own, or whether it represented, as so often happened in such matters, even older Jewish tradition. Did it, perhaps, reflect Hellenistic teaching? Since R. Aḥa's statement does, in fact, constitute a parallel to ideas expressed in a famous passage of the Hermetic writings,[4] and since such teaching would certainly not have entered Jewish thought in Babylonia first, it would not be unreasonable to look for the origin of his ideas in western Jewish circles having extremely close contact with Hellenistic thought.

Now it is quite a remarkable fact that the Hekhaloth literature has preserved among its wealth of magical material a secret name that in later manuscripts is described, expressively, as *Shem ha-Sheminiyuth*, literally, "the name of the *Ogdoas*."[5] This name, already mentioned in the oldest parts of the Hekhaloth, e. g. the Lesser Hekhaloth, is *'Azbogah* (אזבוגה). It is obviously composed of three groups of consonants, each having the numerical value of eight. The considerable age of this secret name is indicated by the fact that in at least one of the Hekhaloth books it is already reinterpreted in an aggadic manner. Originally a secret name of God in his highest sphere, in 3 Enoch 18:22 it is no longer such, but merely a name of one of the celestial rulers, or archons. This archon is:

> *'Azbogah*, the great Prince, glorified, revered, honored, adored, sublime, exalted, beloved, and feared among all the great princes who know the mysteries of the throne of glory. . . . And why is he called *'Azbogah*? Because in the future he will clothe the righteous and pious of the world with garments of life and wrap them in the cloak of life, that they may live in them an eternal life.

'Azbogah is thus taken as a kind of abbreviation for *'ozer bigdei ḥayyim* (אוזר בגדי חיים), which, of course, can only be understood as a homiletical, and not as the original, explanation. The term *bigdei ḥayyim* (the garments of life), incidentally, is precisely the same as

[2] *Achamoth*—rightly explained as a transliteration of the personified *Sophia* (חכמות) in Prov. 9:1.

[3] Kroll, *op. cit.*, p. 307.

[4] Poimandres (*Corpus Hermeticum*, I. 26); cf. R. Reitzenstein, *Poimandres* (1904), pp. 53–54.

[5] MS Munich, Hebrew 346, fol. 116a (from the tradition of the חסידי אשכנז): שם השמיניות אזבוגה. The Hebrew שמיניות is the precise counterpart of the Greek 'Ογδοάς. Cf. שביעיות (The Number Seven) in ספר יצירה, Chap. 4: חיבב את השביעיות תחת השמים ("He loved the number seven under the heaven").

the one presumably used in the Hebrew original on which the Greek translation of the first book of Enoch was based. In Chapter 62:15–16 of this book, the term 'garments of life' also refers to the paradisic garb of the soul.

The older strata of the Hekhaloth, however, retain a fuller awareness of the original meaning. The Lesser Hekhaloth call *'Azbogah* a name of God: *Shem shel Geburah*, literally, 'a name of the Dynamis.'[6] *Geburah*, or 'Dynamis,' was an appellative or metonym of 'The Divine Glory' among the apocalypticists, and with this very meaning entered the Gospels in the famous passage: "You shall see the Son of Man seated at the right hand of the Dynamis [Matthew 26:64; Mark 14:62]." Although in rabbinic sources of the first and second centuries the name 'Dynamis' was widely used as a synonym for God Himself,[7] the esoteric use continued in the circles of the Merkabah mystics.[8] The Life of Adam and Eve, a Jewish apocryphon of the first or early second century, used (§28) the term 'The Great Power' (*virtus magna*) for God or 'The Divine Glory.' This term must have had wide usage, since according to the Acts of the Apostles 8:10 even the Samaritan Simon Magus claimed to be the Great Dynamis: *ἡ δύναμις τοῦ θεοῦ ἡ καλουμένη μεγάλη*. The usage of the Merkabah mystics is characterized by the following passage: "R. Akiba said: 'When I ascended and beheld the Dynamis [*ṣaphithi ba-Geburah*], I saw all the creatures that are to be found in the pathways of heaven.' "[9]

That the 'Dynamis' in the Hekhaloth texts has precisely the same meaning as 'The Divine Glory' can definitely be seen in the Visions of Ezekiel. There it is said that "The Holy One, blessed be He,

[6] MS Oxford 1531, fol. 42b: רבא רבהון דרבייא [ומלכא] מלכהון דמלכיא, ושכינת עוזו בין פיסת יד, ובשם אזבוגה ק' ק' ק' זה הוא שם של גבורה אשרי כל יודעו ומזכירו בטהרה.

[7] Cf. A. Marmorstein, *The Old Rabbinic Doctrine of God*, I (1926), 82; G. Dalman, *Worte Jesu*, I (1930), 164. The image is different in passages such as the prayer in *Berakhoth* 55a: אדיר במרום שוכן בגבורה. G. Widengren, *The Ascension of the Apostle and the Heavenly Book* (1950), pp. 48–52, has collected relevant material about the continuing usage of the term in Syriac (חילא רבא). If the etymology of the name of the Palestinian sectarian Elkesai as חילא כסיא is true, it would point to the same usage: the sectarian prophet considered himself as a manifestation of the hidden dynamis.

[8] In many Hekhaloth texts גבורה and גדולה appear as components in poetic expressions (חדרי גדולה in Appendix C, § 9; אופני גבורה and אופני גדולה in היכלות רבתי 7:1, 8:1, etc.). The benediction ברוך אתה ה' אדון כל הגבורה in the Merkabah text in Appendix C, § 6, is parallel to מרה רבותא (Master of Greatness) in the Genesis Apocryphon from the Dead Sea Scrolls (col. 2, l. 4). The latter term was taken over from Jewish circles by the Mandaeans—a fact now established by the passage in the scroll. (Cf. Reitzenstein, *Das Mandäische Buch vom Herrn der Grösse* [Heidelberg, 1917].)

[9] See the text in Appendix C, § 2.

opened to him [i. e. to Ezekiel] the seven heavens and he beheld the Dynamis." Some lines farther on the same sentence is more or less repeated, but instead of mentioning the Dynamis, it reads: "and he beheld the glory [*Kabod*] of God."[10] Tannaitic sources, too, speak of "seeing the *Kabod*" in the context of esoteric ideas.[11] And in a later Midrash, the *Pesikta Rabbathi*, there is a saying that in the hour of revelation God opened the seven heavens to Israel and they saw the *Kabod*, which sounds very much like the statement on Ezekiel just quoted.[12] As a matter of fact, the two terms, 'The Great Dynamis' and 'The Great Glory,' seem to have been interchangeable even in earlier esoteric terminology. The Greek Testament of Levi (3:4) and the Greek text of Enoch (14:20, 102:3) know of the **μεγάλη δόξα**, corresponding to the Hebrew *ha-kabod ha-gadol*, or, in Aramaic, *ziwa rabba*. The later Aramaic term makes its appearance not only in the Mandaean writings, but also among the secret names of Metatron in the Hekhaloth.[13] The same term must have been used, too, in the original text of the Assumption of Moses 4:3, where Moses beholds a vision of the *majestas magna*. And, finally, it should be noted that the Visions of Ezekiel uses the term 'Name of the Dynamis' as a parallel to the term 'Name of the Creator of the World', and, in

[10] Wertheimer, בתי מדרשות, II, 129: עד שיחזקאל מסתכל פתח הקב"ה לו שבעה רקיעים וראה את הגבורה . . . ופתחו לו שבעה רקיעים וראה כבוד הקו[דש] והחיות ומלאכי השרת וגדודים ושרפים ונוצצי כנף מחוברים במרכבה.

[11] Cf. *Major Trends*, p. 358, on the technical usage of כבוד. To the passages quoted there, the one in ויקרא רבא, Par. II, 8 (parallel to סדר אליהו רבה, ed. Friedmann, Chap. 7, p. 34), should be added. After God had shown the Merkabah to Ezekiel, He said to him: "Son of Man, this is my glory [זהו כבודי]." Cf. also A. von Gall, *Die Herrlichkeit Gottes* (1900), p. 82, and his remarks on the usage of כבוד ה' (δόξα κυρίου) in an apocryphon of a "rabbinic tendency," like Tobith (12:11, 12:15). Von Gall's definitions hold good for the usage in Jewish sources, including the *Shiur Komah*, of which he was not aware.

[12] This passage of the פסיקתא רבתי, ed. Friedmann, 98b, is of great interest: פתח הקב"ה ז' רקיעים ונגלה עליהם עין בעין ביופיו וכבודו ובתוארו ובכתר שלו ובכסא כבודו. In Section VIII, I have shown that this passage uses the same Merkabah terminology as does the hymn in the Greater Hekhaloth, Chap. 24:1. But in a parallel passage, to which S. Lieberman, in his edition of דברים רבה (1940), p. 66, has drawn attention, even the term חדרי המרכבה occurs. R. Joshua ibn Shoeib quotes a passage from מדרש חזית in his דרשות (ed. 1574, fol. 58a), not found in our text of שיר השירים רבה on Song of Songs 2:4: מאי ודגלו עלי אהבה? קרע לי בסיני שבעה רקיעים דכתיב אתה הראית לדעת, והראני שם חדרי המרכבה. The term חדרי מרכבה for the object of the Merkabah vision was current in second and third century traditions of several aggadists; cf. *Major Trends*, p. 359. All these passages do not employ mere poetic figures of speech, but a consistent technical language developed by the Merkabah mystics.

[13] Alphabeth of R. Akiba, in Wertheimer, בתי מדרשות, II, 354: זיווא רבא, נער נאמן, יהוה הקטן על שם רבו, in one sequence. Odeberg's text (p. עב of the Hebrew part) is corrupt: זיו אוכבר instead of זיוא רבא.

addition, say of Metatron that he reflects the secret name (or a secret name) of the Dynamis.[14]

But to return to our discussion of the term *'Azbogah*. The fact that it is introduced into the earlier Hekhaloth as a name of the Dynamis (*Shem shel Geburah*), and into the later texts as the name of the *Ogdoas* (*Shem ha-Sheminiyuth*), in its meaning of the highest sphere of the *pleroma*, would seem to suggest strongly an intimate connection between Jewish and Gnostic concepts; a secret name of the Dynamis is considered to be identical with the secret name of the *Ogdoas*. It is certainly reasonable to assume, moreover, that since the *Ogdoas* speculation (admittedly not of Jewish origin) is independent of Christian elements, it could have entered Jewish circles, like other elements in this realm of thought, before the break between Judaism and Christianity.

The Greater Hekhaloth know of *'Azbogah* as a great "seal" (חותם גדול), which is another term meaning a secret name of God. In the Lesser Hekhaloth we are told that this seal is among those to be shown to the gatekeepers at the second palace, and at the end of the valuable manuscript of the Greater Hekhaloth at The Jewish Theological Seminary of America we are given still more information:

> R. Ishmael said: "One question I have asked R. Neḥuniah ben Hakanah, my teacher, regarding the name of the great seal. Thus I learned it from R. Neḥuniah ben Hakanah, my teacher: צורטק דרע גאת ערד נזיר שורטין ידידיה. This is the great seal by which heaven and earth are sealed. The awesome crown is: אזבוגה אבגדהו זוה וזוה זוה ציה. This is the awesome crown by which one may conjure all the princes of wisdom." R. Ishmael said: "He who makes use of the great seal and the awesome crown and does not say a prayer on each one, will be destroyed at the end."[15]

Whereupon the prayers for the seal and the crown follow in the manuscript, comprising two more Hekhaloth hymns. אזבוגה and צורטק represent, therefore, the most important secret names to be used in the ascent to the Hekhaloth;[16] even though in the later strata of this literature *'Azbogah* becomes, as I have noted, merely another archon.

[14] מטטרון כשם הגבורה.

[15] MS J. Th. Sem. 828, fol. 15a: א״ר ישמעאל שאלה אחת שאלתי את ר׳ נחונייא בן הקנה רבי על שם חותם גדול. כך למדתיו מר׳ נחונייא בן הקנה רבי: צורטק דרע גאת ערד נזיר שורטין ידידיה. זהו חותם גדול שבו נתחתמו שמים וארץ. כתר נורא: אזבוגה אבגדהו זוה וזוה זוה ציה. זהו כתר נורא שמשביעין אותו לכל שרי החכמה. א״ר ישמעאל: כל המשמש בחותם גדול ובכתר נורא ואינו מתפלל תפילה על כל אחת, סופו להסף.

[16] Cf. also in היכלות רבתי, Chap. 12:3, the invocation of צורטג זהרריאל. In Chap. 30:4 (belonging to the שר תורה) we find: ויחזור וישביע אותם ארבעה שרים האחרונים בחותם גדול ובשבועה גדולה בשם אזבוגה שהוא חותם גדול ובשם צורטק שם קדוש וכתר נורא.

It is also worthwhile adding that in another passage of the Lesser Hekhaloth, *'Azbogah*, as a name of the *Ogdoas*, appears together with another name of similar structure, *'Atbaḥ* (אטבח), as the secret name of the *Dekas*. The numerical value of each group of consonants in the latter two names is ten, and both are among the seals to be shown to the gatekeepers of the Hekhaloth.[17]

We find in this passage, too, that the name *'Azbogah* of the *Ogdoas*, like many other names in Jewish magical and angelological traditions, already appears together with the Tetragrammaton as a kind of composite name, אזבוגה יהוה. The same kind of composite name seems to have been taken over by Greek magicians using Jewish and Hellenistic elements confusedly and indiscriminately. In the famous cosmogony of the Leiden Magical Papyrus, which, as is well-known, is heavily tinged with Jewish elements, we find the *Ogdoas* as the name of the Lord, "which is *Ogdoas Theos*, who orders and administers all things" (*τὸ κυρίου ὄνομα ὁ ἐστι ᾿Ογδοὰς ϑεὸς ὁ τὰ πάντα ἐπιτάσσων καὶ διοικῶν*). It seems to me wrong to separate the two words in the manner that Preisendanz and other editors of this text have done.[18] It appears that the combined names *Ogdoas Theos*—a combination that is very bad Greek, indeed!—are nothing but counterparts of the Jewish composite *'Azbogah YHWH* as we have it in the Hekhaloth. In no other Gnostic text is the *Ogdoas* mentioned as a God. According to the Leiden papyrus, all angels, archangels, and male and female demons are subject to the rule of this God *Ogdoas*.

I think, too, that it is a mistake to assume, as Bousset did, that the concept of the *Sophia* as *Ogdoas* preceded that of the Demiurge as *Ogdoas*.[19] The contrary seems to be the case. Basilides, who calls the "world of the Great Archon" (who may be the Demiurge) by the name of *Ogdoas*, and the Leiden papyrus, both point to the same concept of the *Ogdoas* as does the above analysis of the text in which the *Ogdoas* appears as the name of the Divine Dynamis.

[17] MS Oxford 1531, fol. 44a: א"ר עקיבא: חזור ותפוס לך שמות שבעה שרים שומרי שבעה פתחי היכלות, היכל גאוה היכל רוממה היכל נפלאות היכל טהרה היכל שררה היכל פאר היכל קדושה [according to the correct reading in MS J. Th. Sem.] ושמות חיתומיהן ושם כל אחד ואחד אתה מראה לו חותמו והוא מכניס אותך להיכלו. ואילו שמות שבעה השרים . . . [fol. 44b] ואילו חותמיהן אבטח [אטבח] יהוה אלהי ישראל, אזבוגה יהוה אלהי ישראל, זהפנוריי יהוה אלהי ישראל, זבודיאל יהוה אלהי ישראל, אברגהידריהו יהוה אלהי ישראל, נתפדריאילו יהוה אלהי ישראל, שתקייר יהוה אלהי ישראל, רגזאל יהוה אלהי ישראל. The *Ogdoas*, *Dekas*, and *Dodekas* are found in Valentinus' speculations. The reappearance of secret names of both the *Ogdoas* and the *Dekas* in the Lesser Hekhaloth points to some common ground.

[18] Cf. K. Preisendanz, *Papyri Graecae Magicae*, II, 121.

[19] Bousset, *op. cit.*, pp. 17 and 19. Bousset, p. 340, admits that the origin of the *Ogdoas* speculation is not clear at all, and, indeed, it is still a matter of speculation. But we must also admit that it is not Jewish.

A passage in the Leiden papyrus immediately following the one just quoted reads: "Practice thou the Great Name which is *Ogdoas Theos* who administers all things . . . without whom nothing can be achieved." As a secret name of the God of Creation in a Jewish Gnostic sense, such an appellation is not only possible, but as the Hekhaloth prove, in actual existence. Where such composite names are to be found in other passages of the magical papyri, these passages also show strong Jewish influence. A formula such as: "I conjure thee by the God Jao, the God Abaoth, the God Adonai, the God Michael, the God Suriel, the God Gabriel, the God Raphael,"[20] suggests a Hebrew original, which was misunderstood by those who brought this material over into syncretistic circles. Several aggadic sayings state that the angels bear the name of God imprinted on their hearts, and this may explain the custom of the Merkabah mystics to add the Tetragrammaton or one of its many substitutes to the names of the angels. In the *Midrash Tehillim*, R. Levi says: "A tablet with the name of the Holy One, blessed be He, is engraved on the hearts of the angels as a sort of mark [*asteriscus*]."[21] Amoraim of the third century, such as R. Levi and R. Simeon ben Lakish, might well have known of combined names in the form in which they occur in Chapter 18 of the Hebrew Book of Enoch.[22] This last quotation certainly seems to point directly to the interpretation I offer here.

Conversely, what appears as ignorance on the part of some syncretistic users of Hebrew material is sometimes revealed by an accidental find as being grounded in good Hebrew tradition. For example, an interesting detail is found on an amulet of the Ophitic Gnostics that supplements our knowledge of the Jewish sources of Ophitic angelology. Celsus, writing about 178 C. E., reported that Yaldabaoth,[23] one of the seven archons in the Ophitic system of

[20] Preisendanz, *op. cit.*, I, 38–39.

[21] מדרש תהלים, ed. Buber, p. 125 (on Ps. 17): כי שמי בקרבו—טבלרין של הקב"ה חקוק על לבן של מלאכים כמין אסטרי[ס]גוס. For the correct interpretation of the passage, cf. Julius Fürst's remarks, *Magazin für die Wissenschaft des Judenthums*, XV (1888), 51. I have, therefore, departed from the translation offered by William G. Braude, *The Midrash on Psalms, translated from the Hebrew and Aramaic* (1959), I, 205. Cf. on the many parallel passages Buber's notes and Friedmann in his edition of the *Pesikta Rabbathi* (1880), fol. 104. In שמות רבה, Par. XV, we find: טבלא של שם המפורש כתוב על לבם.

[22] The aggadists explain the angelic names like Michael and Gabriel thus: "because His name ['*el*] is combined with the name of the angel [שמו של הקב"ה משותף בשמו של מלאך]." But the fact that the Tetragrammaton is mentioned in this connection leaves place for the other explanation.

[23] The current etymology of Yaldabaoth as 'child of the chaos' (ילדא בהות) is

cosmology, was λεοντοειδής, which should be translated, "Having the face [and not: the figure] of a lion."[24] Why this should be so was not explained in his sources and is, indeed, quite obscure. The amulet,[25] however, contains on its obverse the names Yaldabaoth and Ariel in Greek letters, together with a lion-headed figure, and on its reverse, the names of the seven Ophitic demonic rulers of the universe. That Yaldabaoth was also named Ariel was not known before the publication of this amulet. But Ariel as a lion-headed angel could be only a Jewish conception, Ariel meaning "the lion of God." Ariel seems to have been, therefore, an older name of Yaldabaoth, and the sectarian who designed that amulet was still aware of the original context and meaning of Ariel. The face of the lion was, of course, among the four faces of the Living Creatures bearing the throne of the Merkabah in the first Chapter of Ezekiel.

That Gnostic and Jewish sources can explain each other is not surprising, although relatively little use has hitherto been made of the more out of the way material preserved in Jewish sources. It is equally understandable that Gnostics frequently borrowed such material and deliberately changed it. I will mention one example, which helps shed light on the ways in which even antinomian Gnostics made use of hitherto unknown Jewish sources.

Until now, no Jewish source has been discovered for the early medieval form of the Lilith mythology. Medieval formulae in the form of narratives tell the story of Lilith as a child-devouring female demon.[26] The Prophet Elijah is said to have been walking through a field and, having encountered Lilith (in these magical formulae frequently called by the name Astaribo),[27] asked her where she was

---

nonsense. In imitation of צבאות (Sabaoth), the magicians introduced theophoric *nomina* ending with –ωθ. This syllable becomes the "magic suffix" par excellence, as in ἀωθ, ἀβαωθ, Ιαωθ. It has no connection with the purely hypothetical word for chaos that has been invented *ad hoc*. The Aramaic *behath* means 'shame,' not 'chaos.' There is an analogous development in the Hekhaloth texts: יא or יאי (from יה?) becomes a theophoric suffix in many names (טוטרוסיא, אשרווילּיא, etc.). The possibility is not entirely to be excluded that in some circles the name of the Egyptian God Thot (θώτ) had an additional influence on this prevalent use of the Hebrew ending *–oth* in these names.

[24] Origines, *Contra Celsum*, vi.30.31.

[25] Cf. Campbell Bonner, "An Amulet of the Ophitic Gnostics," *Hesperia, Supplement to Vol. VIII* (1949), pp. 43–47, and Bonner's *Studies in Magical Amulets* (1950), 135–138.

[26] Cf. H. A. Winkler, *Salomo und die Karina* (1931) and the writer's additions from Jewish sources in *Kiryath Sepher*, X (1933), 68–73.

[27] אשטריבו, a misspelling of אשטריגא or שטריגא (*striga*, a sorceress). Cf. the writer's

going. She answered: "I am on my way to drink the blood and eat the flesh of the young children, etc." Although this connection between Elijah and Lilith is not to be found in talmudic and old midrashic sources, it can be shown to have been used and turned upside down by antinomian Gnostics of the third, or at the latest the early fourth, century.

In a passage in Epiphanius' *Panarion*, a Gnostic apocryphon belonging to an antinomian group is quoted.[28] It tells how Elijah meets with a female demon who introduces herself to him as his own *succubus*! Elijah is said by these Gnostics to have come back into the world after his ascent to heaven. Once back,

> There came—they say—a female demon and got hold of him and said to him: "Where are you going? For I have children by you and you cannot ascend and thus leave your children." And he said: "How do you have children by me, and I have lived in holiness?" She said: "Yes, asleep in your dreams you have often been emptied by the flow of the body [by pollutions]. I have received from you the seed and have borne you children."

That this is a corruption of the Jewish formula in which Elijah conquers the female demon (Lilith) is evident. The Gnostics composed a parody calculated to put the prophet Elijah to shame. Instead of Elijah's asking Lilith where she is going, it is now she who asks him the question. Instead of Elijah's conquering her and banning her to the deep sea (as in the Alphabet of Ben Sira),[29] it is she who conquers him. He cannot return to heaven since he must take care of his demonic children! The motif is similar to that of the well-known Aggadah on Adam, of whom it is said that when, after the fall, he desired to live a life of repentance and holiness, female demons came and associated with him and bore him children of a demonic nature.[30]

---

observations in *Kiryath Sepher*, X, 71–72. The Hekhaloth MS Oxford 1531 (written in the 14th century) contains, on fol. 79a, an old charm against Lilith as *striga*:

שחורה אשטריגא, שחורה שחרחורת
דם תאכלי ודם תשתי
כאלוף תגעה, כדוב תנהום, כזאב תדרוס.

Black Striga, black and black,
Blood shalt eat and blood shalt drink;
Like an ox she shall bellow
Like a bear she shall growl
Like a wolf she shall crush!

[28] *Panarion*, xxvi. 13. 5, ed. Holl, p. 293. Dr. Alphons Barb of the Warburg Institute (London) first drew my attention to this curious passage.

[29] *Alphabetum Siracidis*, ed. Steinschneider, fol. 23a–b.

[30] *Erubin* 18b; *Bereshith Rabbah*, Par. XX, 11 (ed. Thodor, p. 195).

What is said about Adam in the talmudic Aggadah is now transferred to the Man of God, Elijah. The Gnostics mentioned by Epiphanius must have known a Jewish formula current in their own time similar to the medieval one and perverted it for their own uses. The tale concerning Elijah's meeting with Lilith, of which we read in the medieval charms, can thus be proven to be much older than hitherto assumed.

It is, moreover, curious that the *Midrash Tanḥuma* has preserved a tale in which the prophet Elijah expresses the opinion (not shared by later Jewish tradition) that the pollution caused by a succubus is not considered as fornication. The story is given as an explanation of Gen. 5:1:

> From here it follows that he who has intercourse with succubi does not thereby commit a sin and this is not fornication. Although he has given of his spermal flow it is considered as similar to a nightly pollution. And the words of the Torah, "Thou shalt not fornicate [Exodus 20:13]," refer to intercourse with men and beasts . . . . And a tale is told of a Ḥasid who encountered a demon in the shape of a woman [a succubus] and she seduced him and copulated with him on the Day of Atonement. Later, the Ḥasid was very much grieved, until he encountered Elijah, who asked him, "Why are you grieved?" He told him all that had happened to him. Said Elijah: "You are free from sin. It was a succubus."[31]

The story is an elaboration of an older one in the Palestinian Talmud that does not mention Elijah at all.[32] The question which presents itself is this: Is it incidental that the Gnostic version of the encounter with Lilith, or the succubus, ascribes to Elijah himself the kind of demonic copulation about which we read in the midrashic story? Or may there not be a connection between the two stories, the Gnostic one laboring its point in a rather derisive way? I do not feel sure about the answer and leave the question open.

[31] *Midrash Tanḥuma*, ed. Buber, I, 20.

[32] *Yerushalmi*, *Shabbath* I, 3.

X

THE THEURGIC ELEMENTS OF THE LESSER HEKHALOTH AND THE MAGICAL PAPYRI

There is one aspect of the Hekhaloth literature that is very puzzling. The question of the place occupied in these texts by theurgical descriptions and prescriptions and the accompanying ever increasing number of magical names and *Ephesia grammata*—all of which give these books a strange resemblance to the magical papyri—has never been sufficiently explored. Indeed, the speculative, religious element in these remains of the Hebrew and Aramaic Hekhaloth books is so closely interwoven with the magical one, that I feel the distinction drawn by many scholars today between Gnostic literature proper and that of the magical papyri is somewhat overstated. It has been argued by Adolph Jellinek that the mysticism of the Hekhaloth was only combined with theurgical elements "in the end," that is to say, at a later stage of development![1] But I hold the contrary to be true. The theurgical element was not a later addition to the texts but a basic component, one which the editors of such books as the Greater Hekhaloth, 3 Enoch, and the *Massekheth Hekhaloth* attempted to minimize or to discard entirely. Yet if it be true that the theurgical element is a basic one, it is equally true that we are faced with what appears to be such a progressive hypertrophy of this material as to amount to a process of degeneration. What Preisendanz said about the magical papyri is evidently also true of some of the Hekhaloth texts:

> As time progressed, the external paraphernalia of incantations, formulae, magic words, etc. in this literature gained continually in volume. What originally constituted a simple theurgical practice, has finally grown into a highly pretentious and elaborate magical apparatus, as it is described and represented in manifold forms by the collections of magical formulae [*Zauberformulare*] known to us.[2]

This process is particularly true both of the Lesser Hekhaloth and of the alternating sayings of R. Akiba and R. Ishmael (see p. 6, no. 5) preserved in several of the manuscripts and sometimes quoted as *Ma'asseh Merkabah.* In Appendix C I have transcribed the latter

[1] Jellinek, in his introduction to בית המדרש, VI, xxviii.

[2] K. Preisendanz, "Zur Überlieferungsgeschichte der spätantiken Magie," *Aus der Welt des Buches, Festgabe für Georg Leyh* (1950), p. 232.

text, which, in its combination of hymnology, prayers, descriptions of parts of the Merkabah world, and sheer gibberish of magical abrakadabra, is most characteristic of this material.[3] I should like, however, to emphasize here the importance of the Lesser Hekhaloth. This text, written mostly in Aramaic and, with the exception of one paragraph, ascribed to R. Akiba, contains none of those hymns which are a distinctive literary mark of the Greater Hekhaloth. Although in its later parts, to be sure, it, too, lists the names of the angels at the gates of the seven Hekhaloth and gives other information which the mystic must acquire for his ascent (thus constituting a close parallel to Chapter 17 of the Greater Hekhaloth), most of the book's content is devoted to descriptions not to be found in the Greater Hekhaloth, and especially to theurgical instructions of considerable age and to fragments of the *Shiur Komah* teaching. The Aramaic, as we read it in the present state of the manuscripts, is a mixture of Palestinian and Babylonian forms. Since later medieval copyists generally tended to substitute the Babylonian for the less familiar Palestinian Aramaic, this is not surprising. The strong Greek element, especially in the magical words, can likewise be adduced in support of a Palestinian original.[4]

What is particularly interesting is the fact that Hebrew material that had found its way into the Greek magical papyri is also to be found here; not, however, in the original Hebrew forms, as we would expect, but as transliterations of the Hellenized forms. Most of these phrases and names have been hopelessly corrupted in the relatively late copies that have come down to us, but often enough the older forms can be easily identified. Thus, for example, at the beginning of the Lesser Hekhaloth we read the names **יאו צבאות**. Instead of the word *Jaho*, which we would expect in Hebrew, we have here a transliteration of the Greek *Jao*. The Greek form *Semiselam*, probably a corruption of the Hebrew *Shemesh 'olam* (Sun of the World), is found here transliterated as **סמוסלם**. These are only a few characteristic examples, but they prove, in my opinion, that the influence worked both ways. Hebrew elements, taken over at some early time by the Greek syncretists, returned in their new Hellenized forms into the circles of Aramaic speaking Jewish esotericists. They were, of course,

[3] R. Eleazar of Worms knew this text as מעשה מרכבה. S. Lieberman, שקיעין (1939), p. 13, has drawn attention to the passage in ס' רזיאל 24a (from Eleazar's ס' סודי רזיא): ומעשה המרכבה אומר: סנדלפון קושר תפלין בראש צור עולמים. The quotation is indeed from this text (MS Oxford 1531, fol. 56a; J. Th. Sem. 828, fol. 33a).

[4] The suffix –os (וֹס) is particularly frequent in these names; cf. מרכבה שלמה, fol. 7b. Only a few of these names also recur in the magical papyri.

supplemented by a great wealth of genuinely Jewish elements and by magical *nomina barbara* that have a definite Semitic ring, as well as by those that sound like an imitation of the Greek.[5] It may also be remarked in passing that the same observations apply to Aramaic inscriptions of the third and following centuries that contain magical incantations and *nomina barbara*.

How strong the theurgical element in the Lesser Hekhaloth actually is can be seen by considering the beginning of the text proper. After some preliminary remarks, which may not constitute an original part of the *Urform* of the book,[6] it begins quite fittingly with a narrative by R. Akiba relating his and his colleagues' journey to Paradise. This narrative closely resembles the version also preserved in *Shir ha-Shirim Rabba* on Song of Songs 1:4. Following that part of the story I have quoted in Section III concerning Ben Azai and Ben Zoma, we read:

> R. Akiba said: "In that hour when I ascended on high, I made marks at the entrances of heaven more than at the entrances of my own house, and when I came to the curtain, angels of destruction went forth to destroy me. God said to them: 'Leave this elder alone, for he is worthy to contemplate my glory.' "[7] R. Akiba said: "In that hour when I ascended to the Merkabah, a heavenly voice went forth from under the throne of glory, speaking in the Aramaic language:[8] 'Before God made heaven and earth, He established a vestibule [בניבה] to heaven, to go in and to go out. He established a solid name to strengthen [or: to design] by it the whole world. He invited Man [to this

[5] See the long lists of such names in Appendix C.

[6] These are the opening three paragraphs in the present state of the text: [§ 1] אם אתה רוצה להתיחד בעולם לגלות לך רזי עולם וסתרי חכמה הוי שונה את המשנה הזאת והוי זהיר בה עד יום פרישתך, אל תבין בה מה שלא הורוך [thus correctly in MS J. Th. Sem. 828] ואל תחקור אמרי שפתותיך. מה שבליבך תבין ותידום כדי שתזכה לצפיית המרכבה, הוי זהיר בכבוד קונך ואל תרד לו ואם ירדת לו לא תהנה ממנו ואם נהנית ממנו סופך להטרד מן העולם; כבוד אלהים הסתר דבר כדי שלא תטרד מן העולם.

[§ 2] בשעה שעלה משה למרום אל אלהים לימדו הקב"ה: כל אדם שיהא לבו שוגה הזכר עליו את השמות האילו בשם בארי אבהאי האי מרמראות סמוסלם אברי ואנכיבון שיתפסו בלבי כל מה שאני שומע ואלמד מקרא ומשנה ותלמוד הלכות ואגדות ולא אשכח לא בעולם הזה ולא בעולם הבא, בא"י למדני חקיך.

[§ 3] זהו השם שנגלה לר' עקיבא כשהיה מסתכל בצפיית המרכבה וירד ר' עקיבא ולמדו לתלמידיו. אמר להם: בני הזהרו בשם הזה שם גדול הוא שם קדוש הוא שם טהור הוא שכל מי שמשתמש בו באימה ביראה בטהרה בקדושה בענוה ירבה זרע ויצליח בכל דרכיו ויאריכו ימיו. ברוך אתה יהוה אשר קדשנו במצוותיו וציונו על קדושם השם.

[7] באותה שעה שעליתי במרום נתתי סימן במבואות הרקיע יותר ממבואות של ביתי, וכשהגעתי לפרגוד יצאו מלאכי הבלה לחבלני. אמר להם הקב"ה: הניחו לזקן הזה שהוא ראוי להסתכל בכבודי. (The talmudic passage parallel to the last sentence reads להשתמש.)

[8] A heavenly voice speaking in Aramaic is quoted in an apocalyptic text from the circle of the Merkabah mystics in MS J. Th. Sem. 828 of the היכלות רבתי, fol. 4a,

pre-established place] to enable him [other reading: And who is he that is able][9]

To ascend on high,	למיסק לעילא
to descend below,	למיחת לתתא
to drive on wheels [of the Merkabah],	למרכב גלגלין
to explore the world,	למחקר תבל
to walk on dry ground,	למהלכא ביבשתא
to contemplate the splendor,	למסתכלא בזיוא
to dwell [?] with the crown,	לאישראה בתגא
to praise the glory,	למשתבחא באיקרא
to say praise,	למימר שבחא
to combine letters,	למדבקא אתיין
to say names,	למימר שמהן
to behold what is on high,	למצפי לעילא
and to behold what is below,	ולמצפי לתתא
to know the meaning of the living,	למידע בפירוש חייא
and to see the vision of the dead,	ולמחזי בחזות מתייא
to walk in rivers of fire,	למהלכא בנהרי נורא
and to know the lightning.	ולמידע בברקא.

And who can explain and who can behold what is before all this.[10] It is said: For man shall not see Me and live [Exodus 33:20]; and secondly it is said: That God speaks to man and he liveth [Deuteronomy 5:21]; and thirdly it is said: I saw the Lord sitting upon a Throne, etc. [Isaiah 6:11].' "

---

and was published in a corrupt form by Jellinek in בית המדרש, V, 168. A correct text would be: בשעה שירדתי שמעתי קול מדבר בלשון ארמי וכך היה אומר:

מקדש קדישא לחורבא / והיכלא לנור דליק
ודירתיה דמלכא לצדיותא / וחדוותיה דמלכא תנטור ארמלתא
ובתולן ועולימן לביזא / ובני מלכא לקטלא
ומדבחא דכיא לאסתאבא / ופתורא דמתקן יבזוניה בעלי דבבא
וירושלים לעיין / וארעא דישראל לזיע.

(This poetic oracle seems to be an elaboration of the Aramaic voice that speaks in a similar vein in *Tosefta Sotah* 13 (ed. Zuckermandel, p. 319, and parallel passages to which S. Lieberman drew my attention—especially מס' שמחות, ed. Higger, p. 153).

[9] עד לא עבד יי שמיא וארקא אתקין בניבה [other readings: בניזבא or בנדבא] לרקיעא למיעל בה למיפק בה [the difficult word is then explained in a glosse as: מבוי] אתקין, שמה יציבה למחשול ביה כל עלמא וזמין בר נשא דיכול [other reading: ומה ברנשא דיכיל]. After this, the formula copied above with my translation follows. A celestial vestibule (מבוי) is in fact mentioned in the text transcribed in Appendix C, § 3.

[10] ומן יכיל לפרושי ומן יכיל לחזויי מן קדמת דנא [Oxford: דנן]. Perhaps the last words should be taken as the opening words of the following sentence: "First it is said . . . secondly, it is said . . ."

The author then proceeds to list some of the names of God in a long sequence of *nomina barbara*, after which, continuing the reference to the prophetic sight of the glory, he proceeds to *Shiur Komah* teachings.

The occult powers acquired by the initiate to the Merkabah are thus considered to be a prelude to the vision of the glory and the knowledge of the measures of its mystical body. The highly formalized description of these powers combines purely magical elements with those of a visionary character. The power of "combining the letters" mentioned here constitutes an early parallel to the talmudic saying that Bezalel, the builder of the Tabernacle (which reflects in itself the structure of the cosmos), "knew to combine the letters by which heaven and earth were created."[11] In the Lesser Hekhaloth, this combination of letters, for which we are given an Aramaic technical term, is mentioned together with the recitation of the secret names of God.

That such knowledge was indeed part of the secret revelations received by the Merkabah mystic is confirmed by a long passage in Chapter 41 (and also in Chapter 13) of the Hebrew Book of Enoch. There, R. Ishmael reports that Metatron, the Prince of the Countenance, said the following to him:

> Come and behold the letters by which the heaven and the earth were created
> the letters by which the mountains and hills were created
> the letters by which the seas and rivers were created
> the letters by which the trees and herbs were created
> the letters by which the planets and zodiacal signs were created
> . . . .
> the letters by which the throne of glory and the wheels of the Merkabah were created
> the letters by which the necessities of the world were created
> the letters by which wisdom, understanding, knowledge, prudence, meekness, and righteousness were created, by which the whole world is sustained.
> And I walked by his side and he took me by his hand and raised me upon his wings and showed me those letters, all of them, that are graven with a flaming style on the throne of glory: And sparks go forth from them and cover all the chambers of *'Araboth.*

The same solemn formula (quoted above on p. 78), each part of which in the Aramaic text consists mostly of two, and at the end of three, words, is almost exactly repeated in another passage of

[11] *Berakhoth* 55a quotes this as a saying of Rab (early third century). למדבקא אתיין is the Aramaic counterpart of לצרף אותיות.

[12] Cf. Odeberg's notes to Chap. 13, pp. 34–35.

the Lesser Hekhaloth.[13] There it appears in connection with, and as a continuation of, a famous Aramaic saying by Hillel the Elder recorded in the *Sayings of the Fathers* (I, 13). However, the new version of Hillel's sentence combines such divers ideas, and juxtaposes them so curiously, that it is perfectly clear that the statement has acquired a new theurgical meaning. The warning note against precisely such theurgical leanings that was sounded in Hillel's original pronouncement contrasts sharply with the context of the Lesser Hekhaloth and its intense theurgical orientation.

Hillel's name is not mentioned in the Lesser Hekhaloth. The anonymous beginning, הוא היה אומר ("He used to say"), however, is identical with the text in the *Sayings*, where, of course, Hillel's name is mentioned as the author of the statement immediately preceding this one—proving that the Lesser Hekhaloth does quote the Mishnah. On the other hand, the Lesser Hekhaloth gives us an addition to Hillel's statement that might refer to the theurgical knowledge described in the subsequent formula, but that might also have a much more simple meaning. The whole paragraph reads:[14]

> He used to say: Who spreads his name loses his name, and who does not study deserves death, and who makes use of the crown [the secret name of God] vanishes, and who does not know קינטמיסא should be put to death, and who knows קינטמיסא will be asked for in the world to come,[15] and who is the man who is able to ascend on high, to descend below, etc. [as the formula quoted above].

I have not been able to find a satisfactory explanation of the obviously Greek word, but Professor Saul Lieberman has kindly told me that he is inclined to take it for the Greek infinitive form *καινοτομῆσαι*, derived from the widely used Greek verb *καινοτομεῖν* (to introduce something new). The aorist infinitive used here is explained by Hesychius, who frequently makes use of Greek technical language used in Egypt and Palestine, as meaning *καινὸν ποιῆσαι* (to do something new). Lieberman assumes that the Greek term reflects a longer version of Hillel's saying, which is extant in several sources and in various readings as, "who does not study deserves death, and who does not develop his own deductions deserves

[13] MS Oxford 1531, fol. 42a.

[14] נגד שמא אבד שמיה ודי לא יליף קטלא חייב ודישתמש בתגא חלף ודי לא ידע קינטמיסא [other readings: קינטאמוסא, קינטמוסא, קינטומסא] מיתקטל, ודי ידע קינטמיסא בעיין ליה לעלמא דאתי, ומן בר נש דיכיל למיסק לעילא למיחת לתתא [וכו'].

[15] S. Lieberman has suggested that this phrase, בעיין ליה לעלמא דאתי, may have the same meaning as נתבקש בישיבה של מעלה in *Baba Metzi'a* 86a, namely: He will be called up to the heavenly world to present his new views or to make decisions. In the present context, however, the more general meaning might be preferable.

manifold deaths."[16] The Greek *καινοτομία*, and the Aramaic סברא (in contradistinction to mere study, גמרא),[17] could then be taken as equivalents. Lieberman's etymology seems to me acceptable, and, in fact, highly illuminating. In the context of the Lesser Hekhaloth it is reasonable to assume that this knowledge of *καινοτομῆσαι* has taken on a magical connotation and is a continuation of the phrase about "making use of the crown" that precedes it. The *Sayings of the Fathers according to R. Nathan* (as I noted in Section VII, note 36) understood this phrase as meaning "making use of the name of God." The quotation from the Lesser Hekhaloth proves that the *Sayings of the Fathers according to R. Nathan* was not the only text from the Amoraic period that retained the theurgical coloring of Hillel's saying—a coloring which afterwards was sometimes obliterated.

Quite in accord with its theurgical orientation, our text contains, among others, an incantation of the Name in which equivalents of the secret names are given as they were allegedly used by Bileam, Moses, the Angel of Death, David, and Solomon.[18] The passage is similar to some in the Leiden magical papyrus, as, for instance: "I call upon thee with the secret name like the Egyptians . . . like the Jews . . . like the Greeks . . . like the High Priests . . . like the Parthians . . ."[19] The sequence of names in the Lesser Hekhaloth, although varying considerably in the tradition of the manuscripts, is more or less identical in character in all of them. Each sequence contains words with a definite Greek sound, possibly derived from some Greek *epiklesis* or invocation. Indeed, it is stated at the end of the particular enumeration to which I refer, that "This is the *Shem ha-meforash* [the ineffable Name] and its interpretations, its explorations and its pronunciations, and its interpretation is Greek."[20]

[16] In the Munich MS of the Talmud: ודלא יליף קטלא חייב ודלא יסבר קטלא קוסמין [צ"ל קטלא קטלין]. Cf. now Lieberman's Hebrew note on קינטומסא in *Scholia, Commentationes de Antiquitate Classica*, III (Jerusalem, 1959), 82–83.

[17] Cf. *Shabbath* 63a: ליגמר איניש והדר ליסבר. Cf. also אדע ואחכם ואסבר ואגמר, in the text published in Appendix C, § 20.

[18] MS Oxford 1531, fol. 41a: ברוך שמו הגדול [הגיבור] והנורא החזק והאמיץ האדיר והאביר שעינינו מייחלות לו ובשמו משביעין: השבעתי עליך מקליטו . . . [ten hopelessly corrupt names follow here] בלעם אמר טוטיפוס פאמון שמו טופי פוסי פיימון שמו. משה אמר אנקלותוס [ἔγκλυτος?] אנקלוותימון שמו פטשייש שמו וכן מלאך המות אמר פטשייש שמו. דוד אמר אנקלותוס אנקלוותימון שמו. שלמה אמר אנקולותות אנקלוותוס אנקלוותימון חסדסיהו יהוסס שמו. ונוקב שם יהוה לכל דייצבי [MS J. Th. Sem.: די יצבי] טקון [other readings: טחגו, טחון, מחון] שהוא שם המפורש וכו'. (The continuation is in note 20.)

[19] Cf. K. Preisendanz, *Papyri Graecae Magicae*, II, 76. Other examples: II, 94, 115, 128.

[20] שהוא שם המפורש ופירושוהי וחיקרוהי וניקבוהי ופירוש שלו [other MSS: ופירוש שמות שלו] יוונית. Cf. also *Shiur Komah* in מרכבה שלמה, fol. 40a, where, after a sequence of names (composed mostly of elements of the Tetragrammaton), another similar sequence

Whether this last remark shows, as it well may do, that the writer was conscious of the original nature of these names, or whether it is simply a statement analogous to those in the magical papyri that characterize some *nomina barbara* as Egyptian, Hebrew, or Persian, without their necessarily being derived from these languages, it would be difficult to decide. I am rather inclined to accept the first explanation. For the Greek element, or at least an imitation of it, continues throughout the long lists of such secret names or words contained in the Lesser Hekhaloth.

The magniloquent promises of theurgical power held out to the initiate are illustrated in still another passage in the following Aramaic proclamation by R. Akiba:

צפית וחמית בתבל כולה
וחזית יתה מה היא
סלקית בעגלא מן נורא
ואיסתכלית בהיכלי ברדא
ואשכחית גרוסקא גרוסקא
וג' אבני לפידא.[21]

I beheld and saw the whole Universe
And perceived it as it is;
I ascended in a carriage of fire
And I contemplated the Palaces of Hail
And I found . . . [an inexplicable Aramaic word twice repeated]
And three torch-like stones.

R. Akiba's ascent in a carriage of fire, בעגלא מן נורא, constitutes a parallel to a statement in the Greater Hekhaloth that the Merkabah mystic goes up from the sixth to the seventh palace בקרון של נוגה, which is nothing but a Hebrew equivalent of the Aramaic in the Lesser Hekhaloth.[22] There follows immediately upon this invocation yet another one, describing for us even more graphically the potency of theurgical power:

דין הוא איסרא וחיתמא
דאסרין ביה ארעא
ואסרין ביה שמיא

---

is introduced with ופרושו בלשון טהרה ("and its interpretation in the language of purity is . . .").

[21] MS Oxford 1531, fol. 42b. I do not know the meaning of גרוסקא.

[22] עגלא מן נורא in our texts seems poor Aramaic, unless we translate "I ascended from the fire in a carriage," which, in the context, makes no sense. A medieval copyist whose mother tongue was French or German (as were the copyists of MSS Oxford and J. Th. Sem.) might easily have slipped and written מן נורא instead of דינורא (*ein Wagen von Feuer*!).

וארעאניידא מניה
ותבל מתרעשא מקדמוהי

. . . .

פתח פום ימא
וסתם מי רקיע
פתח שמיא ומרווי לתבל
עקר ארעא ומערב לתבל.

This is the spell and the seal
By which the Earth is bound
And by which the Heavens are bound
And the Earth flees before it
And the Universe trembles before it

. . . .

It opens the mouth of the sea
And closes the waters [other readings: the hooks] of the firmament.
It opens the Heavens and waters the Universe
It uproots the Earth and confuses the Universe.

But the great spell that is promised is not preserved, and instead we have paragraphs which alternate between *Shiur Komah* fragments and descriptions of the ascent through the seven palaces and cognate matters. If the text of the Lesser Hekhaloth as it is preserved is something of a hodgepodge, it is nonetheless very valuable because of the material it presents for analysis and because of the close resemblance it bears to the world of the magical papyri. The rhythmic prose of some of the Aramaic formulae—the initiates apparently preferred to convey their teachings in rhythmical and highly formalized rhetoric—provides us with striking parallels to the Hebrew style of the Merkabah hymns.

In concluding these observations, I hope to have adduced enough proof to testify to the antiquity of these sources. The analytical study of several points of contact between early talmudic tradition, Jewish Merkabah mysticism, Gnostic teachings, and the magical papyri offered in these pages, should provide us with enough material to set us thinking. The time has come to initiate an informed discussion of these texts, which should be published in critical editions and translated into modern languages. A new evaluation of the inner development of Judaism and its relation to the Gnostic movement should replace the rash and uninformed judgements that have hitherto prevented proper insight into Merkabah mysticism and Jewish Gnosticism.

APPENDIX A

A NEW INTERPRETATION OF AN ARAMAIC INSCRIPTION

The inscription I propose to discuss was first published by M. André Dupont-Sommer in *Jahrbuch für kleinasiatische Forschung*, I (Heidelberg, 1950–1951), 201–217, in a paper called "Deux Lamelles d'Argent à Inscription Hébréo-Araméenne trouvées a Agabeyli (Turquie)." The two amulets referred to in the title are written on thin silver splints, which were rolled and partly damaged. One of these amulets is no more than a fragment containing four lines, whereas the other—lamelle A in Dupont-Sommer's paper—is almost completely preserved and contains an inscription of twenty-two lines. In a short article preceding Dupont-Sommer's paper, the owner of the splints, Madame Muhibbe, gave an account of the circumstances connected with their discovery (*op. cit.*, pp. 199–200) and presented photographs of them. Dupont-Sommer transcribed the texts of both splints from these photographs, to which he added a translation and detailed notes adducing explanations of his interpretation.

Dupont-Sommer ascribed very great value to the longer inscription and called it "a choice piece." His interpretation is indeed a most exciting one and would fully justify his description of the text as one of the most valuable documents of ancient Jewish magic. In fact, his interpretation of this text would make it equally important for the history of Jewish Gnosticism, since according to him it bears witness to the distinction between the Great God and the God of Israel, a basic feature of the heretical forms of Gnosticism in the early Christian Church. Although we know from talmudic sources that some statements about the *Minim* do very probably refer to Jews who had embraced a dualistic Gnostic doctrine, no *documentary* proof for the actual existence of such circles has so far been forthcoming. If we were to accept Dupont-Sommer's interpretation, this situation would be completely changed. It is no small wonder, therefore, that no attention has been paid to the inscription and to the interpretation—and its implications—offered by the French scholar. Erwin Goodenough, in his monumental work, *Jewish Symbols in the Greco-Roman Period*, has so far overlooked the paper.

I have come to form an opinion very different from M. Dupont-Sommer's as to the proper interpretation of this inscription. The text, I think, does justify Dupont-Sommer's high evaluation of it, but in a direction quite different from that taken by my learned contemporary.

Nevertheless, though my views on the salient points differ from his, I remain both grateful and indebted to him for the difficult work in deciphering the inscription.

The transcription of the text as published in the *Jahrbuch* contains several omissions and technical mistakes. I am therefore reproducing Dupont-Sommer's original transcription, which he has kindly put at my disposal:

1 שוי ורחמין מן שמיה
2 לשלו זה בשם מיכאל רפאל
3 עזאל עזריאל אריאל סררו
4 רבה אתת מלאכי הקדש וחד קימי
5 קדם כרסיה דאלה רבה דיתכלון
6 רוחה בישתה וטלניתה ושידה
7 וׄאן דכר ואן נקבה מן שלו זה
8 ברך מיטרין בׄישם . . . ר . ת . . . .
9 שש קופות וסמר וטוש עקר מכמרהׄ
10 סוסגין ברפרון גסאסטר ושבט
11 תחת יהוה בשם דאלה מקדשה
12 דיתכלון רוח בישתה ושידה
13 וטלניתה ומזקה ומחבלה בשם
14 אלה דישראל לרקיעה מליה סלקה
15 בסטר כרסיה דאלׄה רבה חסינה ודחילהׄ
16 מקדשה ומגדלה מארה ומרומה המון
17 תלתהין חדה כפנה ולא אכלה חדה
18 צחיה ולא שתיה וחדה נימה
19 ולא דמכה אמרת לכפנתה למת
20 כפנה ולא אכלה לצחיתה למת צחיה
21 ולא שתיה לנאמת למת נימה ולא
22 דמכה חזי תלתיהן ואמר נדאן

Dupont-Sommer's translation reads as follows:

1 Prix (?) et amour de la part du Ciel
2 pour qui possède ceci! Au nom de Michel, de Raphaël.
3 de 'Azaël, de 'Azariel, d'Uriel, de la Grande Domination (?),
4 épouse des anges de sainteté, et de chacun de ceux qui se tiennent
5 devant le Trône du Dieu Grand! Pour que soient chassés
6 l'Esprit mauvais et la Ténébreuse et le Démon,
7 qu'il soit mâle ou qu'il soit femelle, loin de qui possède ceci!—
8 Bénis une matrice un nom de . . . . .
9 . . . . et cloue, et recouvre une racine . . . .
10 rouge pourpre (?) de talc; et frappe (de ton bâton)

11 en place de Yahwéh: au nom du Dieu sanctifié,
12 pour que soient chassés l'Esprit mauvais et le Démon
13 et la Ténébreuse et le Malfaisant et le Destructeur; au nom
14 du Dieu d'Israël, célèbre (?), parfait, que est monté
15 à côté du Trône du Dieu Grand, Fort et Redoutable,
16 sanctifié et exalté plus que la Lumière et plus que la Hauteur!-Ce
17 (sont) elle trois: une a faim, et elle ne mange pas; une
18 a soif, et elle ne boit pas; et une a sommeil,
19 et elle ne dort pas. Tu (?) dis à celle qui a faim: "C'est pour un mort
20 qu'elle a faim et ne mange pas"; à celle qui a soif: "C'est pour un mort qu'elle a soif
21 et ne boit pas"; à celle qui a sommeil: "C'est pour un mort qu'elle a sommeil et ne
22 dort pas." Regarde ces trois, et dis: "Fuyez!"

Can we accept this extremely bold translation? Because it seems to me that we cannot, I offer my own interpretation below and, following it, my comments upon several points, especially upon those where I depart from Dupont-Sommer:

1 Begging Mercy from Heaven
2 to him to whom this [amulet] belongs. In the Name of Michael Raphael
3 'Azael 'Azriel 'Ariel. The Great Dominion
4 has arrived. The Angels of Holiness stand together
5 before the Throne of the Great God. May they be warded off [lit., destroyed],
6 all evil spirits and shades and demons
7 whether male or female, from him to whom this [amulet] belongs.
8 Blessed be Meta[t?]ron in the Name of LMRBT [?] . . . .
9 ŠŠQWPWT WSMRWTWS 'AQRMKMRY
10 SYSGYN BRPRWNGS 'ASTR YSB[T]
11 Under YHWH. In the Name of the Sanctified God:
12 May they perish—the evil spirit and demon
13 and shade and harmer and injurer, in the Name
14 of the God of Israel. The words ascended to Heaven
15 at the side of the Throne of the Great, Powerful and Awe-inspiring God,
16 Sanctified and Magnified, Glorified and Exalted. Looking
17 are three [she-demons]: One is hungry but does not eat, one
18 is thirsty but does not drink, and one drowses
19 but does not sleep. Say thou to the hungry one: Why art thou

20 hungry but eatest not? To the thirsty one: Why art thou thirsty
21 but drinkest not? To the one which drowses: Why dost thou drowse but
22 sleepest not? Look at all three and say: Begone.

Line 1. Dupont-Sommer's reading, as he himself admits, is very doubtful. The first word, שוי (price, value) does not make sense, and, indeed, is not found there. As the photograph shows, there is a word beginning with שיי, of which the last consonant is illegible. It can, however, be supplemented by looking at the photograph of the second splint, which has the same opening formula. There the first three consonants are completely illegible, the splint having suffered some damage, but the final consonant is clearly recognizable as *Lamed.* I therefore propose to read שייל רחמין, which translates literally as 'Begging mercy,' and makes good sense in connection with what follows.

Lines 2–3. The four angels, Michael, Raphael, Azael, and Azriel, appear together with other names of Hebrew angels in a Greek magical formula; cf. Preisendanz, *Papyri Graecae Magicae*, II, 168. There this list is duplicated with the following additions: apart from Azriel we also find Ezriel, and apart from Azael we also find Aziel. The two forms obviously represent the same original name.[1] There is no reason to read Uriel instead of Ariel, since Ariel as an angelic name is attested to, for example, by the Ophitic amulet discussed in Section IX. It also appears, in addition to Uriel, on the silver splint from Beyrouth, which, in turn, is similar to the half-Jewish text in Preisendanz, *op. cit.*, II, 160–161; cf. the text in *Florilegium Melchior de Vogüé* (Paris, 1909), p. 288, which reads: "Uriel over the rain; Ariel over the snow."

Lines 3–4. Dupont-Sommer's translation here, and his introduction of a heavenly spouse of the Holy Angels designated, as it were, by the name The Great Dominion, seems to me highly fanciful. As a matter of fact, the word סררו starts a new sentence, the predicate of which is אתת; אתת constituting the third person feminine of the present perfect of the verb אתא (to come) and not the *status constructus* of the Aramaic term for wife. Thus Dupont-Sommer's conclusions from this line lose their validity. Instead of וחד קימי, we have to read יחד קימי (the *Waw* and the *Yod* are very similar here). The Aramaic sentence then becomes perfectly clear, reading: סררו רבה אתת, מלאכי הקדש יחד קימי קדם כרסיה דאלה רבה. 'The Great Dominion' might mean the

[1] עזריאל as an archangel, מלאכא רבא, is mentioned in Montgomery's *Aramaic Incantation Texts from Nippur* (1913), p. 154, l. 14.

Glory of God that comes down to the throne. In this case it would be parallel to the term 'The Great Dynamis' (חילא רבה), discussed in Section IX. שררה is frequently used in the Greater Hekhaloth in connection with descriptions of the sublime austerity of the heavenly palaces; cf. there שררה משונה and also שררה של זהיון in Chapters 3:4, 13:4, 16:3, and 18:3. But it also might have the meaning of the angelic hosts of divine 'Dominations.'[2]

In a letter to me (6 March 1960) Prof. Lieberman suggests another reading of these lines, which would be even more in accord with rabbinic tradition. He proposes combining the two words רבה and אתת, and correcting אתת into אתה (the photograph unmistakably reads אתת), to read the whole as one sentence: . . . בשם מיכאל רפאל סררו רבהאתה [=רבוואתה, myriads] מלאכי הקדש יחד קימי . . . , "the Dominion [i. e. the power or the army] of myriads of holy angels standing together before the Throne," etc. This he compares with Papyrus Leiden in Preisedanz, I, 170, that speaks of an *ἐνουράνιος δύναμις ἀγγέλων*, where *δύναμις* is equivalent to the Aramaic חילא, meaning both 'power' and 'army.' The סררו is the same as the צבא השמים, the celestial hosts that stand before God's throne, exactly as in I Kings 22:19, and the writer added to this the synonymous phrase about the myriads of holy angels.

Line 5. On the term אלה רבה, cf. *Sanhedrin* 96a, where it is discussed. It occurs very frequently in Aramaic incantation texts; cf. Montgomery, *Aramaic Incantation Texts from Nippur* (1913), p. 138; p. 145, on the phrase בישמיה דאלהא רבא (partly misread by Montgomery); p. 183; and p. 218.[3]

Line 6. טלניתא: This is the same category of evil spirits that, in the corrupt form שלניתא is mentioned in Montgomery's texts, *op. cit.*, pp. 154 and 190.

Line 8. Dupont-Sommer's reading, מיטרין (or rather, מיטרון), could indeed be interpreted, as he suggests, in the sense of 'blessed be the womb,' if we knew for which purpose this amulet was meant. (Lieberman refers to Gen. 49:25 and *Beresh. Rabbah*, Par. 98, ed. Theodor, p. 1270, where the phrase יתברכון מעייא דהכין אפיקו might prove the existence of a formula corresponding more or less exactly to בריך מיטרין.)

[2] Cf. K. Preisendanz, *Papyri Graecae Magicae*, II, 164, where the angels are invoked as *κύριοι ἄγγελοι*. The same phrase, on a charm from Beroea in Macedonia (seat of a Jewish community!), was published by David Robinson in *Classical and Mediaeval Studies in Honor of E. K. Rand* (1938), pp. 245–253.

[3] אלהא רבא also appears in the conjurations used by the Palestinian (Ebionite?) sectarian Elkesai in the second century; cf. Wilhelm Brandt, *Elchasai* (1912), pp. 33–37.

This, in turn, could be conclusively decided if we knew the character of the three female demons mentioned in the poetic formula at the end of the text. It is, however, equally possible that מיטרון is a misspelling for מיטטרון.[4] A similar misspelling was committed by the writer of this amulet in line 16; cf. this writer's comment on that line. Moreover, the spelling of Meta[t]ron with a *Yod* after the *Mem* occurs in all early sources, as I have observed in *Major Trends*, p. 70. In the context of the present amulet, this interpretation seems to be preferable; it would then call upon Metatron by many magical formulae, stating *expressis verbis* (in line 11) that he is "under God" or "below God"—Dupont-Sommer's unacceptable dualistic interpretations notwithstanding. If this amulet does indeed come from the third or the fourth century C. E., it would contain the earliest mention of Metatron in a Jewish source outside talmudic literature.

Lines 9–10. At the end of line 8, which is partly illegible, there begins a sequence of magical names, the importance of which has escaped Dupont-Sommer's notice. Some of these words ought to be divided differently. I read: ששקופות וסמרוט וש אקרמכמרי סיסגין ברפרונגס אסטר ושבט. In one of Montgomery's texts, *op. cit.*, p. 223, we have a sequence of magical names, all of which seem to be nothing but deteriorated forms of the first two names in line 9 of our inscription. Montgomery's text is already Syriac and the names read: ששביבות אסתר מותא. The name סמרוט may be connected with *soumarta*, a magical word found several times on half-Jewish amulets; cf. Goodenough, *op. cit.*, II, 260. Campbell Bonner has published an amulet from the British Museum in which the two magical words σουμαρτα ἀκραμαχαμαρι appear together exactly as in the Aramaic text before us.[5]

The primary importance of these lines consists, however, in the occurrence of the magical formula, or "logos," AKRAMACHAMAREI SESENGEN BARPHARANGES (with which I deal in Appendix B), in a purely Jewish context and in a Semitic language.

Line 11. I can see no justification for Dupont-Sommer's interpretation of תחת יהוה as: "Le magicien agit comme substitut de YHWH; il s'identifie avec lui." He misunderstood the biblical quotation אני יהוה on another amulet in the same fashion, taking it without any warrant as a formula by which the magician identifies himself with God. The present amulet indicates in a thoroughly Jewish

[4] This mistake was then repeated, or copied (by the same copyist?), in the fragment of the second splint; cf. Dupont-Sommer, p. 211.

[5] Campbell Bonner, "Amulets Chiefly in the British Museum," *Hesperia*, XX (1951), 310.

fashion that Metatron, or those powers called upon by the magical formula, are below God—and I can see no need for further speculation; cf. Ezekiel 10:20: תחת אלהי ישראל.

Line 14. This line is the main source of Dupont-Sommer's dualistic interpretation. According to him, it means that the God of Israel, in His full power, has ascended to the side of the throne of the Most High, thereby implying that the Most High and the God of Israel are two different Divine Beings. I can find nothing of this doctrine in the line. The phrase "in the Name of the God of Israel," concludes the preceding invocation. The word מליה is not the adjective 'full,' but means, quite simply, 'the words,' *millaya*, written in the Palestinian spelling (final ה instead of א) that is used throughout this inscription. סְלִקָה is the feminine 3rd person plural, instead of סלקו. This is the *kethib*, found in similar forms in Daniel (cf. Daniel 5:5: נפקו אצבען, but the *keri* is נפקה; and Daniel 7:20: נפלו, *keri*: נפלה!).[6] The words that ascend to Heaven to the side of the throne of God are nothing but those of the magical formula to be found in lines 8–10. Possibly they could also be the words of Metatron, who speaks these names or utters words of praise. I rather prefer the first alternative. Dupont-Sommer's misunderstanding is connected with his misreading of line 16. In this line the writer of the amulet obviously forgot the consonant *Peh* in the word מפארה and wrote מארה, which gave rise to Dupont-Sommer's interpretation: "exalted more than the light and more than the height." As a matter of fact, the Aramaic words in line 15 are but an Aramaic translation of a biblical phrase, האל הגדול הגבור והנורא (Deuteronomy 10:17), also used at the beginning of the *Shmoneh Essreh* prayer. The rest of line 16 is likewise a perfectly Jewish predication, referring to the God of Israel and not to some unknown Highest God. It reminds us of the well-known formulae in the *Kaddish* prayer, יתגדל ויתקדש (parallel to מקדשה ומגדלה in the inscription) and ויתפאר ויתרומם in the second section of this prayer (parallel to מ[פ]ארה ומרומה in the inscription). According to the photograph, instead of מרומה we have to read מרימה, which is the correct form of the passive participle. The Jewish character of these lines is overwhelmingly clear and no heretical and dualistic theology is implied.

Even less justified is the additional conclusion of Dupont-Sommer that the God of Israel is here identical with Metatron. In the phrase לסטר כורסיה in our inscription, Dupont-Sommer finds additional proof for the etymology of the name Metatron as a combination of the

[6] The correct interpretation of the form סלקה was suggested to me by my colleague, Y. Kutscher.

Greek *μέτα* and *θρόνος* that is offered by several scholars.[7] This widely repeated etymology, in my opinion, has no merit, and I can only repeat the protest I registered in *Major Trends*. It is certainly too much to say that this untenable etymology has been "definitely established" by the formula used in the present inscription. It is a curious coincidence that, according to the interpretation I offered above, this text may indeed contain the name Metatron, a fact of which Dupont-Sommer was not aware. But this does not give any clue to the meaning of the name. The Aramaic בסטר also carries the additional meaning of 'in the direction'; cf. the corresponding use of לצד עילאה in Daniel 7:25. And even if we translate it literally, there is nothing to indicate that Metatron is called by this name simply because his utterances ascend to the side of the throne, as our inscription has it. The ascension of words and names, whether uttered by angels or by any other creature, does not constitute a specific quality of Metatron, a quality by which he could be defined. This is not to mention the impossible use of the Greek preposition *μέτα*—which does not mean what many scholars have made it to mean simply to suit their fancy.

Line 16–17. The last word on line 16 could equally well read חָמְיָן, a feminine plural of the present 'they are looking.' I am, however, not certain of this.[8] Some lines further on, the verb חזי is used. Whether the two verbs, חמא and חזא, are interchangeable within the same sentence, I do not know.

The poetic formula about the three evil female spirits against whom this charm is mainly directed has some sort of parallel in Greek magical texts concerned with the Tantalus motif (cf. A. Barb, "Bois du Sang Tantale," *Syria* [1952], pp. 271 ff.), but no exact equivalent to the present formula is yet known. The Aramaic verbs נים (to nap) and דמך (to sleep) represent different shades of meaning and could, therefore, be used in contrast to each other.

Line 19–21. Dupont-Sommer has misunderstood these lines. He took למת to mean 'this concerns a dead person.' But as my colleague Y. Kutscher has pointed out to me, it is but a combination of למא את, 'why art thou?' We find precisely the same use of *krasis* (contraction

[7] From an hypothetical word, ὁ μεταθρόνιος (he who stands beside the throne); cf. H. Odeberg, *3 Enoch*, Introduction, pp. 136–142, and my remarks in *Major Trends*, p. 69.

[8] Dupont-Sommer reads חמון, which is a masculine form. The photograph reads חָמְיָן, or חָמַין. The latter reading would represent the feminine 3rd person plural form.

of two vowels into one) in the word אמרת in line 19, where Dupont-Sommer gave the right translation although he was uncertain of the explanation. אמרת is אמר and את. Forms of this type are common in Syriac and Babylonian talmudic Aramaic; cf. Carl Brockelmann, *Syrische Grammatik* (5. *Auflage*), p. 38, and C. Levias, דקדוק ארמית בבלית (1930), p. 137. Thus the whole sentence becomes simple and meaningful.

The importance of this inscription lies in the fact that we have here a perfectly Semitic counterpart of the formulae used in the magical papyri. We learn from it how Jewish writers of charms spelled the *nomina barbara* at the time when the magical papyri were composed or copied. I have remarked above, in Section X, that in their theurgical parts the Hekhaloth manuscripts resemble these papyri closely. But these manuscripts present the names in rather deteriorated forms, the result of having been transcribed over a long period of time by many copyists who could not make anything of them and often corrupted them completely. It is interesting to note that the magical bowls from Babylonia present much less *nomina barbara* material than their otherwise close relations to the papyri and related magical sources would lead us to expect. Inscriptions like the present one and like some of those published many years ago by Moïse Schwab[9] stand as testimony to the lively interplay of genuinely Jewish and syncretistic magic. The Greek magicians used Jewish material and the Jewish writers used syncretistic formulae, which, as it seems, they transcribed from Greek originals. It is easy to see, however, that even these Greek formulae often have a Semitic origin, if not necessarily a Jewish one.

It is also easy to see that the misunderstandings of magical inscriptions may lend themselves to far-reaching but unwarranted conclusions. Schwab and Montgomery have provided many saddening examples. Dupont-Sommer discovered a dualism between the God of Israel and the Highest God who is, in turn, described with all the attributes of the God of Israel! Montgomery, forty years earlier, had even discovered a Trinity of Deities in one of the Aramaic incantation texts from Nippur. By misconstructing an Aramaic sentence, he discovered, in a perfectly harmless context, a syncretistic theology in

[9] Many of Schwab's transliterations and translations are more than doubtful and the inscriptions or charms published by him deserve new readings and new interpretations. Only a few of these magical inscriptions have received the benefit of a thorough re-examination by a great expert, such as that given by Jacob N. Epstein in his review of Montgomery's book, in his indispensable article, "Gloses Babylo-Araméennes," *Revue des Études Juives*, LXXIII (1921), 27–58; LXXIV (1922), 40–72.

which the three names of the Great God, אלהא שדי וצבאות, are taken as a representation of a Trinity of Gods. As in the case of the inscription I have just attempted to interpret, the context in this Aramaic text from Nippur is thoroughly Jewish, and, if correctly interpreted, is without a shade of polytheistic or syncretistic ideas. Montgomery's explanation reads like a parallel to Dupont-Sommer's article (*op. cit.*, pp. 207–209).[10]

[10] Cf. Montgomery's commentary to text no. 8 of his collection, p. 149. The difference between singular and plural in the two parallel versions of his text, which misled him, is explained by the fact that the one was written for one person and the other for several persons.

APPENDIX B

ON THE MAGICAL FORMULAE *AKRAMACHAMAREI* AND *SESENGEN BARPHARANGES*

Both formulae, *akramachamarei* (ἀκραμαχαμαρει) and *sesengen barpharanges* (σεσεγγεν βαρφαραγγης), appear on an innumerable number of magical gems, amulets, and splints of Greek, Coptic, and Latin provenience, beginning in the early third century. They are frequently mentioned in the collection of Greek magical papyri edited by Preisendanz and in Campbell Bonner's *Studies in Magical Amulets*. In Preisendanz, *Papyri Graecae Magicae*, I, 200, the *sesengen* logos is mentioned on a half-pagan, half-Jewish charm, which, according to the editor, might date from as early as the second century C. E. This would make it the earliest known source of this formula. (A gem mentioned in note 17 to this appendix would be much older if it were actually from Herculanum.)

The spelling differs widely. The second formula is sometimes combined into one long word, *sesengenbarpharanges*, but is mostly written in two. U. F. Kopp, in his *Palaeographia Critica*, III, 671, mentions no less than ten different spellings of the *sesengen* formula. In some places both formulae appear together, as in the Aramaic inscription discussed in Appendix A.[1] In several sources, both *akramachamarei* and the *sesengen* formula appear together with the well-known magical palindrome *ablanathanalba*,[2] which sounds as if it might be Hebrew or Aramaic, although the explanations hitherto offered are not very convincing and mostly constitute very bad Aramaic.[3] Paul Perdrizet has published in the *Revue des Études Grecques*, XLI (1928), 73–82, a Greek amulet found in Syria on a gold splint. All the magical names it contains are of Jewish character: "I call upon Iao Michael Ouriel Arbathiao Abrathiao Adonai Ablanathanalba Sesengenbarpharanges Akramachamari Semesilamps Laalam Chorbeth Thaubarrabou Thobarimaou Eloai." A very similar sequence of names is mentioned by Perdrizet as existing on a silver splint discovered in Badenweiler. There the text of the charm is in Latin, but the magical names are in

[1] Cf. e. g. Preisendanz, *Papyri Graecae Magicae*, II, 14 (from 4 saec.): Ἰάω Σαβαώθ Ἀδωναι ἀβλαναθαναλβα ἀκραμμαχαμαρει σεσενγεν βαρ[φαρανγης]. The same names in another sequence appear in I, 106.

[2] For other examples see Preisendanz, *op. cit.*, I, 38.

[3] Cf. U. F. Kopp's explanation (as if the name were Christian!) of אב לן את as "Father, come to us," or as C. W. King, in *The Gnostics and Their Remains* (1887), p. 246, translated it, "Thou art Father to us."

Greek letters: **Ια Ια Ια Σαβαωϑ 'Αδωναι 'Αβλαναϑαναλβα 'Ακραμαχαμαρι Σεμεσιλαμ Σεσενγενβαρφαρανγης Ιο Ιο Ιο.**[4] These types of names were also known in Palestine. H. C. Youti and Campbell Bonner have published two curse tablets from Beisan discovered during the excavations by the University of Pennsylvania in 1935–1937[5] and dating from the late third or fourth century. In one of these tablets we read: [Ιω] *ἀβλαναϑαναλβα ιω ἀκραμαχαμαρι ιω σεσενγεν ιω βαρφαραν*[*γης*].

Bonner, in his *Studies in Magical Amulets* (1950), p. 201, has contended that *akramachamarei* is connected mostly with solar symbols.[6] I think that such a connection (which, like many similar statements by him, is highly hypothetical) would be only of secondary character. An examination of charms on which *akramachamarei* appears as a part of longer formulae reveals the fact that it makes its appearance mostly in contexts which betray Jewish influence. A lion-headed God accompanied by the formula *Σεσενγενφαρανγη*, and seen by Campbell Bonner as a sun god, could be interpreted just as convincingly as a representation of the angel Ariel. As a matter of fact, Bonner himself has published such a representation, as I noted above in Section IX, note 25. No less obvious is the Jewish character of those places in which the *sesengen* formula is found. Preisendanz, *op. cit.*, I, 42, contains a prayer in which "Michael Usiris Abriel Sesengen Barpharanges Iao Sabaoth Adonai Lailam" are invoked. Interesting in this connection, too, are the attributes given to the different names in Preisendanz, *op. cit.*, II, 44 (*δὸς μοι . . . τὴν δύναμιν τοῦ Σαβαωϑ, τὸ κράτος τοῦ Ιάω καὶ τὴν ἐπιτυχίαν τοῦ 'Αβλαναϑαναλβα καὶ τὴν ἰσχὺν τοῦ 'Ακραμμαχαμαρει*);[7] and the sexual charm in the same volume, p. 173, that betrays particularly strong Jewish influence. The incantation in this charm is of particular interest in that it invokes, among others, "the Great Michael Zouriel Gabriel Sesengenbarpharanges Istrael Abraam," reminding us of the sequence סיסגין ברפרונגס אסטר retained in the Aramaic inscription discussed in Appendix A. The letters אסטר in this inscription could therefore represent an abbreviation or a corruption of the angelic name Istrael, or Astrael.[8]

[4] Paul Perdrizet, p. 82; A. Wiedemann, "die gnostische Silbertafel von Badenweiler," *Bonner Jahrbücher*, LXXIX (1885), 215–234.

[5] "Two Curse Tablets from Beisan," in *Transactions of the American Philological Association*, LXVIII (1937), 43 ff. The formula is on p. 55.

[6] Also *op. cit.*, p. 191: "a common magical word usually associated with solar deities."

[7] Cf. E. Goodenough, *Jewish Symbols*, II, 200.

[8] Istrael also appears in Preisendanz, I, 128; Astrael in II, 171. Astrael is mentioned as an angel in the magical Testament of Solomon, ed. Chester MacCown

On the other hand, they could also represent the magical word אסתר mentioned, in Appendix A, in my commentary on line 9 of this inscription. (I quote the word there from Montgomery, *Aramaic Incantation Texts from Nippur*, p. 223.) This very name, Aster, is mentioned on a Latin-Jewish seal ring found in Bordeaux.[9]

Akrammachamarei (written with a double M) also reached Coptic Gnostic literature and, in the *Pistis Sophia* (ed. Schmidt, p. 354:12), makes its appearance as the name of the first among the **ἀόρατοι Θεοί**, a divine Triad standing high in its Gnostic hierarchy of deities. Standing at a somewhat lower station, *Akrammachamarei*, as master and ruler of the heavenly firmament, is called upon in one of the curse tablets published by Audollent.[10]

Our second formula, too, has made its way into the Coptic Gnostic texts. *Barpharanges*—the name *Sesengen* has been dropped—appears as the name that purifies the "living waters" (the latter representing a certain stage of emanation in the heavenly word) in the titleless Coptic Gnostic treatise that Charlotte Baynes has transcribed and translated from the Codex Brucianus in Oxford (*A Coptic Gnostic Treatise Contained in the Codex Brucianus* [Cambridge, 1933], p. 180). This book seems to belong to the third century C. E. In even later Coptic Christian conjurations and incantations, *Sesengen Barpharanges* is used as a plural, indicating two or more angels whose protection is called upon by the author of those charms. A. Kropp, in his *Ausgewählte Koptische Zaubertexte* (1930–1931), III, 31 and 77, quotes several examples of this usage.

Hopfner, Perdrizet, Kopp, and Bonner have quoted a great many instances where these names appear and have indulged in speculative explanations of the formula *akramachamarei*. Perdrizet thought that this and similar formulae were "probably invented in the Jewish quarter of Alexandria, whence they spread in all directions."[11] Kopp, whose *Palaeographia Critica*, III, p. 681, is quoted by Hopfner in *Antiker Offenbarungszauber*, § 735, explains the word either as **κραμ ἀχαμαρι**, which he considers as Hebrew for *liga amuletum meum*, or as

---

(1922), p. 70. Preisendanz, in his article "Salomo," in Pauly-Wissowa's *Realenzyklopädie*, supplementary Vol. VIII, col. 678, quotes "Astrael Iao Sabao" from a bronze nail in the British Museum.

[9] Cf. Goodenough, *op. cit.*, II, 217; Frey no. 672.

[10] A. Audollent, *Defixionum Tabellae* (Paris, 1904), p. 325, ll. 7–8: *ὀρκίζω σὲ τὸν θεόν, τὸν τοῦ οὐρανίων στερεωμάτων δεσπότην Ἀχραμαχαμαρει.*

[11] Goodenough, *op. cit.*, II, 204, from *Revue des Études Grecques*, XLI, 82. Goodenough sees (and quite rightly) no reason or evidence for such an assumption and defended the Jewish origin of the formula without being able to explain it.

ἀκραμνι καμαρι, which should be Hebrew for *protegit me amuletum meum*. This seems rather fantastic Hebrew to me.[12]

I think that the spelling in the Aramaic inscription dealt with in Appendix A leaves no doubt as to its actual meaning. It certainly does not come from Alexandria and from Greek-speaking Jews, but from circles where Aramaic was spoken. The Aramaic verb *'aqar* (עקר) means 'to uproot' and is used several times on the magic bowls published by Montgomery in connection with the destruction of evil spirits.[13] The Aramaic מכמרי corresponds precisely to the Greek **μαχαμαρει**, and although it originally meant 'nets,' it was used in magical texts for the net that a magic spell casts upon a person, thereby acquiring the technical meaning of black arts or magic spells.[14] When *makhmarei* was taken over by Greek-speaking Jewish circles, they transcribed it quite sensibly as *machamarei*, indicating by the *Alpha* following the *Chi* the *shwa mobile* under the letter *Kaph*. The whole formula constitutes an imperative—"uproot the magic spells" which might be directed against the bearer of an amulet. The use of the *Ayin* and *Qoph* in the first word, and of *Kaph* in the second one, proves that the etymology of the formula was familiar to the writer of the Aramaic text; otherwise he would mechanically have used an *Aleph* instead of an *Ayin*. The transcription *barpharonges* instead of *barpharanges* is of minor importance, and, as a matter of fact, the *O* instead of the *A* is found in some Latin transcriptions of the name.

The meaning of *sesengen barpharanges* is not clear.[15] Dupont-Sommer read the first element in our inscription as סוסגון, but I think it could equally well be סיסגין. The photograph allows both readings. What is interesting is that this formula was certainly, and perhaps quite rightly, interpreted in Jewish circles as the name of a person,

[12] Alfons Barb, *Klassische Hexenkunst* (1933), p. 15, tried another Hebrew etymology: אקרא ממעמקים (I call from the depths).

[13] Montgomery, p. 24: משמתין ומנידין גוזרין ותבירין, עקירין ומפקין ומבטלין; *ibid.*, p. 154: עקרית ענקתא בישאתא.

[14] אכמרתא is explained as 'magical arts,' by Rich. Stübe, in *Jüdisch-Babylonische Zaubertexte* (1895), pp. 22 and 24 (even in the phrase אכמרתא דאכמרתא). Stübe's own explanation on p. 38 (from כומר, 'priest') is wrong. The same mistake occurs in Jos. Wohlstein, *Dämonenbeschwörungen aus nachtalmudischer Zeit* (1894), p. 29 and p. 37. The word מכמר may be a Hebraic form taken over by Aramaic speaking Jews, but *kamaru* means 'net' in Assyrian, too.

[15] Perdrizet, *loc. cit.*, p. 79, says: "l'étymologie du debut Σεσενγενβαρ fait songer aux *šišim gibborim* [Song of Songs 3:7] . . . le fin est peutêtre le nom Pharaon"!! Kopp, *Palaegraphia Critica*, III, 672 ff., quoted by A. Kropp, *Ausgewählte Koptische Zaubertexte*, III, 126, attempted a derivation from a plant used in the cult of Hecate, which was found, according to Josephus, in the gorge of Baara. The Greek word for gorge is *φάραγξ*. All this is very unconvincing.

a spirit called Sesengen, the son (*bar*) of Pharanges. It has not been noted by the scholars who have dealt with the magical papyri and related subjects that these names are still preserved in old Jewish magical texts published long ago.

Montgomery has published an incantation where the spirit פרנגין בר פרנגין is invoked among other names.[16] We can safely assume that the repetition is but a later corruption of the original name סיסנגין בר פרנגין. When the first name, Sesengen, was forgotten, it was replaced by a duplicate of the second one, Pharanges.[17] Montgomery was not aware of the Greek and Coptic parallels just as the Greek scholars paid no attention to the text published by Montgomery. Montgomery's guess that Pharanges (he reads Pharnagin) represents a Persian name seems quite reasonable to me. A Persian scholar may still be able to explain both names, Sesengen and Pharanges, in a satisfactory manner.[18] That Pharanges has nothing to do with Pharao (as suggested by Perdrizet) seems clear. Rationalizations of this kind serve no purpose.

The name Pharanges, moreover, appears in the oldest manuscript we have of the *Shiur Komah* fragment, which was preserved in the Cairo Geniza and is now in Oxford (C. 65, fol. 1a, l. 9). The secret names of the limbs of the Creator mentioned in the later manuscripts of the *Shiur Komah* are very corrupt, whereas this manuscript, written in the tenth or eleventh century, retains at least some good readings (indicated by a comparison of the understandable parts of the text with later versions). According to this manuscript, the secret name of the right thigh is said to be ששנוסת ופרנגסיי.[19] פרנגסיי and פרנגים are obviously the same name.

[16] Montgomery, p. 146 (l. 12 of the bowl): מפיקנא להון מן הדין ביתא בשום פרנגין בר פרנגין דמן קדמוהי זע ימא ומן בתרוהי זיעין טורין (In the name of Pharangin bar Pharangin, before whom trembles the sea and behind whom the mountains tremble.). (See the characterization above of *Akrammachamarei* as the ruler of the firmament!)

[17] Pharangin instead of Pharanges is a minor variant of the name. Similarly, the name Sesengen is sometimes written Sesenges. Th. Hopfner, *Griechischer Offenbarungszauber*, I, 189, mentions a gem said to be from Herculanum (??) which, in fact, has the name in the same form as the Babylonian bowl: *Σεσεγγενβαρφαραγγην*.

[18] Montgomery followed a suggestion made by D. Myhrman in *Hilpricht Anniversary Volume* (1909), p. 350 (where an almost identical bowl from Upsala was published, pp. 342–351). But Myhrman did not know of the earlier (fully vocalized) forms of the name in the papyri and read the consonants as Pharnagin, which he derived from old Persian *farna* (light). It is highly improbable that, as Myhrman assumes, Pharnagin was "the name of some great magician or some other great man unknown to us, whose name is used as a charm against evil spirits." In a slightly changed form, however, this might indeed be an acceptable hypothesis.

[19] Another version of *Shiur Komah*, in מרכבה שלמה, fol. 32a, reads: שוק הימין

And there is still more. In 1896, Moses Gaster published an old Aramaic-Jewish text on magic, *The Sword of Moses* (חרבא דמשה), which contains many enlightening parallels to the magical papyri. The language is Babylonian Aramaic, but the date is rather difficult to determine. Even if we assume that it was compiled some time between the fifth and the seventh century C. E., a large part of its material is certainly much older. Gaster used a particularly bad manuscript from the sixteenth century[20] (his assumption that it belongs to the fourteenth century is clearly contradicted by the photograph and his own description of the whole codex). On page ix–x of Gaster's text[21] there occurs a long list of names, apparently of spirits, all of whom are called by their own names and the names of their fathers. This excludes the hypothesis that the list is of angels, for according to Jewish angelology angels have no fathers, whereas demons, we learn from talmudic teaching, propagate like men.[22] Later Jewish demonology has even preserved in many cases the genealogies of particularly important demons.[23] Whether the list preserved in *The Sword of Moses* contains just such an enumeration of demonic beings, possibly of Persian origin, remains to be seen; for the time being, all we know is that it is fitted into a Jewish context. At the very top of this list we find, only slightly distorted, two variant forms of the names Sesengen bar Pharanges, namely, ססגנגים בר סרנגיא and ססגן בר ערגגים. I would hesitate to draw a premature conclusion about the original script from which these names were copied, although the double *Gimmel* in the first variant suggests a parallel to the double γγ in the Greek σεσεγγεν. But there are many variants of this kind that do not have a specific historic meaning. Instead of the form Sesengen we sometimes find the form Sesenges, which would come even nearer to the form used in *The Sword of Moses*.

Since writing the above, I was able to consult a microfilm of the Sassoon manuscript of the text in the Ben-Zvi Institute, Jerusalem, and on page 87 it does indeed have the פ instead of the corrupt ע of

---

של הבורא ית' סתמננא שמו, ושל שמאל פרנגסי שמו. One might even read סתסננא and discover in this name of the right thigh our Sesenge[n], had we not the Genizah MS to discourage such speculations! The printed text of the version preserved in the Genizah is found in מרכבה שלמה, fol. 36b (very corrupt).

[20] The only other manuscript of which I know is Sassoon 290, which has not yet been used; cf. D. S. Sassoon, *Ohel David* (1932), p. 443.

[21] Reprinted in M. Gaster's *Studies and Texts*, III (1928), 77–78.

[22] Cf. *Ḥagigah* 15a.

[23] Cf. this writer's papers on Bilar (Beliar), the king of the demons, in מדעי היהדות, I (1926), 112–127; and on Ashmedai and Lilith in *Tarbiz*, XIX (1948), 160–175. In these articles several examples of such genealogies are discussed.

the published edition. The MS reads ססנגן בר פרגים, which is as near to the original form, ססנגן בר פרנגים, as could be expected. The duplicate ססנגנים בר סרנגיא is missing altogether! In the second part of the text, which describes the magical applications of the "names" contained in the first part, these very names are quoted three times in forms which reflect the original spelling admirably. In §174 of the manuscript the first name is quoted as אפורנגים. In §183 it is quoted as ססנג[ן] בי פרנגנו (נו is a common corruption of ס). Thus we get the name SSNGN BY PRNGS almost in its uncorrupted form, and, obviously, in place of פרגים there was indeed the correct form פרנגים in the parent manuscript. In §192 the word ססנגן is fully preserved, but instead of בר פרנגים there is another corruption, ברא טידגנים.

From the single name known to us from the papyri and the Aramaic inscription, we can draw a line of development within Jewish circles that leads first to the Babylonian bowls, and, finally, to *The Sword of Moses*, in which one name has become two names and has begotten quite a "family" of *genii* fashioned after the same pattern. In yet another long sequence of magical words in *The Sword of Moses*, on page xi:9, the name is actually preserved in an almost uncorrupted form: ססנגי פרנגי instead of ססנגין [בר] פרנגי[ס]. But all this, interesting as it is, provides no proof that the origin of the formula was Jewish. Indeed, it might represent anything! Whereas the Semitic origin of *akramachamarei* is clearly established, the true nature of *sesengen barpharanges*, later interpreted (by Jews) as the name of a powerful demonic spirit, or (by Coptic Christians) as the name of a group of angels, still awaits elucidation.

Perhaps the name is that of a mythical figure, the possessor of magical power, like SSM BN PDRŠ, whose magic curse (אלת ססם בן פדרש) against demons of the night we have in an old Canaanite or Hebrew inscription on a gypsum tablet found in Syria and very ingeniously explained by N. H. Tur-Sinai.[24] A mythical name of some ancient protective spirit, who in the old Semitic way was also called by his patronym, might have developed into a formula in itself in the course of time. Such a formula could be invoked against all kinds of evil spirits. Myhrman's theory, mentioned in n. 18, may contain an element of truth after all. The text of the Jewish-Aramaic magic bowl quoted in n. 16 may still retain a vivid memory of Sesengen bar Pharanges as such a mythical figure, "before whom trembles the sea, and behind whom the mountains tremble."

[24] לשון וספר (Jerusalem, 1948), כרך הלשון, 51–52.

APPENDIX C

MA'ASSEH MERKABAH—AN UNPUBLISHED MERKABAH TEXT

Some important collections of Hekhaloth literature, especially those preserved in manuscripts from medieval Germany and France, contain, following the Greater and Lesser Hekhaloth, a text quoted by medieval authors such as Rabbi Eleazar of Worms as *Ma'asseh Merkabah*. A quotation from this little book is among the lost sources mentioned by Professor Lieberman in his study of lost early rabbinic material.[1] Sometimes this title was used to cover a general collection of Hekhaloth books comprising several items. In *S. Shibbolei Ha-leket* (ענין תפלין, No. 20), Chapter 9 of the Greater Hekhaloth is quoted thus: מצאתי במעשה מרכבה. Rashi on *Berakhoth* 51a said of the revelations Rabbi Ishmael is supposed to have received from the angel Suriel: "R. Ishmael ascended to haven by means of a secret name [as recorded] in the Baraitha of *Ma'asseh Merkabah*."[2] The same Baraitha is quoted in his commentary on *Ḥagigah* 13a. Indeed, the manuscript Munich 22 of the Greater and the Lesser Hekhaloth concludes with the following remark on folio 164b: "finished is the book *Ma'asseh Merkabah*" (נשלם ס' מעשה מרכבה). Rashi, furthermore, also had a text before him called *Ma'asseh Merkabah*, or מדרש אגדה [של] מעשה מרכבה, which contained both the Greater Hekhaloth and an additional chapter on the heavenly *Kedushah* — just as we read it in the manuscript of the Hekhaloth at The Jewish Theological Seminary of America (828).[3] In his commentary on Isaiah 6:3, Rashi quotes matters from this book that are to be found only in the addition to the Greater Hekhaloth.[4] Even *Shiur Komah* fragments are sometimes quoted as *Ma'asseh Merkabah*, for example, by R. Judah Ḥayyat.[5] Moreover, even R.

[1] Cf. S. Lieberman, שקיעין, p. 13 and n. 3 on Section X above.

[2] ר' ישמעאל עלה לרקיע ע"י שם בברייתא דמעשה מרכבה.

[3] This additional chapter was published by Jellinek in בית המדרש, III, 161–163, from a quotation in Recanati's commentary on the prayers.

[4] ויקרא זה אל זה: נוטלים רשות זה מזה שלא יקדום האחד ויתחיל ויתחייב שריפה אלא אם כן פתחו כולם כאחד וזהו שיסד ביוצר אור קדושה כולם כאחד עונים וכו' ומדרש אגדה מעשה מרכבה הוא. Cf. my remarks at the end of Section IV above.

[5] In his commentary on מערכת האלהות, ed. Mantua, fol. 24a: מ"ש [מה שכתוב] במעשה מרכבה. S. Wertheimer's explanations of the title, מעשה מרכבה, in his introduction to Vol. II of his בתי מדרשות, p. 6, are all wrong. He did not understand how these texts are collected (and scattered) in the different manuscripts.

Natronai Gaon, who, in one of his responses, uses the oldest quotation from a Merkabah text known to us, calls his source for the quotation *Ma'asseh Merkabah*.[6]

The following pages contain the transcription of the text as I have restored it from the two manuscripts, Oxford 1531, folios 50a ff., and The Jewish Theological Seminary of America 828, folios 29a ff. Both manuscripts are from the circles of the German Ḥasidim, who preserved material that came to them from the Orient through southern Italy. Both manuscripts belong to the fourteenth century, the New York manuscript possibly to the beginning of the fifteenth. I have used the Oxford manuscript as a base for the transcription because in those parts which it contains it has, for the most part, the obviously better readings. But not a few lines, and even complete paragraphs (such as §§ 18–20), are missing in this manuscript whereas they are preserved in the New York manuscript. All additions in brackets are taken from this manuscript. If I have inserted parallel readings from the New York manuscript (also in brackets), I have indicated them by the Hebrew letter נ. The hymns and poetical prayers are set up as such, although in the manuscripts they are written in continuous lines. The paragraph numbers have been added by me in order to facilitate quotations.

[6] S. Assaf: תשובות הגאונים מתוך הגניזה (Jerusalem, 1929), p. 170, where Natronai Gaon mentions: אותיות הניכתבות במעשה מרכבה שתים שתים ויש בהם אלף אלף בית בית גימל גימל. This might well refer to a passage in our Greater Hekhaloth.

[מעשה מרכבה]

§ 1 א"ר ישמעאל שאלתי לר' עקיבה תפילה שאדם עושה כשעולה למרכבה ובקשתי ממנו שבחו של רוזיי יוי אלהי ישראל מי יודע איזו היא. אמר לי: טהרה וקדושה בלבבו והוא מתפלל תפילה:

תתברך לעד בכסא כבוד
אתה שוכן בחדרי מרום
ובהיכל גאוה
כי אתה גילית הרזים ורזי רזים,
הכבושים וכבשי כבושים למשה
ומשה לישראל להיות עושים בהן את התורה
ומרבים בהם את התלמוד.

§ 2 א"ר עקיבא בשעה שעליתי וצפיתי בגבורה ראיתי כל הבריות שיש בתוך שבילי שמים, את שארכן למעלן ורחבן למטן, את שרחבן למעלן וארכן למטן.

§ 3 א"ר ישמעאל והיאך עומדין עליהן מלאכי השרת. אמר לי: בגשר שהוא מונח על הנהר ועוברין עליו כל העולם. כך מונח גשר מראש המבוי ועד סופו ומלאכי השרת סובבין עליו ואומרים שירה לפני טרקליי יוי אלהי ישראל ועומדין עליו זריזי אימה, שלישי יראה, אלף אלפי אלפים וריבי ריבו ריבואות ונותנין שבח [וקילוס] לפני כס יה יהוציה יוי אלהי ישראל. כמה גשרים הם כמה נהרי אש הן כמה נהרי ברד הן כמה אוצרות שלג הן כמה גלגלי אש הן / כמה מלאכי שרת הן. שנים עשר אלפים ריבו [גשרים] ששה למעלן וששה למטן, [שנים עשר אלפים נהרי אש ששה למעלן וששה למטן, שנים עשר אלפים ריבו נהרי ברד ששה למעלן וששה למטן, שנים עשר אלפים אוצרות שלג ששה למעלן וששה למטן], עשרים וארבע ריבו גלגלי אש שנים עשר למעלן ושנים עשר למטן, וסבובין לגשרים לנהרי אש לנהרי ברד לאוצרות שלג למלאכי שרת כמה מלאכי שרת בכל מבוי ומבוי, וכל בירייה ובירייה ועומדין בתוכה [כנגד] כל שבילי שמים. fol. 50b

§ 4 ומה עושה רוזיי יוי אלהי ישראל? אמר ר' ישמעאל[7] היך יכול לצפות בהן [ולחזות מה עושה רוזיי יוי אלהי ישראל]. אמר לי ר' עקיבא תפלת רחמים התפללתי ועל ידי כן הוצלתי, אל זריז יוי אלהי ישראל. ברוך אתה יוי אל גדול גבור בגבורה. ומה עושה רוזיי יוי אלהי ישראל? לפיכך שמע מה אמר לי ר' עקיבא וגילה לי שכל בשר ודם שיש בלבו שבחו של רוזיי יוי אלהי ישראל מתגלי לו[8] רז גדול זה יגמור אותו בכל יום בעלות השחר וינקה עצמו מעוול ומשקר ומכל רע ורוזיי יוי אלהי ישראל עושה עמו צדקות בכל יום בעולם הזה ועומד עליו לכבודו ומובטח לו שהוא בן העולם הבא.

[7] The MSS read: אמר לו לר' ישמעאל, as if Metatron or some other angel were talking to R. Ishmael, but nowhere else in the text do we find this pattern used, although it is familiar from some other Merkabah texts. Perhaps we have to read, as in some of the following sentences: אמר לי ר' ישמעאל.

[8] Perhaps this should be read: ויתגלי לו.

אל רוזיי יוי אלהי ישראל
ברוך אתה יוי אל גדול בגבורה
מי כמוך בשמים ובארץ
קדוש בשמים וקדוש בארץ
מלך קדוש הוא, מלך ברוך הוא
מלך אדיר על כל המרכבה
נטית שמים כוננת כסאך
ושמך הגדול מפואר על כסא כבודך
[רקעת ארץ כוננת בו כסא להדום רגליך
כבודך מלא עולם]
שמך גדול בכל גבורה
ואין מספר לתבונתך
אתה יודע רזי עולם
fol. 51a וחוקר / חכמות ודרכי נסתרות
מי דומה לך בוחן לבות
[וחוקר כליות ומבין מחשבות
אין כל דבר נעלם ממך
ואין נסתר מנגד עיניך]
כל חיים ומות, ברכות וקללות
הטוב והרע נתונים בידך
ושמך אדיר בשמים ובארץ
[שגיא כח בשמים ובארץ
ברוך בשמים ו[ברוך] בארץ
נכבד בשמים ו[נכבד] בארץ
רחום בשמים ו[רחום] בארץ]
קדוש בשמים וקדוש בארץ
זריזות זכרון שמך לעולם
ולעולמי עולמים עד סוף כל הדורות
זה שמך לעולם וזה זכרך לדור דור
חנון ורחום שמך
רחמיך גבורים על העליונים ועל התחתונים
טובים דבריך על אוהבי תורתך
טהורים מאמריך על מקדישי שמך
דרכך ושבילך במים כוננת
כסאך בכח וגבורה, שירה וזמרה
ענני אש, זריזי אימה, שלישי יראה
אלף אלפי אלפים וריבי ריבי רבבות
נותנין שבח וקילוס
לשמך הגדול הגבור והנורא
לפניך עומדים כל הגיבורים
שהן אדירים בשבח ובזמרה
בחדרי תורה ובגנזי ברכה
מערבות משבחין ומרקיע מברכין

מזה ברכה ומזה ברכה
[מזה שבח] ומזה שבח
מי אל כמוך נושא עון ועובר על פשע
מי בשמים שיש כחו לעשות כמעשיך וגבורותיך
גבורתך אש חדרי חדריך אש
[אתה אש אוכלה אש
וכסאך אש וחנותיך [?] אש ומשרתיך אש]
ושמך חצוב באש להבה
[חי יה יהו קדוש ונורא
ברוך אתה יהוה אדיר בחדרי שירה]

§ 5 א"ר עקיבא כיון שהתפללתי התפילה הזו ראיתי שש מאות וארבעים אלף רבוא מלאכי כבוד שעומדין כנגד כסא הכבוד וראיתי קשרת תפילין של גדודיי יוי אלהי ישראל, ונתתי שבח על כל אבריי

עלי לשבח לאדון הכל
לתת גדולה ליוצר בראשית
שלא עשאנו כגויי הארצות
ולא שמנו כמשפחות האדמה
שלא שם חלקי בהם וגורלי ככל המונם
שהם משתחוים להבל וריק
ומתפללים אל אל לא יושיע
ואני מתפלל לפני מלך מלכי המלכים הקב"ה
שהוא נוטה שמים ויסד ארץ
ושכינת עוזו בגובהי מרומים
הוא אלהינו ואין עוד אחר
אמת מלכינו אפס זולתיך
יהוה הוא האלהים, יהוה הוא האלהים, יהוה הוא האלהים
הוא אחד ושמו אחד
יהוה אלהינו יהוה אחד
יהוה יהוה אל רחום וחנון ארך אפים ורב חסד ואמת
על כן נקוה לך יהוה אלהינו
לראות מהרה בתפארת עוזך
להעביר גילולים מן הארץ
והאלילים כרות יכרתון
לתקן עולם במלכות שדי
וכל בני בשר יקראו לשמך
להפנות אליך כל רשעי ארץ
יכירו וידעו כל יושבי תבל
כי לך תכרע כל ברך, תשבע כל לשון
וכל קומה לפניך יהוה אלהינו יכרעו ויפולו
לכבוד שמך יקר יתנו
ויקבלו כולם עול מלכותיך
ותמלוך עליהם מהרה לעולם ועד

כי המלכות שלך היא
fol. 51b ולעולמי עד תמלוך / [בכבוד]
לעולם ולעולמי עולמים קדושים
ואני אקדש שמך הגדול והגבור והנורא
ההד[ו]ר האדיר והמופלא והנכבד

אדרירום יציב גדול טהור מפורש שמו חוצב בשלהביות של אש חי יה יהו יהו קדוש ונורא בראת עליונים ותחתונים במאמרך. ברוך אתה יהוה אדיר בחדרי שירה

§ 6 א״ר ישמעאל וכו׳[9]

א״ר עקיבא מי יוכל להרהר בז׳ הילכות ולצפות בשמי שמים ולראות בחדרי חדרים ולומר אני ראיתי חדרי יה.

בהיכל ראשון עומדין ארבעה אלפים רבבות מרכבות של אש ומ׳ אלפים רבבות שלהביות מתערבין ביניהן.

בהיכל שני עומדין מאה אלפים [רבבות] מרכבות של אש ומ׳ אלפים רבבות שלהביות מתערבין ביניהן.

בהיכל שלישי עומדין מאתים אלפים רבבות מרכבות של אש ומאת אלפים רבבות שלהביות מתערבין ביניהן.

בהיכל רביעי עומדין אלף אלפי רבבות מרכבות של אש וב׳ אלפים אלפים רבבות שלהביות מתערבין ביניהן.

בהיכל חמשי עומדין ד׳ אלפי אלפים רבבות מרכבות של אש וב׳ אלפים אלפים רבבות שלהביות מתערבין ביניהן

בהיכל ששי עומדין מ׳ אלף אלפי רבבות מרכבות של אש וב׳ אלף אלפי רבבות שלהביות מתערבין ביניהן.

בהיכל השביעי עומדין מאה אלף אלפי רבבות מרכבות של אש וב׳ אלפי אלפים רבבות שלהביות מתערבין ביניהן.

בהיכל ראשון מרכבות של אש אומרים ק׳ ק׳ ק׳ יהוה צבאות מלא כל הארץ כבודו.[10] ושלהביותיהן של אש מתפזרין ומתקבצין להיכל שני ואומרים ק׳ ק׳ ק׳ יהוה צבאות מלא כל הארץ כבודו.

בהיכל השני מרכבות של אש אומרים ברוך כבוד יהוה ממקומו וגם שלהביותיהן של אש מתפזרין ומתקבצין בהיכל שלישי, ואומרין ברוך כבוד יהוה ממקומו.

בהיכל שלישי מרכבות של אש אומרים ברוך שם כבוד מלכותו לעולם ועד ממקום בית שכינתו.[11] ושלהביותיהן של אש מתפזרין ומתקבצין להיכל רביעי ואומרין ברוך שם כבוד מלכותו לעולם ועד ממקום בית שכינתו.

בהיכל רביעי מרכבות של אש אומרים ברוך יהוה חי וקיים לעולם ולעלמי עולמים אדיר על כל המרכבה. ושלהביותיהן של אש מתפזרין ומתקבצין להיכל חמשי ואומרין ברוך יהוה חי וקיים לעולם ולעלמי עולמים אדיר על כל המרכבה.

[9] This line is lacking in MS New York.

[10] The reading in MS Oxford is corrupt.

[11] This phrase in Hebrew also appears in ויקרא רבה, Par. II, and in Aramaic in the *Targum* of the *Kedushah*, מאתר בית שכינתיה.

בהיכל חמשי מרכבות של אש אומרין ברוך קדושת מלכותו ממקום בית
שכינתו. ושלהביותיהן של אש מתפזרין ומתקבצין להיכל ששי ואומרין / ברוך fol. 52a
קדושת מלכותו ממקום בית שכינתו.

בהיכל ששי מרכבות של אש אומרים ברוך יהוה אדון כל הגבורה ומושל על כל המרכבה. ושלהביותיהן של אש מתפזרין ומתקבצין להיכל שביעי ואומרין ברוך יהוה אדון כל הגבורה ומושל על כל המרכבה.

בהיכל שביעי מרכבות של אש אומרים ברוך מלך מלכי המלכים יהוה אדון כל הגבורה מי כאל חי וקיים שכחו [שבחו?] בשמי שמים קדושת מלכותו בשמי שמי מרום גבורתו בחדרי חדרים מזה קדוש ומזה קדוש ומביעים שירה[12] תמיד ומזכירים שמו של גהוריא [נ׳: גהוזיי] יוי אלהי ישראל ואומרים ברוך שם כבוד מלכותו לעולם ועד ממקום בית שכינתו.

§ 7 א״ר ישמעאל בשעה שאמר לי ר׳ נחוניא בן הקנה רבי רז חדרי היכל המרכבה וגם תורה לא אשכח חדר מהן ראיתי מלכו של עולם יושב על כסא רם ונישא וכל חדרי [סידרי נ׳] קדושת שמו וגבורתו מקדשין שמו בשבחו כעיניין שנא׳ וקרא זה אל זה ואמר ק׳ ק׳ ק׳ יהוה צבאות מלא כל הארץ כבודו.

§ 8 א״ר עקיבא אשרי אדם שעומד בכל כחו ומגיע שירה לפני ברוכיי יוי אלהי ישראל וצופה במרכבה ורואה כל מה שעושין לפני כסא הכבוד שיושב עליו ברוכיי יוי אלהי ישראל ורואה למצוה ולגבורה ולחוקים ולגזירות טובות שיבטל גזירות קשות מן העולם ולא ינדה [?] את חבירו בשם טען טרוגג יוי אלהי ישראל ששמו כגבורתו וגבורתו כשמו, הוא כחו וכחו הוא ושמו כשמו אסבוגג לצרש ששגג גדו הג גדז הון נורא רעד הו יו הד בה י״י י״י אחד אה הה יהו שמו.

§ 9 א״ר ישמעאל שאלתי לר׳ עקיבא כמה שיעור בין גשר לגשר. אמר לי ר׳
עקיבא / ישרות וחסידות בלבבך וידעת כמה שיעור בשמים. אמר לי כשעליתי fol. 52b
להיכל ראשון חסיד הייתי. בהיכל ב׳ טהור הייתי, בהיכל ג׳ ישר הייתי, בהיכל ד׳ תמים הייתי, בהיכל ה׳ היגעתי קדושה לפני מלך מלכי המלכים ב״ה, בהיכל ו׳ אמרתי קדושה לפני מי שאמר ויצר וציוה כל הבריות שלא ישחיתוני מלאכי שרת, בהיכל ז׳ עמדתי בכל כחי נרתעתי ונזדעזעתי בכל איבריי ואמרתי:

א״ת אל חי וקיים אשר יצרת שמים וארץ
זולתך אין צור לעד
זכרך יפארו גדודי מעלה
מעשה ידיך בתבל ארצך
האל הגדול יוצר הכל
אדיר בגדולה אהוב בגבורה
מודים לפניך גבורי כח
שעמלך לפניך[13] באמת וצדק
צדק תעשה בעולמך
ובצדקת שמך תציל אותי
וברכת כבודך אגדיל לעד
ברוך אתה אדיר בחדרי גדולה

[12] Better: ומגיעין שירה. Phrases like להגיע קדושה are current in this literature. In §§ 8 and 31 the MSS read indeed מגיע שירה in a similar context.

[13] New York: שעומדים לפניך.

§ 10 א״ר ישמעאל וכמה שיעור בין גשר לגשר? אמר לי בין גשר לגשר שנים עשר ריבוא פרסאות, בעלייתן שנים עשר ריבוא פרסאות ובירידתן שנים עשר ריבוא פרסאות. בין נהרי אימה לנהרי יראה כ״ב ריבוא פרסאות. בין נהרי ברד לנהרי חשך ל״ו ריבוא פרסאות. בין חדרי ברקים לענני ניחומים מ״ב ריבוא פרסאות. בין ענני ניחומים למרכבה פ״ד ריבוא פרסאות. בין מרכבה לכרובים קס״ח ריבוא פרסאות. בין כרובים לאופנים כ״ד ריבוא פרסאות. בין אופנים לחדרי חדרים כ״ד ריבוא פרסאות. בין חדרי חדרים לחיות הקודש מ׳ אלפי׳ ריבוא פרסאות. בין כנף לכנף י״ב ריבוא פרסאות, ורוחבן כמו כן. מחיות הקודש לכסא הכבוד ל׳ ריבוא פרסאות. ומרגל כסא הכבוד עד מקום שהוא יושב עליו קדוש מלך רם ונישא אנפרא [נ׳ אנפקה] יוי אלהי ישראל מ׳ אלפים ריבוא פרסאות ושמו הגדול מתקדש שם.

§ 11 א״ר ישמעאל אני הייתי בן שלש עשרה שנה ורחש לבי בכל יום ששרוי [הייתי] בתענית. כיון שגילה ר׳ נחוניא בן הקנה שר של תורה נגלה סווריא[14] שר הפנים אמר לי שר של תורה יופיאל שמו וכל מי שהוא מבקש עליו ישב ארבעים יום בתענית יאכל פתו במלח ולא יאכל כל מיני זוהמא. ויטבול כ״ד טבילות ולא יסתכל[15] בכל מיני צבעונין עיניו ויכבשון בארעא. ויתפלל בכל כחו ויכוין לבו בתפילתו ויחתום עצמו בחותמות שלו ויזכיר שנים עשר דברים: אתה אל חי בשמים החקוק כספיסטוס טמסטוס עקניפוס ענבי בגאה ועפפפא חוכמת פדוך סרט פרטתא אגניטינטון הדרת זוף ואה סרכי ונאין שבעין דינין שבים יזכור דימספא בה בא וה בדירא סות פני אות פיו אניון יזז כוכי הדריה שם החכמה וירדו אצלי שבעים מלאכים ושקדהוזיי מלאך הפנים עמהן. ויזכיר אותיות שלא יתנזק זייף פחף זרץ שמף תירגב בב פימף יה לשמור.[16]

fol. 53b אתה אל חי בשמים שנתתה רשות לגדודי כבודך שיזקקו לבני אדם בטהרה אני מזכיר שמך שהוא אחד על כל הבריות סבר דראי אדיר אדיר דריאם יחפס דרסיי חותם קדוש דש קדש יהו בדף בראייה לעולם עפמעופפפא יהו קדוש וב״ש [וברוך שמו?] חותם למעלה מראשי.

רז יסרז מעל הרזין הגן [?] בוב יה ית שי ישתקעו מזיקים רעים ואדירות גאוות תהא חותם על איבריי בשמך צרוגג צרפף זהתיאג יה יה יהו מי כמוך גדול ונורא. ע״א.

אדירי חכמה יצרתה שיש להן רשות שיורידו סתרי חכמה מרשות שמך שאתה מלכו של עולם בכן אני מזכיר לפניך שם שקדהוזיה עבדך קייץ דדי זזא שבכץ וחביאל סגרץ בחר גיא ארשום פילו מיפטון ארוץ חמם נקב גם תקדרון זרזיאל זעזיאל הגבץ אדרץ נסגיואל זריואל יהוה גדיתיאל יהוה אל יה אלהי חז יילא חילא יהוה ששמו מעולה על שם יוצרו שם שקדהוזיה עבדך הזכרתי שיהיו לי ניסים ונבורות נפלאות רבות אותות ומופתים גדול ונורא בחדרי חכמה ובסתר בינה ואשורר לפניך כמה שנ׳ מי כמוכה באלים יי׳ וגו׳ ברוך אתה יהוה אדון ניסים וגבורות שומע מקדישי שמך ומתרצה ליודעי שמך. וישא עיניו לשמים שלא ימות ויעמוד ויזכיר שם ויפאר כדי שתהא מחוקק בכל איבריו

[14] On this form of the name סוריא, see my article in ס׳ אסף (1953), pp. 470–471.

[15] Perhaps: יסתכלו.

[16] In MS Oxford, the third part of a page is left empty (for other magical names?).

חכמה וחקר בינה בלבבו ויקדים ויתפלל אותו בשמו ויעשה לו עוגה ויעמוד בה
כדי שלא יבואו המזיקין וידמו לו כמלאכים ויהרגוהו.

§ 12 א"ר ישמעאל אמר לי ארפדס מלאך הפנים כל מי שרוצה להשתמש ברז
גדול זה יתפלל אותו בכל כחו שלא ישכח ממנו דבר אחד [שאם שכח] כל
fol. 54a איבריו בהשחת / ויקרא אותם ג' שמות ואני אֲרַד: סדיר תיגרי אם יביא
ביהו סווץ דוף רוף דחם.

§ 13 א"ר ישמעאל שאלתי לר' נחוניא בן הקנה רבי היאך חכמתו של שר
התורה. אמר לי בשעה שאתה מתפלל הזכר ג' שמות שמזכירין מלאכי הכבוד זץ
טיץ זרזיאל תית תופילטי רבת יפא ארחר זיעא עיזוז בגבורה. וכשאתה מתפלל
הזכר בסוף ג' אותיות שמזכירין חיות בשעה שצופין ורואין בארכס יוי אלהי
ישראל גלי איי ארדר יה אל זך בביבא. וכשאתה מתפלל תפילה אחרת הזכר
ג' אותיות שמזכירין גלגלי המרכבה שאומרי' שירה לפני כסא הכבוד הץ פזיפא
הף יאו גהוא שביבא זו היא קנין חכמה שכל אדם שהוא מזכירן קונה חכמה לעולם
וכי יכול אדם לעמוד בו אלא שלש אותיות כתב משה ליהושע בכוס ושתה אם
אין אתה יכול לעמוד חקוק אותם בחוק ואל תצטער בדברי גיבורים. זפק קנידר
הוווא הבא שבון קן טבב צבו הץ הר יט הדרו הדר הוזה שכון ואל תשכח
אזקמף אופופי ידדר אורנוד אב נורא לזריזות חכמה ולאדירות בינה.

§ 14 א"ר ישמעאל ישבתי שנים עשר יום בתענית כיון שראיתי שאינני [יכול]
השתמשתי בשם של ארבעים ושתים אותיות וירד פדקרס מלאך בזעם. אמר לי
בן טיפה סרוחה איני נותן עד שתשב ארבעים יום. מיד נזדעזעתי והזכרתי
ג' אותיות ועלה זה בארעא ביה גדולת אתית ביה[17] וישבתי ארבעים יום והתפללתי
שלש תפילות בשחרית ושלש תפילות בצהרים ושלש בערב והזכרתי י"ב דברים
על כל אחד ואחד וליום אחרון התפללתי ג' והזכרתי שנים עשר דברים וירד
fol. 54b פדקרס מלאך הפנים ועמו מלאכי רחמים / והשכינו חכמה בלב[י]. ר' ישמעאל[18]
מי יוכל לעמוד בתפילתו, מי יוכל לצפות בפדקרס מלאך הפנים משעה שקיים
רז זה. אמר לי פנקרס[19] יוי אלהי ישראל רד וראה אדם דומה לך אם לא ירד
מרשות פנקרס יוי אלהי ישראל השחיתו.

§ 15 א"ר ישמעאל ז' חותמות חתמתי עצמי בשעה שירד פדקרס מלאך הפנים.
ברוך אתה יהוה שבראת שמים וארץ בחכמתך ובתבונתך לעולם שמך חי אוף
סיסי פייאו לו סס בי כיי תגיי שם עבדך אורים ססתיי על רגלי, אבג בגג על לבי
ארים תיפא על זרוע ימיני אורים תסי יאה על זרוע שמאלי, אבית תל בג אר
ייו דיואל על צוארי, אוף אף קיטר סס אחד ידידיה לשמירת גופי, ולמעלה
מכולם אוף פת יהו חיו יו זהו יהו תיתם מעל ראשי מר גוג גדול הף יף הף טהור
הה ייו ההי הה הה הזכרות עולם תתברך אדון החכמה שכל הגבורה שלך. ברוך
אתה יהוה אדון גבורה רם ונישא גדול בממשלה. אתה הוא מלך מלכי המלכים ב"ה.
תתברך אתה לבדך כי אתה אחד לבדך הוכח שמך אווזא זוהוואה שמך רם כי
יד אזי שמך אביץ יהו שמך, זיהא יה טיראי שמך, גחוף שמך, עותתיאה שמך חכבוידהא
שמך, להבת גברת רם זה זיו אדון כל המרכבה לעולם תתקדש מלך הקדוש
קדושתך בשמים ובארץ ברוך אתה יהוה האל הקדוש.

[17] Corrupt. [18] To read: אמר ר' ישמעאל.
[19] It seems that פדקרס מלאך [scil. מלאך הפנים] and פנקרס יוי אלהי ישראל are identical.

אתה מלך הכבוד דרכם [!] כבוד ודבריך קדוש שמך כבוד גדול וקדוש
לעולם ולעולמי עולמים רם יהו עיזוז חיי גיבור דרכיי אהדיץ ריוא לך ברואה
fol. 55a זהרי והא הו ביהו אל פב דריאם יראה חבבא ההגו יא הם תם יתת / הף פא
גה יהו יהו תתקלס מלך העולם שנתת רשות להזכרות שמך בעמידה ובישיבה
ובשאר כל גדולת החכמה יף שתת אד יה סבי אף אראה יוף יה הפוף ביפא
נבטס חיה זו חי וארם עדי עד ישתבח מלך שבח ששמך גדול בשבח ושמך[20]
רם ונישא ברוך אתה יהוה גדול חי בגבורה.

והזכרתי שלשה שמות זייף פסף ארץ משמו שלא יגע בי [בהשחת וכשעלה
הזכרתי שלש אותיות שלא יגעו בי] מלאכים ומזיקים. רדנו יאה סהרי יואי
אכבכי איס תכי כויוא האל הב ואשכיר והמזיקין דע כ"ב ביניין אריס מדרס
קדומה אלף איס יהא יזה מביא אוף הף יה יד יה הו חותם גדול.

§ 16 א"ר ישמעאל אמר לי ר' נחוניא בן הקנה אדם המבקש להשתמש ברז
הגדול הזה יזכיר מלאכים העומדים מאחורי (ה)חיות הקודש מקלס אסגד נוסס
ויתפלל תפילה שלא ישחיתו אותו שהן זעופין מכל צבא מרום. ומה היא התפילה

ברוך אתה יהוה אלהי ויוצרי גדול ונורא
חי העולמים אדיר על כל המרכבה
מי כמוך אדיר במרום
הצליחה לי בכל איבריי
ואהגה בשערי חכמה ואחקור בדרכי בינה
ואצפה בחדרי תורה ואהגה בגנזי ברכה
ויהיו גנוזות לי כי חכמה לפניך
והצל אותי מכל זעופין שעומדין ויהיו לי אוהבים לי לפניך
ואדע כי קדושתך לעולם
ואברך קדושת שמך לעולם
ואקדש שמך הקדוש והגדול
ויהי חותם גדול על כל איבריי דג' [דגופי?]
ככתוב ואקרא ק' ק' ק' יוי צבאות מלא כל הארץ כבודו
ברוך אתה יהוה חי העולמים

§ 17 ושוב אמרתי לר' נחוניא בן הקנה בשעה שהזכיר י"ב דברים היאך יכול
fol. 55b לצפות / בזיו השכינה. אמר לי תפילה התפלל בכל כחו ושכינה אהובה לו
ונותן לו רשות לצפות ואינו ניזוק.

§ 18 א"ר ישמעאל[21] דין עובד חכמה ובינה דכל דעביד ליה חכים ובני בשם
יה יה יהו יהו יהי יהי הי הי הו הו אהו אהו אה יה אהיה
אהיה אהיה ברוך ברוך קדוש קדוש שדי שדי יהוץ יהוץ פץ
פץ פץ רחום רחום חנון חנון. מפרש שמיה בארבעין ותרין אתון
דמאן דעביד ליה חכים וחכמתא מתמלא. זה שמי לעולם וזה זכרי לדור דור.

[20] MSS: ושמח.

[21] The three paragraphs, 18–20, are omitted in MS Oxford. They are found in MS New York on fol. 32b–33a.

ברוך שם כבוד מלכותו לעולם ועד אא"ס. ובנחה יאמר שובה יהוה רבבות אלפי
ישראל.

§ 19 א"ר ישמעאל תלמיד המבקש להשתמש ברז זה הגדול ישב בתענית
מראש חדש סיון ועד עצרת ולא יאכל אלא מן רישא דפסקת מן כלהו ולחש
ירח[ש?] או מייתי חמרא ואפי חדא ריפתא בידיה. אזיל לנהרא וטביל ואף
הנך תשעה יומי צפרא ופנייא טביל וביומא בתראה כד בעי למפא טביל ובתר
דאפי לה טביל וכד בני [?] לה טביל ובתר דאכיל לה לא צריך. וכי בעי
למיכליה לייתי כודא דחמרא מפום דנא ומני עליה ט' זמנין וטביל ושתי ומשתמש
במני חדיתי. ולא לישכוב לחודיה כי היכי דלא לתנזק.

§ 20 א"ר ישמעאל לר' עקיבא טרף תאנה וטרפי זיתא וכסא דכספא וחמרא
וביצה. אמר לי על כולם ששאלת לקדושה וטהרה ישרות וחסידות בלבבך ואתה
עומד בכחן. טרף תאנה. אשבעית עלך סנדלפון מלאכא דהוא קטר תגא למריה
דתיסק ותימר ליה תרין מלאכייא מטטרון ועגמטיא דאינון[22] חכמתא בלבא
דיליה פלוני ואדע ואחכם ואסבר ואגמר ולא אשכח, ואיליף ולא איתנשי,
דאתו קדמאי ודאתו בתראי, עלי לא יחלפון, בשום פץ מפץ מפץ צאה ציאה שק
בקק אה יה ואזמר כגון [נגון?] הוא גמר כגון [נגון?], אברכיניה בשום אה
ואה באה יהו יהו אה יאה האי מעתה ועד עולם. טביל פנייא ולמחר תענית
וכתוב עלי טרף תאנתא ואכול ושתי חמרא בתרה וגני על דרעך. טרפי זיתא.[23]
מסומסנך כמוסמא כמוקמא אין סמך גאה קמא פניפיאל מספו יה ואי יא אילין
שריא דבזעו ית רקיעא ויהבו ית אורייתא למשה על ידי יהו יהו והה. אשבעית
עליכון בשמיה דדרין רבא דתנטרון ית אורייתא בלבא דילי. כתוב על תלתא
טרפי זיתא. מחוק ביין ושתי כתוב הקמיע ותלי בזרוע שמאלי כסא דכספא דיו
ואברין קנתים ואפרכבם (?) האהתיתן ואטוטו ילקוט ואסדרד אל סידרי
אלין סידרי מיכאל אישרצו[24] רבא דישראל תנטרון יתיה לאולפנא דאורייתא
בליבא דילי אא"ס הללויה. כתוב בכסא דכספא מחוק ביין וישתה ומני
עשרין וארבעה זימני שמע בקולינו וזימנא דמסיים אומר שומע תפילה. חמרא.
נבט כגתא דיתיב כליבא וסמך זיזא[25] דיתיב על פומא דקורקפנא מליי מיני
והשליכו בי מקרא ומשנה ותלמוד / ואנהר ית לבי בדברי תורה ולא אתקל fol. 33a
בלישני בכל מה שאלמוד בשם יהואל ואל ובשם האל הגדול יה יהו יה יה אלי [New York]
אל ובשם האל הגדול יה יהו יה יה אל האלהים שם המפורש והנכבד אא"ס.
אמור ארבעין וחד זימנין על חמר מפום דנא במעלי שבתא כדגני ושתי ולמחר
יתיב בתעניתא. ביצה. לאיגנסס כפסה פי אנה הוא איסרא רבא דאורייתא דהוית עם
משה בטורא דסיני ועטרתיה כל ביה (!) כל מה דיליף וכל מה דשמעו אזניה
דתיכול ותיתי לוותי ותעדי אבן מליבי בעגלה ולא תתעכב אא"ס כתוב על

[22] The verb is lacking. Perhaps it is דאינון יהבי. On Metatron as a prince of wisdom, cf. Section VII above. עגמטיה is unknown, as are several of the angelic names in this piece.

[23] The verb is lacking. 'Take' or 'write on'?

[24] The reading is not clear. New York: אי שרא.

[25] The copyist wrote זיקא and added a ז above the line. The whole sentence seems corrupt. The word כנתא might also read רגתא.

ביצה בת יומא דזגתא אוכמת מְטַוֵי לך להאי ביצה ובתר דטוי לה קליף לה וכתי' עלה האי ביצה הדא מילתא והדר אכיל לה. ולא לישתי בתרה. וההוא יומא ליתיב בתעניתא ובין תיבה [צ"ל: וביית בה].[25*]

§ 21 א"ר ישמעאל אמר לי ר' נחוניא בן הקנה רבי בן גאים בשעה שציפיתי בצפיית המרכבה ראיתי הדר גאוה חדרי חדרים הדורי אימה[26] ברורי יראה בוערין ומבוהלין, בערתם מבערה ובהלתם בהלה.

§ 22 א"ר ישמעאל כיון ששמעתי מר' נחוניא בן הקנה רבי השמועה הזו עמדתי על רגלי ושאלתי ממנו כל שמות שרי החכמה ומשאלה ששאלתי ראיתי אור בלבבי כימי השמים.

§ 23 א"ר ישמעאל כיון שעמדתי על רגליי וראיתי פני מאירות מחכמתי והתחלתי מפרש כל מלאך ומלאך שבכל היכל והיכל.[27]

בהיכל ראשון [עומדין] זהופיאל ועזפיאל גהוריאל ורציציאל וסטפאל בזתאל עוזפיאל ועוזבזביאל.

בפתח היכל ב' עומדין גבריאל קצפיאל רהביאל שבזריאל שתקיאל והרביאל קשראל עובמיאל ערפאל.

בפתח היכל ג' עומדין הדריאל זבדיאל זדוריאל סרנאל עמתיאל עממאל ועמתליאל נודריאל ורודיאל.

בפתח היכל ד' עומדין סנסגאל אסראל הילופי והילופתי אלמון גלמון קדוש הקם גדר אגבס בסוס אברמוס פסוי מדור גבריאל זעים זעה אורע יורדע.

בפתח היכל ה' עומדין דהרהיאל אידראל דרגיתאל גהציצא יצוציאל ריפיון חגי זיווי פסק כיסאל רבדלדיאל גאל אפקיאל ייגד ייקד.

בפתח היכל ו' עומדין אבגבג אצהצה אצפצף הדסדגדוי רזוזיאל עטופיאל נרגות סבסא הדוריאל צען דיראל איזעיאל זעזאל צדיעאל קדקדאל רעדאל שוראל פססיאל גהואל ביפיאל.

בפתח היכל ז' עומדין אסמכים קמנמן אמילפטון שמיניאל לפטון אלת קרתיון אבריאל גדודיאל סרפסיון הללביאל עיפפי להבה זעזע שלהביתה שבוביאל פחדיאל חוקיאל / רוט פסיסיאל אספסיסיאל געגע כי עור יקרתה היכלי
fol. 56a (היפלי?) מופליאל יסולדיאל שר הפנים שהוא רואה דמות זהרריאל יוי אלהי ישראל ולמעלה מכולם יושב מלכו של עולם על כסא רם ונישא ומלאכי כבוד מרננים בשירות ומצהילי צהלה ומדברי גבורותיו עומדים מימינו ומשמאלו. ואלה שמותם. עגיון עדיאל עפפיאל צבוציאל ואיבוריאל אשכניזכאל גרוסקסופאל פנוכיאל אגכגדיאל עדריאל עוזרים צץ ופפי נגד גהיראל גהודרי זרזדיאל הדורתיאל ומקיף אדרגחי ודאי יופי ופסיבגד גהוראל גהוריי זרזריאל מלאך הפנים וסנדלפון קושר תפילין בראש צור העולמים[28] יוי אלהי ישראל יתברך

25* This emendation has been suggested by Prof. Lieberman who refers to *Ta'anith* 24b: ביתו כולי עלמא בתעניתייכו.

26 Oxford: אדירי אימה.

27 The names of the angels in MS New York frequently have different readings.

28 This is the sentence quoted by S. Lieberman in שקיעין, p. 13, from the writings of R. Eleazar of Worms. New York reads בראש צור עולמים.

שמו האל הגדול הגבור והנורא האדיר והאביר האמיץ החזק האל הנערץ הנפלא הנשגב היושב במרחבי מרום והעושה רצונו בעולמו ואין מי יאחר.

§ 24 א"ר ישמעאל אמר לי זבודיאל מלאך הפנים בן גאים מה זכות לאביך ולאמך שזכית לעמוד על רז זה שאין כל העולם כולו לא זכו[29] ואני ור' עקיבא זכינו להשתמש בו.

א"ר ישמעאל אמר לי שקדחוזיא מלאך הפנים בן גאים אל תתגאה מכל חביריך ואל תאמר אף אני זכיתי מכולם שלא מכחך ומגבורתך היא אלא מכח גבורה של אביך שבשמים אבל אשריך בעולם הזה וטוב לך לעולם הבא, ואשריך וטוב לך לעולם ולעולמי עולמים. ולכל בני אדם המחזיקים בו ואומרי' משחרית לשחרית בתפילת כמוך.

§ 25 א"ר ישמעאל כיון ששמעתי משקדחוזיה מלאך הפנים עמדתי בכל כחי וזרזתי עצמי ועמדתי ונתתי קדושה מלפני מלכו של עולם ואמרתי יוי אלהי
תתקדש לנצח, תתגאה על החיות ועל המרכבות עוז תתהדר תתברך שאין / כמוך, fol. 56b
תתקדש שאין כמעשיך, ששמי שמים מגידים צדקך, נוראים מספרים כבודך, שרפי מעלה ומטה משתחוים לפניך, כי גדול ונורא אתה, ואין עולה ושכחה לפני כסא כבודך. ברוך אתה יהוה יוצר כל הבריות באמת.

§26 א"ר ישמעאל כיון ששמע ר' נחוניא בן הקנה רבי שעמדתי כלפי שמים ופרשתי כל מלאך ומלאך שיש בכל היכל והיכל, אמר לי מפני מה פירשת מלאכים שהן עומדין על פתח היכלות. אמרתי לו לא לקילוס עצמי עשיתי אלא לשבח מלכו של עולם. א"ר ישמעאל אמר לי ר' נחוניא בן הקנה רבי תורת אמת שקנה לך אהרן הכהן היא עמדה לך ולא היה לך צער על רז זה. אבל אם אתה מבקש להשתמש ברז זה, החזק עצמך בח' [בחמש נ'] תפילות שאני אומר לך באותה שעה סדר לפני תפילות וכל תפילה ותפילה שתים עשרה אותיות משם האל אל חי וקיים, האל הנערץ והנקדש היושב במרחבי מרום.

א"ר ישמעאל כיון שסדר לפני ר' נחוניא בן הקנה רבי תפילות הללו בכל יום הייתי מתפלל לכל אחת ואחת בשמות שלה בירידה ובעלייה[30] והיה ריוח לכל איבריי.

§ 27 תפילה ראשונה שהיה מתפלל אותה זעופיאל שר גיהנם בשעה שרואה הצדיקים ויחדיי[31] יוי אלהי ישראל בגן עדן עמם ואמר לי רבי: היה מתפלל אותה שתנצל לעצמך מדינה של גיהנם:

תתברך אל גדול וגבור חזק מלך המתגאה בהדר אדיר בכבוד אתה אמרת והיה העולם ברוח שפתיך כוננת רקיע ושמך הגדול טהור ומרומם על כל עליונים ועל כל תחתונים זכות ארץ שמך וזכות שמיך שמך ועומדים מלאכים
בשמים וצדיקים בטוחים בזכרך ושמך מעופף על הכל / וזכרך מגודל על כל fol. 57a
בני בשר. ברוך שמך לבדך, ברוך שמך לבדך.[32]

[29] New York: לפי שכל העולם כולו לא זכו.

[30] Here the terminology of ירידה למרכבה is used, in contradistinction to the usage in the earlier paragraphs; cf. § 2. In § 33: עליתי להיכל (the ascent to the היכלות is never called ירידה?).

[31] New York: ויסדרו.

[32] New York does not repeat the sentence.

אש שהוא יקוד נור דליק זען אפספא אש אכלת אש זיעס זעופה יראת
שרפים זע צור כסף צפצפס ממשלת אופנים חיזקת דלוקה זעופה דלוקה
דפוסה דכר מחקק דחקיה אבץ אבץ בץ בבץ ברוך לבדך לבדו זעוס
ורסוס יפס יפץ עפץ זהיר לצדש זיוהיון דס זבוד בבא זבדייה יהו יה יה
צבאות תתקדש אשר יצרת שמים וארץ זכרך יפארו כל גדודי מעלה ומעשה
ידיך מתבל ארצך אלהינו יוצר כל אדיר בגדולה ואהוב בגבורה מודים גבורי
כח שהם עומדים לפניך באמת ובצדק. ברוך אתה יהוה הדר העולמים ואדון
כל הממשלה.

§ 28 תפילה שנייה: תתקדש אלהי שמים וארץ, אדון אדונים אדיר אדירים,
אל הכרובים רוכב כרובים י״י צבאות וממשלתו על צבאות אל משרתים ושמו
מקודש על משרתיו הוא שמו ושמו הוא הוא בהוא ושמו בשמו שיר שמו ושמו
שיר זעופה זעף זועי זיע אהסי הוהסין רמיי יהה הוא רגש ברך אטגאה הוא
חילאה אהי אה הוא הואב הרי עיל דהי רס על דרו זריז יש׳ ויש׳ זריז עין
בעין כח בכח גבורה בגבורה גדולה בגדולה סעד בסעד רש ברש [?יש
ביש נ׳] צל בצל שדי יתלונן תתקדש מלכו של עולם שהכל תלוי בזרועך והכל
שבח מגידים לשמך כי אתה אדון העולמים אין כמוך בכל עולמים. ברוך
fol. 57b אתה י״י הקדוש במרכבה רוכב כרובים. /

§ 29 תפילה שלישית: ברוך שמך קדוש שמך מלך חזק אדיר על רזי מעלה
ומטה אדון ניסים אדון גבורות אדון נפלאות אדון פרישות נותן חכמה לחכמים
ומדע ליודעי בינה אלהי האלהים ואדוני האדונים האל הגדול הגבור והנורא
אל עליון יושב בסתר עליון עושה ניסים וגבורות ונפלאות רבות אדיר חזק
נורא ומפורש אל גדול וגבור על כל נוראותיו וגבורותיו [?][33] י״י אחד
חק שמו אחד יה חסף בחיל חביב חק חדרי ברעותיה מגרס אפטליון רקד
נשיא זה זה הף הף רב מץ יה מפוס אדפס כיטאה איה אפופי אפפי חי יהוה
אלהי העולם. אתה אחד ושמך אחד אדון הכל אדר כל העולם מי כמוך חי
יהוה מלכי ויוצרי מי ככבודך אל חי וקיים כבודך מלא הוד והדר קדושתך
טהרה וענוה. על כן גבורי שמים לך מקלסין ואדירי ארץ לך מפארין כי
אין כמוך בשמים ובארץ. ברוך אתה י״י אדון כל הנשמה.

§ 30 תפילה רביעית: אדיר שמך בכל הארץ כוננת כסאך מושבך שמתה
בגובהי מרומים מרכבך שמתה בעליות זבולך בערפלי טוהר מפארין לזכרך
גדודי אש מהללין שבחך שרפי אש עומדין לפניך האופנים וחיות הקודש ואופני
הוד ושרפי להבה וגלגלי מרכבה בקול רעש גדול ורעם ורעש אומרי׳ הזכרה
בשם בשם טטרוסי י״י מאה וי״א [וי״ב ?] פעמים ואומרי׳ טטרסי טטרסיף
טטרסיע טטרגיס טטמופב טיטרכסי טטריג טרי אכתרי גהץ גיקקא אגהגיה
אפיפביה בעיר טרכסי טריס אזבד סטיטיי אדוה אביבה אהיהה אז הן יחף
טחן טיפי יטי עטר סייה טרפסס תירסיו טיטרפוס רחפין רדנן אגיעץ גחץ
fol. 58a ארסס יה פיהף יה ההה יפיפף יקדקדא יהצץ רוצץ / רהף רהוף רהץ דחצב
חצב אש חק בחק אבג בזג בקק יבקק רך יהגז טטרסוף חפצץ יהגץ יפוף הפף

[33] New York: על כל נוראי׳ וגיבורי׳.

ארכי חפצי מנוסי עתי עפעוף עופינף זביד סבב סבה ירגה טר גריר דלספפסים
יה ימץ צמץ הצהוה זיו רב עשבב יהץ יהף יהק קיר הופכלפס אאג גבג בוג
אגיד דיגרא אסקנים פספיא טטריסג י״י טטריסג הגגא הגיגא הי הוי הוא הוא
הי׳ והוא ווי הגיא תגיא נדק ענר גוג איבד תרפסיסא חד חוד ואדבה הגגא
מהגיא הטלתיה כונס אנגים זה נבוס מקטל הפקתפהי נדוס בתל ברך יפף
רגשת דבב בפת לא אבזק פדק חקק מרקק אכסוף אחסר אהגה אהיגא אהיפבנא
עבתיה טבטיב טוב טבי יהוה הליה הף יהגג מרסיע י״י עייועי היגי ומהגי הוה
גלי יה גר סברה שלט גיד שבי ברוף עיפעיף אעיפעיף אבי הגא יה קרקך הוהו
טטרסיה י״י קדוש שמך בשמי שמים רם ונישא על כל כרובים יתקדש שמך
בקדושתך יתגדל בגדולה יתגבר בגבורה וממשלתך עד סוף כל הדורות כי
גבורתך לנצח נצחי נצחים. ברוך אתה יהוה אדיר בכח גדול בגבורה.

§ 31 תפילה חמשית: יהוה אלהי גדלת מאד הוד והדר לבשת ומי כמוך
אדיר במרום אשרי׳ בך מברכין משבחין ומפארין מקלסין מחבבין לשמך הגדול
הגבור והנורא מגיעים לפניך ברכה שירה וזמרה קילוס תודה תהילה תורה
זכות ואמת צדק קדושה טהרה ניקוי ונקיון צהלה גילה ריעות ישרות מלכות
ענוה גדולה גבורה אדירות / עריצות ששון ושמחה ריצה הוד והדר כבוד fol. 58b
תפארת לך אל קדוש מלך רם ונישא מלך הדור מלך אדיר מלך הדר מלך ירום
זירדיאל טופריאל [צורטק] טופגר טטרסיף זבודיאל ברוניא טעצש אשרוולון
טורטביאל הדרירום אדרירום יהי שמך מבורך לעולם ועד ומלכותך לעולמי
עולמים, מושבך לנצח כסאך לדור ודור נצחך בשמים ובארץ ממשלתך על
העליונים ועל התחתונים והכל מגיעין לפניך שיר ושבח והלל יהוה שמך
צדיק מכל, אתה צור עולמים.
א״ר ישמעאל אמר לי ר׳ נחוניא בן הקנה כל המתפלל תפילה זו בכל
כחו יכול לצפות בזיו השכינה ושכינה אהובה לו.

§ 32 א״ר ישמעאל כך אמר לי ר׳ עקיבא אני תפילה התפללתי וצפיתי
השכינה וראיתי את כל מה שעושין לפני כסא כבודו ומהי התפילה.
ברוך אתה יהוה גדול שמך בגבורה י״י אחד שמך ואין זולתך ברומי
שמים כוננת כסאך לעולם בחכמה אדיר אתה ברחמים. אדיר אתה בחכמה בבינה
ובתבונה בראת עולמך באדרתך בראת כרובים [?] ברורין וגדודין דמומין
עומדין לפני כסא כבודך קבעת תבל [הכל נ׳?] גיאה וגיאות וכוננת בכבוד
והלל שיר הילול ומפואר וכל גדודים שרפים שעומדין לפניך מהללין ומפארין
לשמך וגלגלי מרכבה משוררין שירה לפניך וכוננתה כסא כבודך זמרה
וזכייה. ומלאכי שרת שעומדין מקדישין לקדושתך ומגדלין גבורתך ואומרים
חי י״י צבאות שדי יהו לעולם מלכותך מסוף העולם ועד סופו. ולשמך מזכירין
כל מה שבראתה בעולמך מי כמוך גדול שמך לעולם קדושתך לעולם גבורתך על
כל המרכבה אדירותך על חיות הקודש כי אתה חי וקיים לעולם כל עולמך.
טהור אתה ורחמיך / מתגלגלין על מנצחי חיות [?] לנצח נצחים ידיד ויחיד fol. 59a
אתה אהבת מי זרחת בכל העולם ואמת וצדק שמך כסאך הוד והדר כבוד
ותפארת קדושה וטהרה מסלסלין לפניך ניקוי ונקיות תפארת ונצח. תתגדל
ותתקדש לעולם מלך אל קדוש רם ונישא כי אין כמוך בשמים ובארץ בים

ובתהומות במרומי שחק כסא כבודך משורר וערבות רקיע שם כסאך כוננת בהם מלאם אדירות ועריצות מסלסלים לפניך ששון ושמחה אופני הודו וכרובי קודש משוררין שירה ענני ניחומה חיות הקודש ממללין בזמרה ברד פיהם כנפיהם מים ויה זיהיון מגיעין לשמך צור עולמים. קק״ק יוון ייה יהי הו הי חי שלימין יה הויה והו יהיה קדוש שמך ומשרתיך קדושין י״י אחד אל רם ונישא רנה ויראה מלא כסא כבודך תתברך תשתבח תתפאר תתרומם תתנשא תתגדל תתקלס תתקדש תתהדר תתחבב כי אתה כוננת בכסאך שירה זמרה שיר שבח והלל ותהילה ותפארת ונצח ואתה יודע רזי מעלה ומטה גלויין לפניך ומי יוכל לספר שבח מרכבך לעולם תתברך מכל צבא מרום תתהדר מאופני הדר תתקדש מכרובי קודש תתהדר מחדרי חדרים תתפאר מגדודי אש תתחבב מחיות הקדש תשתבח מכסא כבודך שעומדין לפניך ומשוררין לפניך בכל יום ומגיעין קילוס לשמך הגדול הגבור הנורא כי אין כמוך בשמים ובארץ.
fol. 59b ברוך אתה יהוה האל הקדוש. /

§ 33 א״ר ישמעאל אמרתי לר׳ עקיבא היך יכול לצפות למעלה מן השרפים שעומדין למעלה מראשו של רוזיי יוי אלהי ישראל. אמר לי כשעליתי להיכל ראשון תפילה התפללתי וראיתי מהיכל רקיע ראשון ועד היכל ז׳ וכיון שעליתי להיכל שביעי הזכרתי שני מלאכים וציפיתי למעלה מן השרפים ואילו הן סריד הגלין. וכיון שהזכרתי שמותם באו ותפשוני ואמרו לי בן אדם אל תתירא מלך הקדוש הוא שהוא [קדוש] על כסא רם ונישא ובחור הוא לעולם ואדיר על המרכבה. באותה שעה ראיתי למעלה מן השרפים שעומדים למעלה מראשו של רוזיי יוי אלהי ישראל.

ואיזו היא התפילה.

ברוך אתה יהוה אל אחד
בורא עולמו בשמו אחד
יוצר הכל במאמר אחד
ברומי שמים כוננת כסאך
ומושבך שמתה בגובהי מרומך
מרכבך שמתה בעליית מרום
גבולך נטעת באופני הדר
מפארין לזכרך גדודי אש
מהללין לשבחך שרפי אש
כולם טעונים דממה דקה
שבח אומרים בהליכתן
באימה מהלכין ביראה מעטפין
עמוסין בגאוה לפאר ליוצר כל
מלאים עינים על גביהן
מראיהן כמראה בזק
זיוום נאה חיכם [מתוק]

זה לעומת זה נושאין ומביעין[34]
נושאות חיות טהורות ק׳ ק׳ ק׳
מלאכי שרת אומרין לפניך
גלגל חמה צבע פניהם
מבהיק זיוום כזוהרי רקיע
כנפיהן פרושות ידיהן פשוטות
כקול מים רבים קול כנפיהן
לפידי אש טורדין ויוצאין מגלגלי עיניהם
בקול רעש גדול משוררין שירה לפניך
זיו מלאים נוגה מפיקים
זיון נאה בצאתם ששים בביאתם שמחים
זוהר נאה לפני כסא כבודך
באימה ביראה עושין רצונך / fol. 60a
מגיעין שבח לשמך הגדול הגבור והנורא
פאר וכבוד מזכירין לזכר מלכותך
צהלה ורנה כי אין כמוך
ואין ככהניך ואין כחסידיך
ואין כשמך הגדול לעולם ולעולמי עולמים.
זועף בים ויבש צופה בארץ ורעשה
מגבורתך מתרעש כל העולם
מחייה מתים ומעמיד המתים מעפרן
גדול שמך לעולם, אדיר שמך לעולם, קדוש שמך לעולם.
י״י אחד י״י אחד יה יה הו יהו יה חי לעולם
הו יהו שמך י״י שמך לעולם י״י זכרך לדור ודור

שרטף זען זעפי יה מקמא נקס ננקון יערדד אבג בג הוי הגג הג חו יו לעולם גבורתך לעולם קדושתך לעולם מלכותך בשמים ובארץ. לפיכך נקרא שמך, נברך לגבורתך נסלסל ונגיע קילוס לפני כסא כבודך כי אין כמוך בשמים ובארץ. ברוך אתה יהוה צור העולמים.

[34] To read ומגיעין. Cf. note 12.

APPENDIX D

משנת שיר השירים

מאת שאול ליברמן

לזכר החתן אלחנן בן פנחס בַּר
קינה במקום שיר

שנינו במשנת ידים ספ"ג: אמר ר' עקיבא וכו' שאין כל העולם כלו כדאי כיום שניתן בו שיר השירים לישראל, שכל הכתובים קודש ושיר השירים קדש קדשים. ובמסורת א"י של המדרשים: שכל השירים קודש[1] ושיר השירים קודש קדשים. לפי פשוטו, שיר השירים הוא קדוש משירת משה.[2] ולא עוד אלא שלר' עקיבא היה „יום" מתן שיר השירים,[3] דוגמת „יום" מתן תורה. ובשה"ש זוטא הוצ' בובר, עמ' 4, הוצ' שכטר, עמ' 5: ר' עקיבא אומר אלו לא נתנה שיר השירים בתורה כדאי היתה לנהוג את העולם,[3א] ועיי"ש בהוצ' שכטר, סוף עמ' 49.

אין להבין את הדברים, אלא אם נניח שר' עקיבא סובר ששירה זו נאמרה בסיני. ואפשר שלדעתו הקב"ה בעצמו אמרה. ואמרו בריש שה"ש זוטא: ר' נתן או' מלאכי השרת אמרו אותה[4] וכו', רבן גמליאל אומר הקב"ה אמרה, שנ' שיר השירים, השיר הנבחר

1 עיין מ"ש במבוא לתוספת ראשונים ח"ב, עמ' 9, בהערה. ויש להוסיף גם מחזור ינאי, עמ' רפ"אי ועיי"ש, עמ' רע"ה.

2 המפרשים פירשוהו שהוא קדוש מכל השירים שאמר שלמה, עיין בפירוש הראב"ע ומ"ש בתוספת ראשונים הנ"ל. וכן מוכח ממשלו של ר' אלעזר בן עזריה בשהש"ר פ"א סוף פסוק א', הוצ' ראם, ג' ע"ד. אבל עיין בהמשך הדברים שם. ובשה"ש זוטא שם, הוצ' בובר, עמ' 9, שכטר, עמ' 10: עשר שירות הן וכו', שירת משה וכו' ושיר השירים משובחת מכולם וכו', אמר ר' אלעזר בן עזריה משל וכו' כך הקב"ה סילת את הנביאים מתוך התורה, ואת הכתובים מתוך הנביאים, ושיר השירים נסלתה מכולם. ועיין שם בהערות בובר ל"ב ול"ד, ובהערות שכטר, עמ' 53, והעירו שם גם על תרגום שה"ש במקומו. ועיין בדרשות ר"י ן' שועיב, ליום אחרון של פסח, דפוס קראקא, מ"ב ע"א, שהעיר על התרגום.

3 בגליון של משנת ידים מכת"י הגניזה (לפי פורת, לשון חכמים, עמ' 184, הערה 1) הגירסא היא: כיום שנשתנה בו שיר השירים (עיין מש"ש בשמי). ונראה שיש כאן גירסא אחרת, ולא פירוש לגירסא „ניתנה בו שיר השירים", כלומר, שניתנה בו מגילת שה"ש. לפי גירסת הגליון הכוונה ליום ששנו את משנת שה"ש (עיין מ"ש ע"ז להלן בפנים בהמשך דברינו). וכ"ה הסיגנון בספרי· שופטים פיס' ק"ס, הוצ' ר"א פינקלשטין, עמ' 211: משנה התורה שעתידה להשתנות. ובכי"א שם: להיות שונין אותה על פה (עיי"ש בשנו"ס. ועיין מאירי סנהדרין, עמ' 74), כלומר ביום הקהל. והנוצרים פירשוה לפי דרכם, עיין בספר חרב פיפיות ליאיר בן שבתי, הוצ' רוזנטל, עמ' 63, וכיוון שם לספרי הנ"ל.

3א עיין מ"ש במחברתי מדרשי תימן, עמ' 14, הערה 1, ומ"ש גיסי ר"א הלקין בסה"י לכבוד מרכס (החלק האנגלי), עמ' 393, הערה 21. ועיין הסיגנון בברייתא של אבות, פרק קניין תורה, בתחילתה. ובמשנה עצמה מתקבל פירושו של הלקין.

4 ועל פיו פייט במחזור ינאי, עמ' רפ"א, ועיי"ש, ועמ' רע"ה.

מכל השירים. ובשהש"ר פ"א, ב', מוחלפת השיטה, עיי"ש. ועיין בבלי שבועות ל"ה ב'. ולפי שיטות אילו אין שיר השירים מקלס את מעשה הים ומעשה סיני לאחר זמן, אלא אף הוא באותה שעה נאמר.

ובשהש"ר פ"א, ב': היכן נאמרה (כלומר, שירה זו), ר' חיננא בר פפא אמר בים נאמרה, המד"א (שה"ש א', ט') לסוסתי ברכבי פרעה. ר' יודא ברבי סימון אמר בסיני נאמרה וכו', ר' יוחנן אמר בסיני נאמרה וכו', ר' מאיר אומר באהל מועד נאמרה וכו', רבנין אמרין בבית עולמים וכו', ועיין בפירוש מהרז"ו שם. ובאמת כל השיטות הללו של תנאים הם, וכל אחד טרח לפרש את המגילה בעקביות ע"פ שיטתו הוא. וכן במכילתא דרשב"י, הוצ' אפשטין־מלמד, עמ' 143: ועליהם מפורש בקבלה (שה"ש ב', י"ד) יונתי בחגוי הסלע בסתר המדרגה, ר' אליעזר אומר, אין דבר זה אמור אלא על הים, הראיני את מראיך וכו', ומראך נאוה.[5] ויאמן העם. ר' עקיבה אומ' אין דבר זה אמור אלא לפני הר סיני, הראיני את מראיך (שה"ש שם). ועיין גם במכילתא דר' ישמעאל, מס' דבחדש פ"ג, הוצ' הורוביץ, סוף עמ' 214 ואילך. ובשהש"ר פ"ב, י"ד, הובאו דברי ר' אליעזר ור' יהושע (בשינויים), ואח"כ אמרו: ר' הונא וכו' פתרי קרייה על דעתיה דר' מאיר באהל מועד וכו', אינון פתרון לה על דעתיה דר' מאיר באהל מועד, אף אנא נפתרינה על דרבנן[6] בבית עולמים וכו'. הרי לך שכל אחד טרח לפתור את הפסוקים ע"פ שיטה קבועה.[7]

וכן בשהש"ר פ"ב. ב': כשושנה בין החוחים וכו'. ר' אליעזר[8] פתר קרייה בגאולת מצרים וכו'. ובמכילתא בא רפ"ז, עמ' 22: אבא חנן משום ר' אליעזר אומר זה חפזון שכינה, אף על פי שאין ראיה לדבר זכר לדבר. קול דודי הנה זה בא מדלג על ההרים מקפץ על הגבעות (שה"ש ב' ח'), ואומר הנה זה עומד אחר כתלנו (שם ט'). ובמדרש תנאים, עמ' 91: אבא חנין אומר משום ר' אליעזר זה חפזון שכינה, אע"פ שאין ראיה וכו' קול דודי דופק (שה"ש ה' ב'), הנה זה עומד אחר כתלנו.

ובשהש"ר פ"א, י"ב: ר' אליעזר ור' עקיבא וכו', ר' אליעזר אומר עד שהמלך במסיבו, עד שמלך מלכי המלכים הקב"ה במסיבו, ברקיע, כבר הר סיני מתמר באור, שנאמר וההר בוער באש (דברים ד', י"א). ר' עקיבא אומר עד שמלך מלכי המלכים הקב"ה במסיבו ברקיע כבר וישכן כבוד ה' על הר סיני (שמות כ"ד, ט"ז). והמפרשים נדחקו מאד לפרש את ההבדל בין ר' אליעזר ור' עקיבא. ועיין בחידושי הרש"ש שם שעמד על הלשון „מתמר", ועיין גם בפירוש מהרז"ו שם,

5 בשהש"ר פ"ב, י"ד: ר' אלעזר (צ"ל: אליעזר) פתר קרייה בישראל בשעה שעמדו על הים וכו', ומראך נאוה. שהיו ישראל מראין באצבע, ואומרים זה אלי ואנוהו. ועיין מ"ש להלן הערה 15.

6 בדפוסים חדשים: על דעתיה! ועיין מ"ש על סיגנון זה בגנזי קדם של לוין ח"ה, סוף עמ' 184 ואילך.

7 וכן ר' יוחנן שסובר ששה"ש נאמרה בסיני (עיין מ"ש לעיל בפנים) הרבה לפרש כמה פסוקים בשיטתיה, עיין שהש"ר א' ב' (הוצ' ראם, ד' ע"ד), ד' ד' (כ"ג סע"ד), שם (כ"ד ע"א), ספ"ה (ל"ב ע"ג) ועוד.

8 וכצ"ל גם בוי"ר פכ"ב, ב', הוצ' ר"מ מרגליות, עמ' תקכ"ז, כגירסת כי"י, עיי"ש בשנו"ס. ותקנו ר' „אלעזר" מפני המחלוקת של האמוראים להלן שם, אבל באמת אינה עניין כלל לדברי ר' אלעזר, עיי"ש.

ודבריהם דחוקים מאד. ובדרך אולי ושמא נראה שצ"ל בדברי ר' אליעזר: הי'[8א] סנה (במקום „הר סיני") מתמר באש, שנאמר והסנה (במקום: וההר) בוער באש (שמות ג', ב'). ובמדרשות לפסוק זה:[9] מיכן אמרו האש של מעלה מעלה לולבין. ופירשו ביפה תואר וברד"ל שדרשו ב„לבת אש" שבפסוק זה. ובקטעים מתנחומא כ"י ועוד[10] גורס שם: מעלה לובלבין, כלומר הסנה מעלה לובלבין ומפריח באש, כמפורש בתרגום המיוחס ליונתן שם בנוסח כ"י.[11] וכן במדרש הגדול שם, הוצ' ר"מ מרגליות, עמ' מ"ו: שראה את הסנה והוא מלבלב ועולה מתוך האש וכו'. והסנה כשהוא מלבלב, וורדים הוא מלבלב, כמפורש בשמו"ר פ"ב ה'. ולפ"ז מתפרשים יפה דברי ר' אליעזר, וכוונתו עד שהמלך עדיין ברקיע, לפני מתן תורה, וכבר היה סנה מתמר באור, ועושה תמרות ולובלבין ונותן ריחו („נרדי נתן ריחו").[12] ואף שדברי ר' עקיבא סתומים, מ"מ ברור שבא להוציא מדברי ר' אליעזר, ומפרשו במתן תורה בסיני, עיין בדברי ר' פנחס בשם ר' הושעיה להלן בשהש"ר שם, והשוה מכילתא, בחודש פ"ג, עמ' 214, ד"ה ויהי ביום השלישי. נמצאנו למדים שאף כאן התנאים בשיטתם; לר' אליעזר רומז כאן לסנה, ושיבחו כן בים, ולר"ע הכל בהר סיני.

וכן סובר ר' פפייס באבות דר"ן נו"א פכ"ז, מ"ב ע"א: כנסת ישראל היתה משבחת (כלומר, על הים) על סוס רכב פרעה וכו', כדבריו[13] במכילתא, ויהי פ"ו, עמ' 112 (ובמקבילות, עיין בציונים שם): לססתי ברכבי פרעה (שה"ש א', ט'). רכב פרעה על סוס זכר וכו', א"ל ר"ע דייך פפוס וכו'. ומפסוק זה הרי הוכיח ר' חיננא בר פפא בשהש"ר פ"א, ב' (בתחילתו) ששיר השירים נאמר על הים. ולפי דרכנו למדנו שכבר נחלקו התנאים, ר' אליעזר ור' עקיבא, היכן נאמרה השירה; לדברי ר' אליעזר נאמרה על הים (ואף פפוס סובר כן), ולר' עקיבא נאמרה בסיני. ובשה"ש זוטא (בובר עמ' 9, שכטר, עמ' 10): וחכמים אומרים מהר סיני נתנה.

ובשהש"ר פ"ב, ט': במצרים ראו אותו וכו', בים ראו אותו וכו' בסיני ראו אותו וכו'. ועיי"ש פ"ג, ז'. דברים הללו עיקרם בברייתות בדברי תנאים, עיין מ"ש להלן. ובדב"ר הוצ' ליברמן, עמ' 14: א"ר חייא הגדול לא המלאכים היו עושין כן, אלא הקב"ה בכבודו (כלומר, היה כביכול מטפל בתינוקות שנולדו במצרים) וכו', והיו מתגדלין ונכנסין בעדרים לבתיהם וכו', והיא (כלומר, אמו של התינוק) שואלתו ואומרת לו, מי היה מגדלך, והוא אומר לה בחור אחד קווץ נאה שאין כיוצא בו, ועיי"ש בהערות. ועיין מדרש שה"ש הוצ' גרינהוט, י' סע"א ואילך. ובשמו"ר פכ"ג, ח': אמר ר' יוחנן מיד היה יורד הקב"ה בכבודו כביכול וכו', והיו אומרים להם בחור אחד נאה ומשובח היה יורד ועושה לנו כל צרכינו, שנאמר (שה"ש ה', י') דודי

8א =היה, ובכ"י אי אפשר לפעמים להבחין בין רי"ש ויו"ד, עיין מ"ש בתוספת ראשונים ח"ג, עמ' 154, שם, עמ' 124 ועוד.

9 שמו"ר פ"ב, ה, תנחומא סי' ט"ו.

10 עיין מ"ש במאמרי חזונות ינאי ב„סיני", שבט תרצ"ט, עמ' רל"ג, ובצופה האנגלי, סדרא חדשה, חל"ו (1946), עמ' 318.

11 עיין מ"ש בצופה האנגלי שם.

12 בקצת דוחק אפשר לפרש את המדרש גם בלי הגהה. וכוונת ר' אליעזר להר סיני, חורב, שהוא הסנה. ובפרקי דר' אליעזר פמ"א, הוצ' הרד"ל, צ"ו ע"ב: ר' אליעזר אומר (כגירסת כ"י ג', עיין חורב ח"י, ניורק תש"ח, עמ' 219, ובהערות שם, עמ' 281) מיום שנבראו שמים וארץ נקרא שם ההר חורב, ומשנגלה הקב"ה על משה מתוך הסנה, על שם הסנה נקרא סיני, הוא חורב. ולענייננו הכל אחד, אבל מחוור יותר, כמו שהגהנו.

13 והוא פפוס הוא ר' פפייס שבאבות דר"ן, עיין בשנו"ס במכילתא.

צח ואדום דגול מרבבה. וברור שאף „קווץ" שבדב"ר הנ"ל הוא רמז לאותו פסוק: קוצותיו תלתלים.[14]

וכן ר' אליעזר הסובר ששיר השירים נאמר על הים (עיין מ"ש לעיל), אף הוא אומר שראו אותו כביכול ממש, כמפורש במכילתא, שירה פ"ג, סוף עמ' 126: זה אלי ואנוהו (שמות ט"ו, ב'). ר' אליעזר אומר מנין אתה אומר שראתה שפחה על הים מה שלא ראו ישעיה ויחזקאל וכו', אלא כיון שראוהו הכירוהו, פתחו כולן פיהן ואמרו זה אלי ואנוהו. ועיין במכילתא דרשב"י, עמ' 78, ובספרי וזאת הברכה פיס' שמ"ג, סוף עמ' 398, ומדרש תנאים שם עמ' 211. ומספרי התנאים גם במדרשי האמוראים, דוגמת דב"ר הוצ' ליברמן הנ"ל, עמ' 15: לפי כשבאו לים וראו אותו היו מראים לאמותם באצבע,[15] ואומרין להן זה אלי ואנוהו, זהו שגדלני וכו'. ובמכילתא, שירה פ"ד, עמ' 129: לפי שנגלה על הים כגבור עושה מלחמה וכו'. ובמכילתא דרשב"י, עמ' 81: לפי שכשנגלה ה[קב"ה על הים] נראה להן כבחור עושה מלחמה. ובנספח לאגדת שה"ש של שכטר, עמ' 87: ראשו כתם פז (שה"ש ה', י"א). זה ממה"מ (=מלך מלכי המלכים) שנראה לישראל ברוב דמיונות, שנגלה עליהם על הים לעשות מלחמה עם פרעה נגלה כבחור, מפני שבחור נאה למלחמה, שנ' ה' איש מלחמה (שמות ט"ו, ג').[16] וכשם שראו אותו כביכול, כן ראו אף את המרכבה שירדה לים,[17] ואמרו בשהש"ר פ"א, ט': אמר ר' יודן מבין גלגלי המרכבה שמטן הקב"ה והטיסן על הים. אמר ר' חנינא בר פפא (והוא סובר שם פ"א רפ"ב שהשירה על הים נאמרה) בשר ודם שהוא רוכב על טוענו, על דבר שיש בו ממש, אבל הקב"ה אינו כן, טוען את רכובו,[18] ורוכב על דבר שאין בו ממש וכו'. והם מפרשים „אפריון עשה לו שלמה" (שה"ש ג', ט') על כסא הכבוד והמרכבה, עיין שהש"ר לפסוק זה.

מאידך גיסא הסוברים שהשירה נאמרה בסיני, אף הם אומרים שראו אותו כביכול ממש, וכן בשהש"ר פ"א, ב': [ישקני מנשיקות פיהו]. ר' יוחנן פתר קרייה בישראל בשעה שעלו להר סיני וכו', תני ר' שמעון בן יוחאי, כך תבעו, אמרו רצוננו לראות כבוד מלכנו. ועיין שה"ש זוטא פ"א, ב', הוצ' בובר, עמ' 10, שכטר, עמ' 11. ובמכילתא, שירה פ"ד, עמ' 129: נגלה בסיני כזקן מלא רחמים, שנ' ויראו את אלהי ישראל (שמות כ"ד, י'). ועיין מכילתא דרשב"י, עמ' 81, ובנספח לאגדת שה"ש של שכטר, עמ' 87, ובבלי חגיגה י"ד א'.

ואף את המרכבה ראו שם,[19] כמו שאמרו בפסיקתא דר"כ, בחודש השלישי, ק"ז ע"ב (ובמקבילות): אמר ר' אבדימא איש חיפה, שניתי במשנתי שירד הקב"ה בסיני בעשרים ושנים אלף כתות של מלאכי השרת וכו'. ד"א רכב אלהים רבותים אלפי שנאן (תהלים ס"ח, י"ח), מלמד שירד עם הקב"ה עשרים

14 וכ"ה רמוז („קווצים") בספרי וזאת הברכה פיס' שמ"ג, הוצ' ר"א פינקלשטין, סוף עמ' 398, עיי"ש בשנו"ס. ועיין בערוגת הבושם ח"א, עמ' 11.

15 עיין לעיל הערה 5, ומ"ש בסה"י לכבוד שוקן, עלי עי"ן, עמ' 78. ועיין שמו"ר פכ"ג, ה', שם פ"א סוף סי' י"ב, בבלי סוטה י"א ב', פרקי דר"א פמ"ב, הוצ' הרד"ל, צ"ט ע"ב.

16 ועיין במה"ג ואתחנן (הסגלה של הרמ"ז חסידה, חי"ח, עמ' 52), תנחומא יתרו, הוצ' בובר סי' ט"ז (ובמקבילות), בבלי חגיגה י"ד א'.

17 עיין מ"ש להלן הערה 24.

18 עיין מ"ש בתרביץ שכ"ז, סוף עמ' 186 ואילך.

19 ועיין לעיל הערה 17.

ושנים אלף מרכבות, וכל מרכבה ומרכבה כמראה שראה יחזקאל. רכב אלהים. מכת[20] שעלה (צ"ל: שעלת) מבבל אמרו שירד עם הקב"ה לסיני כעשרים ושנים אלף מרכבות, כך שנה אליהו זכור לטוב וכו'. ועיין בפסיקתא רבתי פכ"א, הוצ' רמא"ש, ק"ג ע"ב.

וכבר הראינו לעיל שעיקר גילוי הקב"ה כביכול בדמותו ובמרכבתו על הים ובהר סיני מסורת של תנאים היא, ומשניות הן. ושיר השירים משבח ומקלס את הקב"ה ואת דמותו כביכול, ומפרש גם את המרכבה, עיין להלן, ועיין שהש"ר פ"א ד' (הביאני המלך חדריו), תוספתא חגיגה פ"ב ה"ד (ומקבילות) ובבלי שם ט"ז א'. ועיין שהש"ר פ"ג, ט', י"א, וירושלמי ר"ה פ"ב ה"ד, נ"ח ע"א. ובשהש"ר פ"א ב' (הוצ' ראם, ד' ע"ג): אמר ר' ברכיה שנה לי ר' חלבו, הדבור עצמו היה נחקק וכו', ועיין לעיל שם בשם רשב"י, ובספרי וזאת הברכה פיס' שמ"ג, עמ' 399. וכן להלן בשהש"ר פ"א, י"ב: [עד שהמלך במסבו נרדי נתן ריחו] וכו', אלא מסטתא[21] עלתה בידם מן הגולה, ושנו בה, שקפץ להם מעשה העגל, והקדים להם מעשה המשכן.[22] ומכאן שכמה עניינים ממדרש שה"ש משניות הן, ושתי פעמים אנו מוצאים בעניינים שעלה להם כן מן הגולה, ושנו בה,[23] כמו שהבאנו לעיל. והתנאים היו עקביים בפירושיהם, ודרשו את שה"ש כל אחד לפי שיטתו, אלא שהאמוראים פירשו לפי דעות תנאים חולקים.[24]

20 בילקוט המכירי תהלים ס"ח, קס"ז ע"א: מרכבת. ובמדרש תהלים שם, הוצ' בובר, ק"ס ע"א: משום כת. וכן העתיק יעללינעק בבית המדרש ח"ה, עמ' 73. ובפסיקתא רבתי, הוצ' רמא"ש, ק"ג ע"ב: במסורת (וכ"ה גם בד"ר שם, ל"ז ע"ג). וקשה להאמין שגירסא פשוטה זו נשתבשה בכל המקורות בפנים שונים. ועיין תנחומא יתרו, הוצ' בובר סי' י"ד, הערה ע"ו. ואף משם ברור שהשמיטו מאמר זה משום שלא הבינו אותו, עיי"ש. ועיין בהערות רמא"ש לסדר אליהו רבה, סוף עמ' 119 ואילך, וסדר אליהו זוטא, עמ' 179, ודבריו אינם מחוורים כלל. ועיין לעיל עמ' 5 הערה 9. ועיין להלן הערה 21.

21 כ"ה בד"ר. ובאות אמת: נ"א מסורת. ובמתנות כהונה שם: ובספר ישן גרס וכו' מסורת. ועיין מ"ש לעיל הערה 20. ושמא צ"ל: מסטורא, עיין ערוך ערך מסטר.

22 הנכון הוא בפירוש מהרז"ו שם. ודבריו מקויימים ע"י סדר אליהו זוטא פ"ד, הוצ' רמא"ש, עמ' 179. ועיין בבלי שבת פ"ח ב'.

23 אף שהגאונים קראו גם למדרשי אגדה „משניות", עיין גנזי שכטר ח"ב, סוף עמ' 88 ואילך. ועיין אוה"ג תענית, עמ' 8. וכן רגיל בספרי קבלה „במתניתא", וכדומה. אבל בנידון שלנו הכוונה למשניות ממש, לברייתות של תנאים, שאף להן קראו „משניות".

24 בשמו"ר פ"ג, ב', פמ"ב, ה', פמ"ג, ח', תנחומא כי תשא כ"א, אמרו שעשו את העגל ע"פ השור שבמרכבה שראו בסיני. אבל היה קיים מדרש אחר לשה"ש שדרשו בו שעשו את העגל ע"פ המרכבה שבים, עיין מ"ש במחברתי „מדרשי תימן", עמ' 17 ואילך, וסמכוהו לפסוקים בשה"ש. ומדרש זה הוא בשיטת ר' אליעזר ששיר השירים נאמר על הים. ועיין במדרש שה"ש הוצ' גרינהוט, י"ג ע"ב, ומכילתא בא פי"ד, עמ' 51, שם, ויסע פ"א, עמ' 153 (ור' יהודה שנה את משנת ר' אליעזר, כתוספתא זבחים ספ"ב ומקבילה), ספרי בהעלותך פיס' פ"ד, עמ' 82 ומקבילות. ועצם האגדה שעשו את העגל ע"פ שור המרכבה, אגדת תנאים היא, כפי שראה לנכון ר"ל גינצבורג בספרו אגדות היהודים ח"ו, עמ' 52, הערה 271. וכבר בא ר' פפייס להוציא מלבות האומרים כן, עיין מכילתא בשלח פ"ו, סוף עמ' 112, ומקבילות.

ומן המדרשים שלנו לשה"ש השמיטו תכופות את עניין העגל, שכן כותב המיוחס לרס"ג (לשה"ש א', י', גאון הגאונים של רש"א ווערטהיימער עמ' פ"ה): דע כי פירוש נאוו לחייך, ותורי זהב, ועד שהמלך, וצרור המור, ואשכול הכופר דודי, הם (כלומר פ"א, י'–י"ד) סמוכים, בפירוש אלו החמשה פסוקים הוא מספר עבודת העגל וכו'. ולפנינו במדרשות נדרש פסוק י"א („תורי זהב" ו„נקודות הכסף") על מעשה העגל במדרש שה"ש הוצ' גרינהוט, י"ג ע"א ואילך, ופסוק י"ב („נרדי נתן ריחו") נתפרש בשהש"ר ובמקבילות למעשה העגל. ומן התרגום לשה"ש ולקח טוב שם מוכח שהיו לפניהם מדרשים שדרשו את הפסוקים בפ"א, י"ב–י"ד על מעשה העגל. ועיין גם

מעתה מקובלת עלי הנחתו של שלום שהמשנה (עיין להלן) של שיעור קומה הוא מדרש קדום לשה"ש פ"ה, י'–ט"ז, שהיה כלול במדרש שה"ש עתיק. שיעור קומה הוא קילוס ושבח להקב"ה בצורה שדרכה נפלאת מאתנו. ובמכילתא בשלח, שירה פ"ג, עמ' 127: [זה אלי ואנוהו וכו']. ר' עקיבא אומר אדבר בנאותיו[25] ובשבחיו של מי שאמר והיה העולם בפני כל אומות העולם וכו', וישראל אומרים להם לאומות העולם מכירים אתם אותו, נאמר לכם מקצת שבחו, דודי צח ואדום דגול מרבבה (שה"ש ה', י'). כיון ששומעים שכך שבחו אומרים לישראל נלכה עמכם וכו'. וכ"ה (סתם) בספרי וזאת הברכה פיס' שמ"ג, עמ' 399, אלא ששם הובאו כל ראשי הפסוקים משה"ש ה', י'–ט"ז. לא גילו לנו רז"ל את מהות השבח שיאמרו לאומות העולם, ומה ישפיע עליהם עד שיאמרו „נלכה עמכם". אבל ברור שהפסוקים הללו כללו את השבחים בהי"א הידיעה. ועיין גם במכילתא, שירה פ"א, עמ' 120.

ובפירוש ר' עזרא לשה"ש שם (כ"ב סע"ב): אחז"ל במדרש שיר השירים דודי צח ואדום, דמותו מאודם, משחור, מירוק, מלבן, כך דמותו של הקב"ה (יחזקאל א' כ"ח) כמראה הקשת אשר יהיה בענן.[26] ובמשנת חגיגה פ"ב סמ"א: וכל מי שלא חס על כבוד קונו רתוי לו שלא בא לעולם. ובבבלי שם ט"ז א': מאי היא? ר' אבא אומר זה המסתכל בקשת וכו', דכתיב כמראה הקשת אשר יהיה בענן וכו'. ובשיעור קומה קרוב לסופו:[27] א"ר ישמעאל כשאמרתי דבר זה לפני ר' עקיבא, אמר לי כל מי שהוא יודע שיעור זה של יוצרנו ושבחו של הקב"ה שהוא מכוסה מן הבריות מובטח לו שהוא בן עולם הבא וכו', אני ור' עקיבא ערבין בדבר זה שכל מי שהוא יודע שיעור זה של יוצרנו ושבחו של הקב"ה מובטח לו שהוא בן עולם הבא, ובלבד שהוא שונה אותו במשנ' בכל יום ויום. וכבר הסמיכו הגאונים (עיין אוה"ג חגיגה, סוף עמ' 18 ואילך) את הברייתא של שיעור קומה למשנתנו הנ"ל, ועיין בתוספות רי"ד חגיגה ט"ז א' ד"ה כל. ואף ר' עקיבא לא אמרו אלא על מי שיודע „שיעור זה של יוצרנו ושבחו", כעין שאמרו בבבלי מגילה כ"ה א': סיימתינהו לשבחיה דמרך? ובירושלמי ברכות פ"ט ה"א, י"ב ע"ד: לך דומיה תהילה אלהים בציון (תהלים ס"ה, ב') וכו', למרגלית דלית ליה טימי, כל שמשבח בה פגמה. ובפירוש לשה"ש למחבר תימני:[28] אמ' לפני רבן גמליאל אם אין לבריות רשות להגיד אמתתו של בורא, יש להן רשות להגיד שבחו, היך דכת' (שמות ל"ג, כ') כי לא יראני האדם וחי, חיים תלויין בשבחו, אבל אמתתו מסותרת וכו'. שיעור קומה הוא השבח של אמת, ואין

בקטע ממדרש שה"ש שפרסם מאן בשנתון של צינצינטי חי"ד, עמ' 335. ולפנינו בשהש"ר פ"ג ה', וכן בדב"ר פ"ז, ח', במ"ר רפ"ה, תנחומא ויקהל סי' ז', אין רמז למעשה העגל. והוא משום שדעת ר' יהודה היא שאין דורשין שה"ש לגנאי (שהש"ר פ"א, י"ב, פ"ב, ד'), אעפ"י שגם בשהש"ר שלנו נשרדו הרבה דרשות לשה"ש במעשה העגל. ומדרש שה"ש צורף וזוקק יותר משאר מדרשים. ועיין גם באבות דר' נתן פ"כ, ל"ז רע"א.

[25] עיין ערוגת הבושם הוצ' ר"א אורבך ח"א, עמ' 11, הערה 11. אבל גם בספרי וזאת הברכה פיס' שמ"ג 399: כיון ששמעו אומות העולם נאותו ושבחו. ובמס' סופרים פ"ג הי"ז, היגר 133: הרבות בנאות אלו.

[26] בפירוש האגדות שלו, עמ' 70, מעתיק כן בשם מדרש שה"ש, וממשיך עד סוף הפרק. וספק גדול הוא אם ההמשך הוא מאותו מדרש, עיין בפירושו לשה"ש שם. ולעצם העניין עיין בתוספ' רי"ד חגיגה ט"ז א' ובפתח עינים להחיד"א שם.

[27] מרכבה שלמה, ל"ח ע"ב.

[28] סה"י לכבוד שטיינשניידר, עמ' 58, עיין מ"ש ב„מדרשי תימן", עמ' 12 ואילך.

לבריות רשות להגיד אמתתו שהיא מסותרת ומכוסה מן הבריות, ועיין מ״ש ע״ז להלן.

ספר עתיק זה היה מקודש באומה, וכשנשאל יהודי צרפתי במאה האחת עשרה לספירה הרגילה מה היא דעת היהודים בצרפת על האגדות של שיעור קומה, ענה: כמפי הגבורה.[29] ויש רגלים לדבר שספר זה היה ידוע גם לר׳ אליעזר הקליר, וקראו בשמו.[30] והגאונים החשיבו ספר זה (עיין אוה״ג חגיגה, עמ׳ 11 ואילך), ואף ר׳ סעדיה לא פסל אותו (עיין אוה״ג ברכות, התשובות, עמ׳ 17). וקרוב לוודאי בעיני שאף הרמב״ם האמין בו בימי ילדותו, שהרי כן הוא בפיה״מ שלו לסנהדרין פ״י, היסוד השביעי: ושנבאר בתחילת מציאות המלאכים ושינוי מעלותיהן, מן הבורא השם יתברך וכו׳, עד שנדבר בצורות שזכרו הנביאים שראוי לבורא ולמלאכים, ויכנס בזה שיעור קומה ועניינו. ולא יספיק בעניין זה לבדו, ואפילו יהיה מקוצר בתכלית הקיצור מאה דפים וכו׳. ואשר לתשובת הר״מ בהוצ׳ רא״ח פריימן זצ״ל סי׳ שע״ג, עמ׳ 343, הרי נעלם ממנו (וממני ב„שקיעין”, עמ׳ 12) שהמקור הערבי נתפרסם ע״י גאטטליעב (פיה״מ להר״מ סנהדרין, הנובר 1906, עמ׳ 97), והנוסח שם (לפי תרגומו של הנ״ל): אנשי מערב שאלו את רבינו משה ז״ל מה דעתו בשיעור קומה, האם יתקיימו דברי האומרים שהוא חיבורו של אחד הקראים, ומסרו כך מפי הדרתך, או הוא סוד מסודות החכמים, תוכו דברים במה שלמטה ובמה שלמעלה, כמה שכתב רבי חייא בספר מספריו. ושכרך כפול. תשובת רבי משה בי רבי מיימון ז״ל אל אנשי מערב: מעולם לא הייתי סבור שהוא לחכמים. חס להם. שוב חס להם. אינו אלא חיבורו של אחד הדרשנים בין הרומים, לא דבר אחר וכו׳. התשובה, כנראה, אף כאן משובשת במקצת, ומתוך התשובה המרוגזת של הר״מ „מעולם לא הייתי סבור וכו׳” משמע לכאורה שייחסו לו את הדברים, ושאלו: ומסרו כך מפי הדרתך, או שהוא סוד וכו׳, כלומר, אף זה מסרו מפי הדרתך. והנוסח הנכון בתשובה הוא כבהוצ׳ פריימן הנ״ל: איני רואה כי הוא מן החכמים וכו׳. אבל בילדותו האמין הר״מ בקדושת שיעור קומה, ונמשך אחרי ספר יסוד מורא של הראב״ע, שער א׳, ט״ז ע״א, שהשפיע הרבה על הר״מ,[31] ואח״כ חזר בו ומחק את המלים „פי דלך שיעור קומה ומענאה”,[32] כרגיל בפיה״מ שלו, ולפנינו, וכן בארבעה כי״י, נשרדה לנו המהדורא קמא של הספר. והרי הר״מ רגיל לכתוב דברים קשים נגד הפירושים של עצמו בפיה״מ מהדו״ק, עיין מ״ש במבוא לה׳ הירושלמי להר״מ, עמ׳ ז׳ (לפיה״מ כלאים פ״ט מ״ח), ועמ׳ י״ב ד״ה לאורן. ובחיבורו פ״ג מה׳ תשובה ה״ז פסק שהאומר שהוא גוף ובעל תמונה הרי זה מין. ושום כרכורים של גאטטליעב לא יועילו לשבש את

29 עיין במחברתי שקיעין, עמ׳ 11 ואילך.

30 בפיוטי בן קליר שפרסם פרנקל בסה״י לכבוד צונץ, עמ׳ 212: כדמות בוראו היות דמותו, כּשִׁיעוּר קוֹ (כ״ה בכ״י, עיי״ש הערה 13) קומתו, כאימת יוצרו על כל אימתו. ולפי בקשתי הודיע לי ידידי פרופ׳ שלום שפיגל שבכ״י קנטבריא (TSH 3:10) הגירסא היא: כשיעור קומה קומתו. ועיין מ״ש פרנקל בסה״י הנ״ל (החלק הגרמני), עמ׳ 171. ומכאן ש„שיעור קומה” כבר היה בזמנו של הפייטן שם קבוע למדות יוצרנו כביכול.

31 כבר הוכיח הרי״פ פערלא בהקדמתו למניין המצות של הרס״ג, עמ׳ 15 ואילך, שהרמב״ם שאב בקביעות מספר זה. ועיין גם בפירושו לשמות ל״ג כ״א.

32 אבל הן ישנן בשני כת״י, עיין בהוצ׳ גאטטליעב (שהזכרנו בפנים), עמ׳ 51, הערה ג׳, וכ״ה בכ״י ישן נושן (קובץ ענעלאו 290) 37 רע״א, ובכ״י תימני של אדלר בביה״מ כאן. ועיין מ״ש גאטטליעב שם. עמ׳ 98, בשם העתקת חריזי כת״י. ורק בשני כת״י חסרות המלים הללו. ועיין בהקדמת הר״מ לפרק חלק, הוצ׳ האלצער, עמ׳ 24, ועמ׳ 38, הערה 160.

הנוסח שבפיה"מ המקויים ע"י ארבעה כתי"י. ומתשובת הר"מ אין ראייה, כמו שכתבנו לעיל. ובמחברתי שקיעין, עמ' 12, הראיתי על הברייתא בבכורות מ"ד א': חוטמו גדול וכו', תנא כאצבע קטנה. ופירש הר"מ (בניגוד לרש"י): ושיעור חוטמו אמרו שהוא כשיעור אצבע קטנה שבידו. ובס' שיעור קומה:[33] אורך החוטם כאורך האצבע קטנה, עיין מש"ש, ועיין מ"ש[34] G. Sarton ב־Isis חל"ג (1941), עמ' 72.

סוף דבר, מחוץ לפתרון שה"ש כפשוטיה היה קיים בישראל פירוש מגילה זו „רשום בכתב אמת", כפי שכבר כתבו המפרשים של ימי הביניים, עיין בפירוש הראב"ע בתחילת שה"ש, ועוד. ויפה סיכם ר"י ן' שועיב בדרשה „ליום אחרון של פסח, והוא מדרש שיר השירים":[35] כי דברי זה השיר סתומים וחתומים מאד וכו', ולכן דנוהו קדשי קדשים, כי כל דבריו הם סתרי המרכבה ושמותיו של הקב"ה וכו', ואעפ"י שדבריו סתומים וחתומים יש בו נגלה וכו', ורבותינו ז"ל פירשו בדרך נגלה כי החתן הוא הקב"ה, והכלה כנסת ישראל. ועל שה"ש פ"ה, י"—ט"ז הוא כותב:[36] ועל דרך הקבלה הם עניינים נעלמים שאפילו המחשבה אסורה בו, הם המרכבה העליונה למעלה ממרכבת יחזקאל, והן הספירות וכו'. ובדרך זו תאר אותו גם המפרש התימני:[37] אשרי כל חרש ושונה[38] בו ויודע בענין מכתבו, נתיחד עם מלך במסבו וכו'. ולהלן שם (עמ' 53): וחכמ' אומ' מותר לקרות שיר השירים על פשטיה, ואין מורין בו דבר חכמה (כלומר, חכמת אמת) אלא לדיין או לראש העיר. ובבבלי חגיגה י"ג א': ולא במרכבה ביחיד. אין מוסרין ראשי פרקים אלא לאב בית דין וכו', ע"ש. ומכאן שפשטיה של שהש"ר הוא בניגוד לסוד המרכבה. ושה"ש נדרש על דרך הפשט ועל דרך האמת המסותרת.[39] ובמחזור ינאי, עמ' רע"ב: שיר השירים אמת וודיי, אין כל העולם בה כדיי. וכן מפורש בשהש"ר פ"א, י"א: נקודות הכסף (שה"ש א', י"א). זה שיר השירים. מלה חתומה ומלה מסיימה, כלומר דבר חתום ודבר מסויים,[40] והיינו שעניינה חתום, סתום ורשום מצד אחד, ומסויים וגלוי מצד שני, פירוש על דרך הסוד, ופירוש על דרך הפשט, כשם שהנקודות („נקודות הכסף") שעל גבי האותיות שבתורה מורות על פירוש אחר שאינו כפשוטו.[41]

וכשר' יהושע רצה להסיע את ר' ישמעאל לדבר אחר, שאל אותו היאך אתה קורא כי טובים (כלומר, מנשיקות פיהו כי טובים), דודיך—מיין (שה"ש א', ב'), או כי טובים דודיך.[42] ובארו בירושלמי שם[43] שרמז לו לריש הפסוק: ישקני מנשיקות

33 ס' רזיאל, ל"ח רע"א, מרכבה שלמה, ל"ח ע"א.

34 ד"ר שלמה גנדז המנוח העירני בשעתו על מאמר זה.

35 ד' קראקא של"ג, מ"ב ע"ב ואילך.

36 מ"ג סע"ב.

37 עמ' 50, עיין לעיל הערה 28.

38 כנראה שזו היא מליצה ע"פ ב"מ ק"ז א': כריב ותני.

39 כמו שהעתקנו לעיל (עיין הערה 28, ובפנים שם): אבל אמתתו מסותרת. ועיין מ"ש להלן בפנים.

40 בדרשות ר"י ן' שועיב שהבאנו לעיל, מ"ב ע"ב: ואעפ"י שדבריו סתומים וחתומים יש בו נגלה כדברי שלמה שיש בהם משל ומליצה וכו', היה אומ' דבריו נגלה ונסתר. ואפשר שכתב ע"פ המדרש כאן, ופירש שיש בה במגילה דברים חתומים ודברים נגלים. אבל לפי פירוש זה קשה מה עניינו ל„נקודות" הכסף.

41 עיין מ"ש בספרי (באנגלית) הילניסמוס בא"י היהודית, עמ' 45 ואילך.

42 משנת ע"ז פ"ב מ"ה, ותוספתא פרה פ"י ה"ג, ואני מבטל מ"ש בתוספת ראשונים ח"ג, עמ' 248 ואילך, והפירוש הנכון הוא בלקוטים מהגר"א בסוף שנות אליהו סדר זרעים, ופירושו מוכרח מסוגיית הירושלמי ומדרש שה"ש.

43 ע"ז פ"ב ה"ח, מ"א רע"ד.

פיהו, יש דברים שמשיקין עליהן את הפה, ועיין גם בשהש"ר שם במקומו. וכע"ז גם בבבלי ע"ז ל"ה א'. ובירושלמי ובשהש"ר שם הביאו גם את הפסוק כבשים ללבושך (משלי כ"ז, כ"ו). ובבבלי חגיגה י"ג א': ליגמרון מר מעשה מרכבה. אמר להו תנינא בהו דבש וחלב תחת לשונך (שה"ש ד', י"א) וכו'. ר' אבהו אמר מהכא כבשים ללבושך.

ובירושלמי ובשהש"ר הנ"ל אמרו שר' יהושע לא גילה לו לר' ישמעאל את טעם הדבר, מפני שהיה קטן, ורמז לו בפסוק ישקני מנשיקות פיהו. ואח"כ הביאו את הפסוק ממשלי הנ"ל: כבשים ללבושך ומחיר שדה עתודים, ודרשו: בשעה שתלמידים קטנים כבוש לפניהן דברי תורה, הגדילו ונעשו כעתודים גלי להם רזי תורה. ובוודאי שר' ישמעאל לא היה קטן ממש, שהרי קרא לו שם „ישמעאל אחי",[44] ולא „ישמעאל בני", אלא שלא הגיע לבגרות גמורה.[45] ובבבלי חגיגה י"ג א': א"ל ר' יוחנן לר' אלעזר תא אגמרך במעשה המרכבה. א"ל לא קשאי. ופי' ר"ח: כלומר, איני בן חמשים שנה, ועיין בבלי קדושין ע"א א', ובחידושי אגדות למהרש"א שם. ועיין מ"ש בספרי הירושלמי כפשוטו, עמ' 458.

מעתה נאמנים עלינו דברי המפרש התימני הנ"ל[46] שכתב: מעשה שדרש ר' עקיבה בשיר השירים, וכשהגיע לפיסוק ישקני מנשיקות פיהו בכה רבן גמליאל, אמ' לו תלמידיו, ר' למה בכית, אמ' מפני שאין דורשין במעשה מרכבה אפלו ביחיד. אמ' ר' עקיבה לפניו, רבינו אין רשות לקורא לקרות בספר תורה עד שחזן הכנסת קורא לפניו תחלה,[47] מיד שתק רבן גמליאל ואמ' וכו'. וכנראה, שהכוונה שר' עקיבא דרש תחילה בפסוק ראשון של שיר השירים, שהוא המקודש שבכל השירים, ושנאמר בהר סיני ע"י הקב"ה, ו„כל שלמה האמורין בשה"ש קדש, שיר למי שהשלום שלו, חוץ וכו'",[48] וכדומה. וכשהגיע לפסוק השני בכה רבן גמליאל וכו', והשיב לו ר' עקיבא שאפילו בתורה אין קוראין בלי רשות, ומכל שכן במעשה מרכבה, עיין תוספתא חגיגה פ"ב ה"א („אמ' לו תן לי רשות"), ואינו מתכונן לדרוש יותר.

והוא מדרש שה"ש, הוא מעשה מרכבה, הוא שיעור קומה.

ואם עדותו של אוריגינס נכונה (עיין לעיל עמ' 38) הרי החמירו ביחזקאל ובשה"ש יותר מן הפסוקים שנקראין ואינן מתרגמין ושאינן לא נקראין ולא מתרגמין. והרי שנינו בתוספתא מגילה פ"ג (פ"ד בכי"ע) הל"ח: לא נקראין ולא מתרגמין. והסופר מלמד כדרכו. ולא נזכר בשום מקום שאסרו לסופר ללמד שיר השירים וכדומה. וכנראה שיש לפנינו חומרא שהעם קבל על עצמו שלא מדעת חכמים.

44 עיין מ"ש בתוספתא כפשוטה ח"א, עמ' 5, הערה 17.

45 מעין עדותו של אוריגינים (עיין לעיל עמ' 38) שהיהודים נהגו שלא ליתן רשות להחזיק ספר שה"ש לבני אדם שלא הגיעו לבגרות גמורה. אבל מכאן אין ראייה אלא שלא דרשו בשה"ש לצעירים.

46 סוף עמ' 52, עיין לעיל הערה 28.

47 תוספתא מגילה פ"ד הכ"א, עיין מ"ש בתוספת ראשונים ח"א, עמ' 237.

48 בבלי שבועות ל"ה ב' ומקבילות.